SATAN
AND HIS FRIENDS

A MINIMALIST APPROACH FOR BELIEVERS

SATAN AND HIS FRIENDS

EDMON L. GALLAGHER

Abilene Christian University Press

SATAN AND HIS FRIENDS

A Minimalist Approach for Believers

ACU PRESS

ISBN 978-1-68426-322-6 | LCCN 2025003741

Printed in the United States of America

Throughout this book, in the author's writing and in Scripture quotations, the term YHWH, a representation of the name of the God of Israel, is used rather than "Lord" or "LORD." Other Greek and Hebrew words are also retained in Scriptures, rather than following the English translations.

LIBRARY OF CONGRESS CATALOGING-IN-PUBLICATION DATA

Names: Gallagher, Edmon L. author

Title: Satan and his friends : a minimalist approach for believers / Edmon L. Gallagher.

Description: Abilene, Texas : ACU Press, [2025] | Includes bibliographical references.

Identifiers: LCCN 2025003741 (print) | LCCN 2025003742 (ebook) | ISBN 9781684263226 paperback | ISBN 9781684268191 ebook

Subjects: LCSH: Devil—Biblical teaching | Good and evil—Biblical teaching

Classification: LCC BS680.D56 G35 2025 (print) | LCC BS680.D56 (ebook) | DDC 235/.47--dc23/eng/20250407

LC record available at https://lccn.loc.gov/2025003741

LC ebook record available at https://lccn.loc.gov/2025003742

Cover design by Greg Jackson, Thinkpen Design | Interior text design by Sandy Armstrong, Strong Design

For information contact: Abilene Christian University Press, ACU Box 29138, Abilene, Texas 79699

1-877-816-4455 | www.acupressbooks.com

25 26 27 28 29 30 31 // 7 6 5 4 3 2 1

For Evelyn Gallagher,

Friend of Jesus

CONTENTS

PREFACE

When I told Jodi, my wife, that I was thinking of naming this book *Satan and His Friends*, she feigned concern and imagined someone asking, "Am I Satan's friend?" Only at that moment did I realize the different ways that "friend of Satan" could be interpreted. I had been thinking of the phrase in reference to the spiritual forces described in Christian tradition as working alongside Satan or under his authority—fallen angels, demons, Beelzebub, and so on. But Jodi immediately thought of human beings under the influence of Satan, whether willingly or not. If Abraham was a friend of God because of his faithfulness (Isa. 41:8), then Judas (cf. Luke 22:3!) could be considered a friend of Satan. A book on Satan and the people under his control would probably be classified under "spiritual warfare," and it might help readers identify the evil spiritual beings at work in their lives and how to combat them. This is not that book.

Let me explain why I have not written the book many readers may be expecting and wanting. It's not that I doubt the reality of evil. Christian Scripture—not to mention the evidence of my own eyes—assures me of its existence.[1] The New Testament warns readers about a supernatural being usually called Satan or the devil that not only has power to mislead or

[1] Or something like that. Maybe evil does not exactly "exist" but is instead the absence of good. See §2.1 of Calder, "The Concept of Evil," online at https://plato.stanford.edu/archives/win2022/entries/concept-evil/.

harm people but also enjoys the help of other spiritual entities. Believers are told to resist this power. "Resist the devil, and he will flee from you" (James 4:7). According to 1 Peter 5:8, the devil walks about like a roaring lion, "seeking whom he may devour," and in the next verse readers are told again to "resist" him (KJV). Peter does not explain what it means for the devil to "devour" people or how to resist him. The passage is not altogether comforting.

The premier "spiritual warfare" passage in the New Testament is undoubtedly Ephesians 6:10–20, which begins with the well-known (to Christians, anyway) admonition to "be strong in the Lord, and in the power of his might" (KJV). This is the passage that insists that the Christian is engaged in a battle against forces not so mundane as "flesh and blood" but rather "spiritual wickedness in high places," which Paul also describes as "principalities" and "powers" and "the rulers of the darkness of this world" (Eph. 6:12 KJV). To combat such celestial enemies, what should one do? Paul tells the Ephesians that they need to put on the armor of God, but how can one do such a thing? Where is this armor to be found? The passage continues by describing the individual pieces of armor that the believer should wear (belt, breastplate, helmet, sword, etc.), but these turn out to be metaphors for regular Christian practices and commitments. While Paul uses exalted and memorable language here, his advice seems to boil down to meditating on Scripture, praying, practicing righteousness and peace, and maintaining one's commitment to God and his grace—all things that can be done without worrying overmuch about demons lurking around corners or on my shoulder. There are no incantations to learn, no special prayers to memorize, no need to draw a pentagram on the floor. The way to resist the evil powers has little to do overtly with those evil powers. I would summarize Paul's instruction as "act like a Christian"—not an easy thing to do, but not made easier (to my mind, at least) by ruminating on demons.

Paul seems to have thought about demons much less than later Christians have; the word *demon* appears in his thirteen canonical letters in only two passages (1 Cor. 10:20–21; 1 Tim. 4:1), and even the chief of the demons, Satan, shows up infrequently in those missives. The grandest presentation of the gospel in the New Testament mentions the devil only once, at the very end, when Paul assures the Romans of Satan's doom (Rom. 16:20). Granted, Paul sometimes refers to evil spiritual beings without using the terms *demon* or *evil spirit* or such, as he does in Ephesians 6:12 (see Rom. 8:38; perhaps 1 Cor. 2:8, possibly echoed already by Ignatius, *Ephesians* 19.1), but even so, Paul talks about these evil spiritual beings infrequently, and they never serve as the focus of his discourse. It seems that the apostle thought that Christians should know about the cosmic battle into which their allegiance to Christ had thrust them, but there was no need to give much attention to the principalities and powers.

Perhaps readers will scoff at my description of Ephesians 6 as the premier "spiritual warfare" passage in the New Testament, since the Gospels contain vivid episodes centering on Jesus's war against evil spirits. Who can forget Jesus vs. Legion (Mark 5:1–20) or the temptation scene pitting Jesus against Satan (Matt. 4:1–11)? Even if the other Gospel reports of exorcisms are not quite as dramatic (Mark 1:21–28; 7:24–30; 9:14–29), still they show that Jesus regularly fought demons—and that's not even to mention the healings Jesus performed and the role of evil spirits in causing sickness (see Luke 13:16; Acts 10:38). Should modern Christians consider the accounts of Jesus's battles with demons as examples for imitation?

No.

That's the short answer. The long answer is the rest of this book.

Let me try here for an intermediate answer with some nuance. Christian Scripture does not lead inexorably to a view of spiritual warfare such that the believer ought to give any more attention to evil spirits than did Paul in his letters. I say that Christian Scripture does not lead inexorably in this direction. There are Christians in the twenty-first century who do routinely talk about evil spirits at work in their lives and how to combat them, and I will not gainsay them; if they find such a perspective helpful for coping with life under the care of God, wonderful! But not every believer finds this perspective helpful, and I aim to establish—or, at least, to argue—here that an approach to Christian living that affords little attention to Satan and his friends coheres perfectly well with the Bible, certainly the Old Testament but also the New Testament. If you want to view Jesus's encounters with demons as models for your own battles with evil spirits, more power to you (you'll need it!). But I find it perfectly reasonable to view the increased presence of demons within the ministry of Jesus—unusual within the context of the Bible—as a special case; without question, what Jesus did to those demons, the power he demonstrated, was a special case. At least, I have never seen someone (or even heard someone claim to) exercise power over demons in the manner of Jesus. (I admit that neither have I seen someone that I would guess had a demon afflicting him or her.) There is a reason Jesus gained a reputation for having remarkable authority (see Mark 1:27). He gave similar authority to specific delegates of his (Mark 6:7), but I remain unconvinced that anyone today enjoys such power.

The Christian religion does not need a major role for evil spirits. The basic story of the Bible is not about God against evil spirits, or even God's battle with Satan, but about God's relationship with humans. In the Bible one encounters frequently the tension between good and evil, but the evil almost always resides within people and is not attributed to non-human spiritual beings. In this book I argue that Satan, or the devil, is a minor character in the New Testament and is never mentioned in the Old Testament—or never in the Hebrew Bible, though he does make a few appearances (improperly, in my view) in most English translations of the Old Testament. The same can be said for demons: minor characters in the New Testament, probably never mentioned in the Old Testament. If some believers feel comforted or helped in some way by imagining a more robust role for Satan and his spiritual allies than what I have just described, that is fine with me and coherent with the New Testament; I insist only that the New Testament does not require that view. I think my approach falls neatly in between the "two equal and opposite errors into which our race can fall about the devils" that C. S. Lewis mentioned in the preface to *The Screwtape Letters*, since I am promoting neither disbelief in their existence nor "an excessive and unhealthy interest in them."[2]

I am a Satan-minimalist. I find Satan in the Bible only when he is named—named in the original texts, not in English translations. Let me be more precise: I find Satan in the Bible only when it seems likely to me that the original authors of the various texts making up the Bible were trying to describe a wicked being who was opposed to God. And it turns

[2] Lewis, *Screwtape Letters*, 15.

out, if that is the criterion, Satan appears in Scripture much less frequently than believers have typically imagined, and the biblical testimony about Satan—and demons, too—is not very informative. Most of what we think we know about Satan and his friends comes not from Christian Scripture but from Christian tradition.

And that is why I have not written a book about Satan's attacks on you. Such books are probably useful in some ways; certainly I find *The Screwtape Letters* immensely helpful, though, admittedly, its usefulness in my mind lies not in what it says about the nature of demons but in its insights into the nature of humans. Human nature as revealed in *The Screwtape Letters*, and in Christian Scripture, and in history, is characterized by grace and sin, joy and suffering. The Bible sometimes talks about demons in connection with these themes, but rarely. According to the Bible, evil spiritual forces can tempt people toward sin, but Scripture prefers to concentrate on encouraging people to develop virtues, filling their lives with the things of God so as to crowd out evil. The Bible warns about wicked spirits who cause suffering, but suffering can also be a gift from God (see Phil. 1:29) for the testing and refinement of one's faith (1 Pet. 1:6–7), resulting in joy (Rom. 5:3; Heb. 12:2; James 1:2).

Can people be friends of Satan? Perhaps. People may want to follow a path that the Bible associates with wickedness. I assume as axiomatic that a Christian believer concerned that he or she may be a friend of Satan is not one. The graver danger here for believers is in characterizing our enemies as friends of Satan. At the quarter mark of the twenty-first century, demonizing one's opponents is all too common, and it may be that some Christians consider themselves to be reflecting good biblical theology in identifying the evil forces working with their adversaries. Probably the biggest problem with this practice is the self-delusion involved, the confidence on display insisting that the other team is acting in concert with demons and not we ourselves. It probably also represents a misunderstanding of the scriptural testimony on wicked spiritual forces, and I hope this book can contribute to informing readers and provoking thought.

Enough about the book I did not write. The book I have written aims to trace the development of beliefs about Satan and his friends—the demons and fallen angels that aid Satan in his work of temptation and torment—from Christian Scripture through Christian tradition. I am interested in which elements of these traditions are grounded in the Bible. In my experience, among the evil beings that inhabit Christian theology, Satan is the most fully developed in people's minds. Most churchgoers know at least vaguely about fallen angels and demons and perhaps other evil spirits, and some churches have quite sophisticated teachings on these beings. Still, Satan exists in most Christians' imaginations as more than a vague idea, but as a fully fleshed-out force (usually without the flesh), with clearly defined goals and motivations and strategies. This book has two objectives: to investigate the origins of these depictions of Satan, and to show that, in large measure, Christian Scripture allows for but does not require such interpretations of this being.

Some form of Satan-minimalism (as I defined the term earlier) is very popular today among biblical scholars, though I am, even among biblical scholars, on the minimalistic side of the spectrum (but not at the outer edge), finding Satan in the Bible comparatively infrequently.[3] My view stands in distinction to a popular view among Christians—in antiquity and still today—that could be labeled "Satan-maximalism," such that the wicked being Satan is alluded to in Scripture much more often than he is named.[4] I cannot say for sure that Satan-maximalism misreads Christian Scripture, but I want to show that Satan-minimalism is a sensible and faithful interpretive approach.

I am interested in faithful interpretation—faithful to the major aspects of the Christian tradition, faithful to Christian Scripture, and ultimately faithful to the God revealed in those writings that I consider sacred. I write as a Christian believer with a high view of Scripture. This perspective determines some of the questions I ask and some of the answers I promote. Part of what I think it means to be a faithful interpreter of Christian Scripture is to attempt to account for my own myopia and prejudices, and to this end I am a big fan of critical biblical scholarship. In this book I am attempting to study the evil spirits of the Bible using the methods of critical

---

[3]The outer edge could probably be represented by Kelly, *Satan*, who never finds God's enemy in the Christian Bible but only in postbiblical tradition.

[4]A modern representative here, and increasingly influential (if my anecdotal evidence can be trusted), is the late Heiser, *Unseen Realm*.

scholarship. For this reason, I believe readers who do not share my theological perspective will be able to profit from this book if they are interested in biblical interpretation and the history of the Christian tradition.

This book regularly uses a few terms in Hebrew, the language of Jewish Scripture. In many of the quotations found in this book (from the Bible and other ancient texts), I retain those Hebrew, Greek, or Latin words in place of their English translations. They are always explained, I believe, at their first appearance—except for the most important one. That is the term YHWH, a representation of the name of the God of Israel. Sometimes this same name is spelled Yahweh, but not in this book. The name appears in the Hebrew Bible some six thousand times, and it never appears with its proper vowels. (Remember that most Hebrew vowel markers are a later addition to the text of the Hebrew Bible, which was originally written with consonants only.) Because the Hebrew Bible does not contain the proper vowels (out of respect for the name), I have mimicked this practice by spelling the name YHWH, both in my writing and in verses quoted herein. Readers will usually discover that their own English Bibles do not contain the name YHWH at all but the substitute word Lord (in all or small caps). The substitution is itself a venerable tradition, starting centuries before the birth of Jesus, but this ancient practice risks obscuring the fact that we are dealing with a personal name.[5]

[5] For more, see Gallagher, *Book of Exodus*, chapter 2.

ACKNOWLEDGMENTS

This book has been in the incubator for a long time. I think I first started putting this material together in 2018, at the request of some people at my church, the Sherrod Avenue Church of Christ (Florence, Alabama). The more I studied, the more questions I had—a common predicament. Eventually, I presented some of this material in a series of chapel lessons at Heritage Christian University in the fall of 2022, but still there was research and writing to do, and other scholars insisted on continuing to produce excellent and important studies germane to my topic. Along the way, I received much encouragement from various sources, none so persistent as Jamie Cox, the librarian at HCU, who has for years now been waiting to see my material on angels and demons. Jamie supported this work in the most productive way anyone could: by keeping the library stocked with books.

My wife, Jodi, has lived most intimately with this book over the years. I am grateful for her daily example of endurance, humility, and love. Thank you to my children: Miriam, Evelyn, Josiah, Jasmine, Marvin, and Ellie. You all have provided much joy, education, and distraction, with not too much frustration. I love you all.

I dedicate this book to my daughter Evelyn on the occasion of her transition from high school to college. At around the same time that this book is published, Jodi and I will be dropping Evelyn off at the university where she will study pharmacy, the same career as my parents and my sister. Though she has not (yet?) chosen to follow my educational path (theology or biblical studies) or to pursue a career in law (as I have incessantly encouraged her—she argues well), perhaps she will still find useful all that Latin I made her learn. It has been my pleasure to live with her for eighteen years and to witness her becoming an amazing woman. Truly, I could not be more proud of her—unless, of course, she decides to switch her major to theology or law!—and I know she will bring great glory to our family, as she already is doing. I love you, Evelyn.

ABBREVIATIONS

//	Indicates parallel passages in the Gospels
ANF	*The Ante-Nicene Fathers*. 10 vols. Edited by Alexander Roberts and James Donaldson. Christian Literature, 1885–1887.
DDD	*Dictionary of Deities and Demons in the Bible*. 2nd ed. Edited by Karel van der Toorn, Bob Becking, and Pieter W. van der Horst. Brill, 1999.
DJD	Discoveries in the Judean Desert. 40 vols. Oxford University Press, 1955–2010.
EBR	*Encyclopedia of the Bible and Its Reception*. 23 vols. Edited by Constance M. Furey, Peter Gemeinhardt, Joel Marcus LeMon et al. De Gruyter, 2009–2025.
KTU	*Die keilalphabetischen Texte aus Ugarit*. Edited by M. Dietrich, O. Loretz, and J. Sanmartín. Neukirchener Verlag, 1976.

INTRODUCTION

PORTRAIT OF A MATURE SATAN

Better to reign in hell, than serve in heaven.
—Satan, *Paradise Lost* 1.263

The mature Satan cuts an impressive figure. In the mid-twentieth century, Mick Jagger channeled a Satan who described himself as "a man of wealth and taste" who was involved in many of the major events in world history. This earworm from the Rolling Stones may not engender in listeners any genuine sympathy for the devil, but he does demand our courtesy and respect. Jagger's Satan is introspective, but if we are looking for such a depiction of Satan, we could hardly do better than turn to John Milton, whose portrait of Satan in his seventeenth-century epic poem *Paradise Lost* both summed up previous traditions and pushed those traditions in new directions. Milton probably gave the English-speaking world the most mature Satan of all, so mature, in fact—so fully developed—that readers have often considered Satan the real hero of *Paradise Lost*, the character who rejects the authoritarianism of God, insisting on thinking for himself and (in the modern vernacular) following his heart and being his own master. Milton's Satan will be nobody's slave, not even God's. One wonders whether this interpretation of Satan in *Paradise Lost* has influenced at all the modern Church of Satan, which defines Satanism as "a philosophical position that promotes individuality, liberty, joy, and self-expression."[1] Those characteristics could, perhaps, describe Satan in *Paradise Lost*, though the hardest to justify would be *joy*, and one would need to add *evil*. At any rate, whether this "positive" interpretation of Milton's Satan is what Milton himself intended—some readers (famously, William Blake) have considered Milton to belong to Satan's party, while others have dissented—certainly the legend of Satan is developed in *Paradise Lost* far beyond what we can find in Scripture or in ancient Jewish literature.[2]

In *Paradise Lost*, the angel Raphael tells Adam the story of Satan's fall in books 5–6. According to Raphael's account, Satan was one of the most eminent archangels, "great in power, / in favour and pre-eminence" (5.660–61).[3] His original name was not Satan but something else that is "heard no more in heaven" (5.659). We elsewhere learn that his original name was Lucifer (see, e.g., 5.760; 7.131; 10.425). After his fall, Satan is proud of his new name that identifies him as "Antagonist of heaven's almighty king" (10.387). Why did Satan fall? Before the creation of the world, God the Father presented to his angels the divine Son (5.600–615) and commanded everyone to worship him. This order engendered jealousy in Lucifer/Satan (5.661–62), so he led away a third of heaven's host (5.710) and headed to "the palace of great Lucifer" (5.760) where he claimed equality with God, making a speech to his subjects that disclosed his envy (starting at 5.772).

Only a single angel in Satan's camp objected to the burgeoning rebellion. Abdiel reminded Satan that it was through the Son that the Father had made all things, even Satan (5.835), but Satan disputed this assertion as a strange, new doctrine (beginning at 5.853).

[1]These are the words of Peter H. Gilmore, high priest of the Church of Satan, based in Hell's Kitchen, New York, as recorded for Episode #666 of the radio program *This American Life*. The episode is called "The Theme That Shall Not Be Named," available at https://www.thisamericanlife.org/666/the-theme-that-shall-not-be-named. Gilmore's description of Satanism comes at the 32:30 mark.

[2]William Blake made the comment about Milton's belonging to Satan's party in his work *The Marriage of Heaven and Hell*, originally written in the 1790s and available in many editions. The comment comes near the beginning of the work, in a note on a section called "The Voice of the Devil." For a full exposition of a heroic Satan in *Paradise Lost*, see Forsyth, *Satanic Epic*. For a view dissenting from Blake's description, see Lewis, *Preface to Paradise Lost*, chapter 13.

[3]Thomas Aquinas also argued that Satan had probably been the chief archangel; see Bonino, *Angels and Demons*, 207–9.

The story of the ensuing war in heaven occupies book 6. It was a fairly even fight between Satan's forces and the forces of Michael the archangel, until the Son of God got involved and easily routed the evil forces, who threw themselves out of heaven in order to escape the Son's wrath.

> headlong themselves they threw
> Down from the verge of heaven, eternal wrath
> Burnt after them to the bottomless pit. (6.864–66)

After a fall of nine days, they wound up in hell (6.867–92). All of this story of the war in heaven is told in flashback. *Paradise Lost* begins in book 1 at the point when the battle is finished, with Satan and his minions defeated, having just arrived in hell. And it was all due to Satan's pride.

> his pride
> Had cast him out from heaven, with all his host
> Of rebel angels, by whose aid aspiring
> To set himself in glory above his peers,
> He trusted to have equalled the most high,
> If he opposed; and with ambitious aim
> Against the throne and monarchy of God
> Raised impious war in heaven and battle proud
> With vain attempt. (1.36–44)

From this point on, Satan is "the Prince of Hell" (4.871). He is also "the infernal serpent" (1.34), "apostate angel" (1.125), leader of seraphim (1.129), "arch-fiend" (1.156), "lost archangel" (1.243). His second-in-command (rather than an alternative name for himself) is Beelzebub (1.81), who is himself a "fallen cherub" (1.157).

Satan has no interest in repenting from his rebellion (1.94–96; contrast 4.32–113), which he perpetrated "from sense of injured merit" (1.98). He now wants to grieve God (1.167), see "how we may henceforth most offend / Our enemy" (1.187–88). Now he counsels his army that they should "work in close design, by fraud or guile / What force effected not" (1.646–47). That is, Satan has learned from the disastrous battle in heaven that he cannot defeat God by force of arms, so he devises other means: fraud or guile. Eventually the evil angels settle on the plan of tempting God's new favorite creature, mankind, into evil in order to pain God. Thus Satan became

> The tempter ere the accuser of mankind,
> To wreak on innocent frail man his loss
> Of that first battle, and his flight to hell. (4.10–12)

Milton presents a fascinating and compelling portrait of Satan, one based on a reconceiving of many biblical and postbiblical elements.[4] The depiction of Satan in *Paradise Lost*, at least in broad outline, is probably familiar to most of my readers, especially those with more than a passing interest in the Christian tradition. Milton did not invent the major aspects of the character Satan for *Paradise Lost*, and throughout this book we will find much in Jewish and Christian tradition with parallels to Milton's epic poem. To what extent is such a depiction of Satan found in Christian Scripture? That question proves challenging to address, both because the Bible's depiction of Satan is often ambiguous and because this traditional portrait of Satan has exerted an enormous influence on Christian readings of Scripture. Something like Milton's mature Satan has long featured in popular accounts of the nature of evil within Christianity and has become established doctrine in some circles.

The *Catechism of the Catholic Church* (1997), easily found online, provides an interesting point of comparison. Under the heading "The Fall of Angels," we find the following description:[5]

> (391) Behind the disobedient choice of our first parents lurks a seductive voice, opposed to God, which makes them fall into death out of envy [Gen. 3:1–5; Wisd. of Sol. 2:24]. Scripture and the Church's Tradition see in this being a fallen angel, called "Satan" or the "devil" [John 8:44; Rev. 12:9]. The Church teaches that Satan was at first a good angel, made by God: "The devil and the other demons were indeed created naturally good by God,

---

[4]Evans, *Paradise Lost and the Genesis Tradition.*

[5]§1.2.1.7.2. The online version is at https://www.vatican.va/archive/ENG0015/index.htm.

but they became evil by their own doing" [Lateran Council IV (1215)].[6]

(392) Scripture speaks of a sin of these angels [2 Pet. 2:4]. This "fall" consists in the free choice of these created spirits, who radically and irrevocably rejected God and his reign. We find a reflection of that rebellion in the tempter's words to our first parents: "You will be like God" [Gen. 3:5]. The devil "has sinned from the beginning"; he is "a liar and the father of lies" [1 John 3:8; John 8:44].

(393) It is the irrevocable character of their choice, and not a defect in the infinite divine mercy, that makes the angels' sin unforgivable. "There is no repentance for the angels after their fall, just as there is no repentance for men after death."[7]

(394) Scripture witnesses to the disastrous influence of the one Jesus calls "a murderer from the beginning," who would even try to divert Jesus from the mission received from his Father [John 8:44; cf. Matt. 4:1–11]. "The reason the Son of God appeared was to destroy the works of the devil" [1 John 3:8]. In its consequences the gravest of these works was the mendacious seduction that led man to disobey God.

(395) The power of Satan is, nonetheless, not infinite. He is only a creature, powerful from the fact that he is pure spirit, but still a creature. He cannot prevent the building up of God's reign. Although Satan may act in the world out of hatred for God and his kingdom in Christ Jesus, and although his action may cause grave injuries—of a spiritual nature and, indirectly, even of a physical nature—to each man and to society, the action is permitted by divine providence which with strength and gentleness guides human and cosmic history. It is a great mystery that providence should permit diabolical activity, but "we know that in everything God works for good with those who love him" [Rom. 8:28].

---

[6] See *Enchiridion Symbolorum*, ed. Denzinger and Huenermann, §800.

[7] John of Damascus, *On the Orthodox Faith* 2.4 (§18). For Greek text and another English translation, see John of Damascus, *On the Orthodox Faith*, trans. Russell, 104.

While the legend of Satan in the *Catechism* is not nearly as developed as in *Paradise Lost*, they share significant features. What elements do we see in this mature Satan legend? Satan is a fallen angel, and the snake in Genesis 3 was empowered or embodied by—or even identical to—Satan. On these two points, the *Catechism* agrees with *Paradise Lost* and with much Christian tradition. (I acknowledge that the wording of the *Catechism* is nuanced in regard to the identity of the snake of Genesis 3, speaking of a "reflection" of angelic rebellion in the words of the tempter.) *Paradise Lost* also depicts a Satan whose aim in tempting humans is to win revenge against God both for Satan's loss in his primordial war in heaven and for the supposed offense of commanding Satan to worship the Son. The *Catechism* also attributes the sin of the devil to envy (§391). We will find that Christian (and maybe Jewish) tradition posits—similar to *Paradise Lost*—that the original sin of Satan was pride and/or envy, though in these tellings, the object of Satan's envy was not Jesus.

Looking for these familiar elements of the mature Satan in the Christian Scriptures proves substantially more difficult, and we will see in this volume that the biblical account of Satan is open to multiple readings. The questions that people have often asked about Satan (regarding his origins, nature, motivations, etc.) are simply unaddressed in Scripture, at least in any direct way. The Christian tradition has supplied the answers, sometimes multiple answers to the same question.

Satan also has friends, and these friends form an essential element of the presentation of Satan wherever he appears. Satan would be much less intimidating if he did not have evil angels and demons under his control. Milton names many of these friends (e.g., Beelzebub), while the *Catechism* merely references them. Once again, passages in the Bible mention these spiritual beings but answer precious few of our questions about their origins and nature. Might it be, indeed, that demons are identical to the evil angels, another name for the same beings? Such has been a common thought in Christian history. What does the Bible say? And if these ideas are not in the Bible, where did they come from?

PLAN FOR THE BOOK

Most of this book concerns the Hebrew Bible and the history of its interpretation, including its interpretation in the New Testament. One of the points I will argue is that the evil spirits familiar to readers of the New Testament do not make any explicit appearances in the Hebrew Bible. This "Satan-minimalism," as I labeled my position in the preface, is, perhaps, somewhat unusual in the long Christian tradition of biblical interpretation, but it is the consensus opinion—or nearly so—among modern biblical scholars. (There is some discussion among biblical scholars as to whether the wicked Satan appears, e.g., in 1 Chron. 21:1.) If my position is distinctive among biblical scholars, it is probably in pushing my Satan-minimalism somewhat further than usual by claiming that the New Testament authors likewise did not (necessarily) find the wicked Satan in the Jewish Scriptures.

We start not with Satan but with God, or with divine beings. Chapters One and Two introduce readers to what has become over the last few decades a well-accepted aspect of ancient Israelite conceptions of the divine: the existence of multiple divine beings (gods) and the convocation of a council of the gods—usually, or always, presided over by the Israelite God, YHWH. It must be admitted that ancient Hebrew literature does not provide such explicit and sustained depictions of the divine council as does the literature of other cultures, yet the literature of these other cultures has enabled biblical scholars to recognize the brief descriptions of, or allusions to, the divine council in the Hebrew Bible. We will find in these chapters that while these concepts may seem new and strange to modern Bible readers, ancient Jewish and Christian readers sometimes acknowledged the Bible's depictions of multiple gods and an assembly of gods. These ancient readers also regarded some of the gods as having a special relationship to the non-Israelite nations, the subject of our Chapter Three. By surveying some important elements of ancient Hebrew thought on supernatural beings, including possible rebellion or insubordination on the part of some supernatural beings, these chapters will prepare us to consider the role of harmful or evil spirits in Israelite theology.

Chapter Four still does not treat the character of Satan but other spiritual beings mentioned in the Hebrew Bible as agents of the Israelite God, even though these beings bring harm upon people. One of the more familiar examples here is the so-called evil spirit sent by YHWH upon King Saul in the wake of Saul's rebellion against YHWH. This spirit torments Saul in some way, and the king can find relief only through listening to music, particularly via the harp of a young man named David. The job of such spirits employed by God was essentially to bring punishment on sinful people.

In this context, Chapter Five explores the Hebrew term *satan*. Though this term is often translated as a proper name, Satan, in a few passages of the Old Testament (Job 1–2; Zech. 3; 1 Chron. 21:1), I argue—in harmony with many biblical scholars—that the term is never a proper name in the Hebrew Bible and, indeed, never refers to a wicked being at all. Sometimes the Hebrew Bible applies the term *satan* to human beings, sometimes to spiritual beings that are clearly working for YHWH (such as the angel of the Lord), and sometimes—I argue—to a harmful spirit sent from God like those treated in Chapter Four. In other words, the being called *satan* in Job 1–2 is a willing servant of YHWH.

Chapter Six turns to the New Testament, and here we do meet a spiritual enemy of God. The Greek New Testament adopts the Hebrew word *satan* to name this being, the *satanas* (with a Greek ending), still probably not used as a proper name. The *satanas* tempts and torments people, and he has at his disposal a band of demons and wicked angels. Humans who reject Jesus are destined to be punished along with Satan and his spiritual allies.

What are the origins of this Satan that we meet in the New Testament? Why does he care to tempt and torment people? While these questions have ready answers in postbiblical Christian tradition, Chapter Seven shows that Jewish literature from the Second Temple period does not present a coherent portrait of Satan that could have been presupposed by the authors of the New Testament. Are there not passages in the Old Testament that supply answers? Christian tradition routinely interprets the snake of Genesis 3 as an agent or embodiment of Satan; surely this story supplies some clues as to the origins and motivations of Satan? Or what about Ezekiel 28 and Isaiah 14, prophetic oracles that have for many centuries been interpreted as describing the fall of Satan? Chapter Eight investigates the history of interpretation of these passages, showing that they are all subject to alternative explanations and that they were, in fact, not perceived as descriptions of Satan until (probably) the second century AD or later.

Having dealt with Satan over a series of chapters, we turn next to his friends. Chapters Nine and Ten treat in succession the wicked angels and the demons. Aside from the bare mention of evil angels in the New Testament, the Christian Bible has little to tell us about these beings—unless, that is, the odd paragraph at the start of Genesis 6 has something to do with them. Chapter Nine covers the ancient interpretations of the marriages between the sons of God and the daughters of men, as narrated in Genesis 6:1–4, along with the simultaneous appearance of the Nephilim. While the most common interpretation of this difficult pericope involves sinful angels, I argue that the Christian Scriptures do not really point in this direction, though they do allow for it.

The New Testament has a great deal more to say about demons, at least their activities if not their origins, which is the subject of Chapter Ten. We find that demons are not unique to the Bible, being a common trait of many cultures, a fact that in some ways increases the difficulty of determining what the biblical authors may have thought about them.

The final, brief chapter reminds readers of the biblical mandates to fear God and not wicked spiritual powers. While, according to the Bible, these wicked forces do have power, and they did have the ability to harass people, as attested in the New Testament, they have been defeated, "disarmed" (Col. 2:15), through the crucifixion of the messiah. While Paul charges Christians to be aware of the spiritual war in which they find themselves, the apostle's battle instructions amount to practicing the spiritual disciplines of prayer and meditation on Scripture, along with living out the message of Jesus (righteousness, peace), in addition to maintaining faith in the One who guarantees the victory (Eph. 6:10–20). The essential message of the gospel is the proclamation Jesus left to his apostles following his resurrection and thus his decisive conquest of all rulers and authorities: "All authority in heaven and on earth has been given to me" (Matt. 28:18).

CHAPTER ONE

YHWH AND OTHER ELOHIM

What are human beings that you are mindful of them,
mortals that you care for them?
Yet you have made them a little lower than God,
and crowned them with glory and honor.

—Ps. 8:4–5

What are human beings that you are mindful of them,
or mortals, that you care for them?
You have made them for a little while lower than the angels;
you have crowned them with glory and honor.

—Heb. 2:6–7

The writer of Hebrews quoted Psalm 8, where the psalmist had marveled at the lofty position God had granted humans. According to the quotation in Hebrews, God has made humans "lower than the angels." The epistle to the Hebrews was written in the Greek language (as is the entire New Testament), and so it quoted the Greek translation (the Septuagint, or LXX) of the Psalms, which used the word "angels" (ἄγγελοι, *angeloi*) at Psalm 8:5. But the Hebrew text uses the word *elohim* (אֱלֹהִים), usually translated "God" or "god." That's why the NRSV (quoted above) translates the Hebrew text of Psalm 8:5, "You have made them a little lower than God [*elohim*]." In other words, the Hebrew text of Psalm 8:5 says that humans are a little lower than *elohim*, and when this verse was translated into Greek (the LXX), the Greek translation said that humans were lower than *angeloi* (angels), and it is this Greek translation that the author of Hebrews quoted at Hebrews 2:7. Did the LXX mistranslate the Hebrew text? Did Hebrews quote from a mistranslation?

No, that is not the best way of understanding what is happening in these texts. It is better to say that the translator(s) of the Greek Psalter interpreted the *elohim* at Psalm 8:5 not as a reference to YHWH, the God of Israel, but rather to other spiritual beings.[1] This example helps us to see that the Hebrew word *elohim* does not always mean "God" (capitalized). We usually translate this word as "God," as in Genesis 1:1, "In the beginning, God [*elohim*] created the heavens and the earth." But *elohim* can mean other things as well.[2] In English, we use the term "god" (lowercase) to refer to pagan gods, not just the God worshiped by Jews and Christians. In Hebrew, it is the same: *elohim* can mean God or gods. Our use of capitalization to distinguish these two words (God and gods) has no parallel in Hebrew, with its single set of letters (no capitalization), so the word *elohim* looks the same either way.

Let's think for a moment what we mean by "gods." Most people these days do not countenance the existence of these gods, but we frequently use the term when talking about the Greco-Roman gods (Zeus, Hera, Apollo, etc.) or the ancient Near Eastern gods (Baal, Asherah, Marduk, etc.). What do we mean when we use the word "gods" in this way? In the ancient Greco-Roman mind, or the ancient Near Eastern mind, what distinguished Zeus or Baal from a human being? What made them "gods"? We can think of a few characteristics that ancient people attributed to these gods. Zeus and Baal were very powerful—not all-powerful, but quite powerful.[3] They

---

[1]For more on the LXX and its use in early Christian literature, see Gallagher, *Translation of the Seventy*.

[2]See Clines, *Dictionary of Classical Hebrew*, 1:384–96, where different definitions include "other god(s)," "images," "divine being, god, deity," "ghost," "perh. household gods," and "perh. Judges, rulers."

[3]Irenaeus, *Against the Heresies* 2.5.4, at the end of the second century AD, noted that a god who is subject to fate is not an omnipotent god like the one described in the Christian Bible, and he cited *Iliad* 4.43 as demonstrating the power of fate over Zeus.

did not live on earth but somewhere in the sky, or at least on a very tall mountain that reaches to the skies (Mt. Olympus). And they were immortal, not subject to death.

Those characteristics again: very powerful (but not all-powerful), not terrestrial but heavenly (they don't live on earth), and immortal. Do these characteristics apply to anything in the Christian Scriptures? Certainly, and Christians usually call them "angels." From this perspective, you could call angels a type of god, and Augustine in the fifth century recognized that the angels were called "gods" by the Platonists.[4] After all, what distinguishes Zeus (as depicted in ancient Greek literature) from the archangel Michael (as depicted in ancient Jewish and Christian literature)? Well, Michael doesn't receive worship, and he conducts his affairs under the authority of YHWH, but other than those two points, they are pretty similar: very powerful, heavenly, immortal.[5] And in fact, the Hebrew Bible occasionally uses the term *elohim* in reference to what modern believers would probably call angels: supernatural beings in the service of YHWH. Apparently, that is the reason the LXX translated the word *elohim* in Psalm 8:5 as "angels," and that's why some modern English translations (like the ESV) render *elohim* in that verse as "heavenly beings."[6]

The main point right now is that the Hebrew Bible applies the word "god" (*elohim*) sometimes to beings other than YHWH, the God who created heaven and earth. Actually, maybe we shouldn't translate *elohim* as "god" but rather as "supernatural being" or something like that. "In the beginning, the supernatural being created the heavens and the earth"—not a very attractive translation, but possibly more accurate. Modern believers

[4]Augustine, *City of God* 12.25; Sommer, *Bodies of God*, 146–47: "It is thus appropriate to term the supreme being the one God and the other heavenly beings gods or angels." Sommer attributes to the thirteenth-century Jewish scholar Nachmanides the recognition of this basic point. For an example from Nachmanides, see below at note 15.

[5]Even Zeus was not considered all-powerful (see Sommer, *Bodies of God*, 170), and gods sometimes die (such as Tiamat in the Babylonian Enuma Elish).

[6]This terminological shift from "gods" (*elohim*) to "angels" was happening already at the time of the Greek translation in the third century BC. The third-century AD writer Origen recognized that angels are sometimes called "gods" in the Bible; see his *Against Celsus* 5.4. See also the discussion in Haring, "Origen and the Council of YHWH," 482–85.

might not like to talk about multiple gods in the Bible, but usually they would acknowledge the depiction of multiple supernatural beings in the Bible. From this perspective, YHWH would be one of the *elohim*, in fact, the most powerful (all-powerful) and only eternal *elohim*, the one *elohim* that created all the other *elohim*.

A COUPLE OF HEBREW WORDS: ELOHIM AND ELIM

Let's review the two Hebrew words that are primarily translated "God" or "god" or "gods."

El (אֵל) and Its Plural Elim (אֵלִים)

This word appears 240 times in the Hebrew Bible and a whole bunch of times outside the Bible (e.g., over five hundred times in the Dead Sea Scrolls). It can refer to YHWH, as in the compound term *El Shaddai*, often translated "God Almighty," but *el* can refer to YHWH without the addition of *Shaddai*. *El* can also refer to pagan gods (e.g., Deut. 32:12; Ps. 44:21). In Exodus 34:14, *el* appears twice, once in reference to YHWH and once in reference to other gods: "You shall worship no other *el*, because YHWH . . . is a jealous *El*." The LXX usually translates *el* with *theos* ("god"), but not always.[7] There was also a god named El acknowledged at Ugarit as the king of the gods.[8]

Eloah (אֱלוֹהַ) and Its Much More Common Plural Elohim (אֱלֹהִים)

The singular appears in the Hebrew Bible fifty-seven times—the vast majority in the book of Job—and only a handful of times in the Dead Sea Scrolls. The plural appears in the Hebrew Bible more than 2,600 times and more than two hundred times in the Dead Sea Scrolls. *Eloah* (the singular) usually refers to YHWH (Deut. 32:15; Ps.114:7) but can refer to a pagan god (Dan. 11:39).

In the Hebrew Bible, *elohim* also usually refers to YHWH, even though it is plural in form and YHWH is singular. This is strange, and I don't have a great explanation for it. Maybe the plural *elohim* refers to the singular

---

[7] Herrmann, "El," *DDD*, 274–75.

[8] For texts in translation and an introductory discussion, see Coogan and Smith, *Stories from Ancient Canaan*.

YHWH because *elohim* emphasizes the majesty or power of God?[9] Despite a common Christian interpretation of this use of the plural, the explanation for it is probably not that YHWH is Trinity, because the Israelites most likely did not understand their God in this way. At any rate, when *elohim* refers to YHWH in the Hebrew Bible, it takes a singular verb. We can compare the English sentence "The deer is eating acorns"; the fact that the verb used is "is eating" tells you that the word "deer" (which can be singular or plural) must be singular here. We could also say "The deer are eating acorns" for multiple deer. Likewise, the Hebrew verb form, in certain contexts, tells us that *elohim* (even though it looks plural) must be functioning as a singular noun. For instance, "In the beginning *Elohim* created the heavens and the earth" has a grammatically singular Hebrew verb translated "created."

Just to cover all my bases, let me acknowledge that occasionally in the Hebrew Bible a plural verb is used with *elohim* even when the reference is YHWH.[10] Maybe these plural verbal forms are just instances of mistakes in the transmission of the texts.[11] When *elohim* refers to pagan gods, one would imagine that a plural verb should be used (such as at Judg. 2:12), showing that the word should be translated "gods" (plural), but occasionally a singular verb is used (Judg. 11:24; 1 Kings 11:5, 11:33).

ELOHIM/ELIM THAT ARE NOT YHWH

Even though *elohim* almost always refers to YHWH and is translated "God," there are instances in the Bible where *elohim* or *el*(*im*) does not refer to

---

[9] See Kautzsch and Cowley, *Gesenius' Hebrew Grammar*, 398–99, §124g.

[10] Gen. 20:13, 31:53, 35:7; Deut. 5:23; 1 Sam. 17:26, 17:36, 28:13; 2 Sam. 7:23; Jer. 10:10, 23:36. A plural participle is used for God at Ps. 58:11. (Possibly, Gen. 31:53 was intended as a plural, as spoken by the Aramaean Laban; Hendel, "God and the Gods in the Tetrateuch," 246.) On the interpretation of this phenomenon in rabbinic literature, see Segal, *Two Powers in Heaven*, ch. 8, who lists (pp. 128–29) the following passages as particularly problematic for the rabbis, and then goes on to discuss them: Gen. 1:1, 1:26, 11:5, 19:24, 35:5; Deut. 4:7; 2 Sam. 7:23; Dan. 7:9; Josh. 22:22, 24:19; Ps. 50:1.

[11] See David P. Wright, *Inventing God's Law*, 463 n. 78.

YHWH. We have seen an instance in which the LXX translates *elohim* as "angels" (Ps. 8:5). Take a look at the following passages:[12]

> Ascribe to YHWH, O sons of *elim*,
> ascribe to YHWH glory and strength.
> Ascribe to YHWH the glory of his name;
> worship YHWH in holy splendor. (Ps. 29:1–2)

> Let the heavens praise your wonders, O YHWH,
> your faithfulness in the assembly of the holy ones [בִּקְהַל קְדֹשִׁים].
> For who in the skies can be compared to YHWH?
> Who among the sons of *elim* is like YHWH,
> an *El* feared in the council of the holy ones [בְּסוֹד־קְדֹשִׁים],
> great and awesome above all that are around him?
> (Ps. 89:5–7)

> Who is like you, YHWH, among the *elim*? (Exod. 15:11)

> What *el* in heaven or on earth can perform deeds and mighty acts like yours? (Deut. 3:24)

> O YHWH, *elohim* of Israel, there is no *elohim* like you in heaven above or on earth beneath. (1 Kings 8:23)

> For YHWH is a great *el*,
> and a great King above all *elohim*. (Ps. 95:3)

> For you, O YHWH, are most high over all the earth;
> you are exalted far above all *elohim*. (Ps. 97:9)

> The king said to her, "Have no fear; what do you see?" The woman said to Saul, "I see *elohim* coming up out of the ground." (1 Sam. 28:13)[13]

---

[12]For these references and more like them, see Clines, *Dictionary of Classical Hebrew*, 1.352, "אֵל," definition 1a, "god."

[13]This verse is the single example given for the meaning "ghost" in Clines, *Dictionary of Classical Hebrew*, 1.395, "אֱלֹהִים," definition 3b.

That's enough for now. I would not pretend that the interpretation of these passages is simple, or that it's easy to get inside the mind of the ancient Israelites who composed these texts or read them. But, at least on the face of it, it seems that the Bible uses the words *elohim* and *el(im)* for more beings than just YHWH. It has long been recognized that the first of the Ten Commandments, "You shall have no other *elohim* before me" (Exod. 20:3), implies the existence of other *elohim*, or, at least, does not explicitly deny their existence.[14] The thirteenth-century Jewish scholar Nachmanides commented on this verse: "The correct interpretation, even according to the straightforward sense of the text, is that none of the angels or the divine host of heaven are to be our gods."[15]

Christians have traditionally understood that angels were sometimes called "gods" or "sons of God," as the fourth-century Latin writer Jerome said in reference to the fourth person in the fiery furnace of Daniel 3 (see Dan. 3:25).[16] Much later, in *Paradise Lost,* Milton represented God the Father as addressing his heavenly host as "gods" (3.341). Already in the second century AD, Irenaeus felt compelled to issue a caution about such language.

> When, however, Scripture calls those gods who really are not, it does not, as I have already noted, present them as gods absolutely, but with certain modification and indication by which they are shown not to be gods. Thus does David say, *The gods of the nations are idols of the demons* [Ps. 96:5].[17] And, *You shall not bow down to foreign gods* [Ps. 81:10].[18]

Here Irenaeus was concerned to argue against a gnostic theology that posited multiple gods as worthy of our attention, as helpful to directing us

---

[14] For a discussion, see von Rad, *Old Testament Theology*, 1.210–11.

[15] Translation in Carasik, *Commentators' Bible: Exodus*, 157.

[16] Jerome, *Commentary on Daniel*, trans. Archer, 43–44.

[17] Steenberg, who supplied the notes for this translation of Irenaeus (see next note), points out (p. 135 n. 22) that "idols" does not appear in the Hebrew or Greek of the Psalm, but it does appear in Justin, *Dialogue* 55.2, 73.2; *1 Apol.* 4.11 (but not *Dialogue* 73.3, 79.4, 83.4).

[18] Irenaeus, *Against the Heresies* 3.6.3, trans. Unger.

spiritually. He asserted that these other gods mentioned in the Bible were not really gods (though he did not define what they were).[19] Irenaeus's point was that the gnostics were wrong: "There is no other God, nor another Father, nor Profundity [*bythos*], nor Fullness [*Pleroma*] of thirty Aeons, nor Mother called Ogdoad" (3.10.3)—all these being gnostic names for different divine beings.

Another Christian who commented on the varying scriptural uses of the word "god" was Origen in the third century.

> To take another example, the word "God" is used primarily of Him of whom are all things, and by whom are all things, and in whom are all things [cf. 1 Cor. 8:6; Rom. 11:36]; so that it declares plainly the virtue and nature of the Trinity. But by a secondary and so to speak improper usage Scripture describes as gods those to whom the word of God came, as the Saviour affirms in the Gospels [cf. John 10:34; Ps. 82]. And the heavenly powers also seem to be called by this name when it is said: God hath stood in the congregation of gods; and, being in the midst of them, He judgeth gods [Ps. 82:1]. And by a third usage, false rather than improper, the daemonic gods of the Gentiles are so styled when Scripture says: All the gods of the Gentiles are devils [Ps. 96:5].[20]

I have already suggested that we might want to translate *elohim* as "supernatural being(s)" rather than "god(s)." The biblical scholar Jon Levenson suggests that the word *elohim* "functions like the English word *spirit*, which can denote anything from God to an angel, a demon, a ghost, a tone of an organization, or an alcoholic beverage."[21]

---

[19] Irenaeus, *Against the Heresies* 3.6.3–5.

[20] Origen, *Commentary on the Song of Songs*, prologue, trans. Lawson, 34–35. On Ps. 96:5, see also Origen, *Homilies on Numbers* 27.8.

[21] Levenson, *Resurrection and the Restoration*, 57.

What about the statements in the Bible that seem to deny the existence of *elohim* other than YHWH?[22] For example:

> YHWH is the *elohim*; there is no other besides him. (Deut. 4:35; see also v. 39)
>
> There is no *elohim* beside me. (Deut. 32:39)

Despite appearances, these statements probably do not intend to deny the existence of *elohim* besides YHWH; rather, these statements exalt YHWH above all other *elohim*. Compare Babylon's claim that "there is no one besides me" (Isa. 47:8, 10); it is unlikely that the city of Babylon intended this boast to communicate that no other cities existed, but only that no other city compared favorably to Babylon. Same thing for Nineveh (Zeph. 2:15). Same thing for YHWH. The other *elohim* are not comparable to YHWH. He alone is "God of gods" (Deut. 10:17). The other gods, in fact, do not deserve that label at all (Deut. 32:17, 21), for they are mere "breaths" or "puffs of air" (Deut. 32:21).[23]

Later Jewish authors sometimes used this terminology in the same way we have seen in the Bible. One interesting text from the Dead Sea Scrolls (11Q13) conceives of Melchizedek (see Gen. 14:18; Ps. 110:4) as a heavenly being, something like an angel. This exaltation of Melchizedek supplies interesting material for comparison with the description of Melchizedek in Hebrews 7. This Dead Sea Scroll interprets Psalm 82 in

---

[22] See also Isa. 43:10–12, 44:6, 45:5, 45:21–22, 46:9; cf. 2 Sam. 22:32 // Ps. 18:32; 2 Sam. 7:22; 1 Kings 8:60; Hosea 13:4; Jer. 2:28, 11:13. (In this book, I use // to indicate parallel passages in the Gospels.) Some scholars read these texts as denying the existence of other *elohim*; see Friedman, *Exodus*, 149–61, but he seems to be working with a stricter definition of *elohim*. For a better interpretation, see Bauckham, "Biblical Theology and the Problems of Monotheism," in *Jesus and the God of Israel*, 60–106, esp. 68–71. Other cultures sometimes said similar things about their favored gods, without any implication that these cultures denied the existence of other gods aside from their favored one; see Sommer, *Bodies of God*, 160–63.

[23] The Hebrew word here is *hebel*, the same word translated "vanity" in Ecclesiastes and in the King James Version of Deut. 32:21 (the ESV uses "idols" for this latter verse). As some of these verses indicate, there are passages in Scripture that seem less ready to use the label *elohim* for beings other than YHWH. Such reticence has been suggested, for example, in regard to Isaiah and Ezekiel; see Lynch, *First Isaiah*, 15–16.

terms of Melchizedek, so that Melchizedek is called *elohim* and passes judgment on other *elohim*. (I discuss Psalm 82 in Chapter Three.)

In the New Testament, Paul talks about "so-called gods" (λεγόμενοι θεοί) at 1 Corinthians 8:5–6. Paul does not mean to deny the existence of a spiritual reality called "god"; he just means to say that they are misnamed.[24] He does not mean that there is only one θεός ("god") and one κύριος ("lord") in existence, but only one of each that Christian believers care about, that are "for us" (ἡμῖν). "Paul is not saying that God and Christ are worthy of devotion by virtue of the fact that they exist."[25] That is, it is not mere existence that sets apart the Christian God and Christian Lord from others; the reason Paul emphasizes that God the Father and Jesus the Lord are worthy of worship is because they are "for us," because of their love for believers. Paul may be relying on concepts reflected also in Psalm 96:5 (LXX 95:5), which describes the pagan gods (*elohim* in Hebrew, *theoi* in the LXX) as "idols" (*eliylim* in Hebrew) or, in the LXX, "demons" (*daimonia*). In Chapter Three, we will look at the relationship between these other *elohim* and the nations. For now we can simply note that Paul writes as if the gods of foreign nations (Zeus, etc.) have a real, demonic power behind them (cf. 1 Cor. 10:20–21).

YHWH AS THE CHIEF AND CREATOR OF THE ELOHIM

Is this monotheism? Is the Bible a monotheistic book? Is biblical religion monotheistic? It depends on what you mean by monotheism.[26] The complications in that term and concept are now well-known to biblical scholars. One example is Richard Bauckham:

> The essential element in what I have called Jewish monotheism, the element that makes it a kind of monotheism, is not the denial of the existence of other "gods," but an understanding of the uniqueness of YHWH that puts him in a class of his own, a

[24] I am following the interpretation of Williams, *Spirit World*, 153–55.

[25] Williams, *Spirit World*, 154.

[26] A helpful study of the various ways the Hebrew Bible presents YHWH in relation to other *elohim* is Lynch, "Mapping Monotheism."

> wholly different class from any other heavenly or supernatural beings, even if these are called "gods."[27]

Bauckham goes on to identify the "transcendent uniqueness" of YHWH in the following ways: "YHWH alone is Creator of all things, whereas all other things are created by him; YHWH alone is the sovereign Lord of all things, whereas all other things serve or are subject to his universal lordship."

According to Job 38:7, at the creation of the world, "the morning stars sang together and all the sons of *elohim* shouted for joy." In my experience, Christian believers have been happy to interpret the "sons of *elohim*" as "angels," and, in fact, this interpretation is found already in the LXX ("all my angels"). The nearly identical Hebrew phrase (sons of the *elohim*) is used in Job 1:6 and 2:1, where the Septuagint translated it both times as "angels of God."[28] If we accept that the "sons of *elohim*" at Job 38:7 are angels, notice what angels are also called in this verse: "morning stars."

Sometimes the heavenly bodies (stars and such) are represented as supernatural beings (*elohim*, or sons of *elohim*). Or maybe we should reverse that equation: Supernatural beings were sometimes described as if they were stars.[29] This identification of celestial bodies with living supernatural beings is well-known outside ancient Israel. Different cultures in the ancient world attributed divine status to the sun and moon.[30] Most readers will know that the ancient Egyptians worshiped the sun.[31] Plato called the stars "the heavenly kind of gods."[32] In Plato's telling, Socrates

---

[27] Bauckham, *Jesus and the God of Israel*, 86.

[28] The slight difference between the Hebrew wording of Job 38:7 and Job 1:6 and 2:1 is that *elohim* has a definite article ("the") at 1:6 and 2:1 but not at 38:7. The equation of "Son of God" with "angel" is also made by the writer of Dan. 3 (see vv. 25 and 28) and at 1 En. 19.1.

[29] For an interesting argument that Jesus in Mark 12:25 refers to this idea in connection with God's promise to Abraham in Gen. 15:5, see Thiessen, "Buried Pentateuchal Allusion."

[30] For this sort of thing among Israel's neighbors, see Smith, *Origins of Biblical Monotheism*, 61–66. The notion that the stars are divinities was attacked on scientific grounds by John Philoponus in the sixth century AD (*De Opificio Mundi* 6.2). See Scott, *Origen and the Life of the Stars*.

[31] See Assmann, "Re," *DDD*, 689–92.

[32] Plato, *Timaeus* 40a, οὐράνιον θεῶν γένος, trans. R. G. Bury in Plato, *Timaeus, Critias, Cleitophon, Menexenus, Epistles*, 83. Augustine, *City of God* 13.16, notes this opinion of Plato's but refuses to discuss the matter.

defended himself against the charge that he did not believe in the gods by asking rhetorically, "Do I not even believe that the sun or yet the moon are gods, as the rest of mankind do?"[33]

Such concepts are reflected in some biblical passages. Sometimes the biblical authors condemn Israelites for participating in the worship of celestial bodies (as we will see below). But there are also passages in which the biblical authors reflect this notion that the celestial bodies are divine beings of some sort.

> You are YHWH, you alone; you have made heaven, the heaven of heavens, with all their host, the earth and all that is on it, the seas and all that is in them. To all of them you give life, and the host of heaven worships you. (Neh. 9:6)

The host of heaven worships God. Are we talking about living beings here? Apparently, since God makes them live ("To all of them you give life"). The heavenly host, the sun and moon and stars, are represented as living beings that worship YHWH. They are supernatural beings. YHWH created them and receives their praise.

> Praise YHWH!
> Praise YHWH from the heavens;
>   praise him in the heights!
> Praise him, all his angels;
>   praise him, all his host!
>
> Praise him, sun and moon,
>   praise him, all you shining stars!
> Praise him, you highest heavens,
>   and you waters above the heavens!
>
> Let them praise the name of YHWH,
>   for he commanded and they were created. (Ps. 148:1–5)

[33] Socrates, in Plato, *Apology* 26d, in the translation of Harold North Fowler, *Plato*, vol. 1, 99. See also, e.g., Plato, *Republic* 508a, where the sun is called one of "the gods in heaven" (ίοεθ ῷναρὺο νὲ ίο).

Perhaps the biblical authors are just borrowing the common language of celestial bodies as divine in order to exalt YHWH. In the New Testament, when we read that Jesus is the morning star (2 Pet. 1:19; Rev. 22:16), it seems unlikely that this equation was supposed to communicate that the morning star was, in fact, Jesus. Yet the Jewish philosopher Philo, contemporary with the New Testament, did state that "the stars are souls divine."[34] Whatever the biblical authors thought about these ideas, the point I want to make right now is that this language about stars and the other celestial bodies sometimes refers to angels or spiritual beings, so that when the Bible says that God created the heavenly bodies, one thing such an assertion means is that God is the creator and ruler of the other *elohim*. Even though there may be other *elohim* besides YHWH, there is no creator besides YHWH.

Deuteronomy forbids Israel from "going to serve other *elohim* and worshiping them—whether the sun or the moon or any of the host of heaven" (Deut. 17:3). According to Jeffrey Tigay,

> Heavenly bodies were worshiped in Syria and Canaan before the Israelites settled in Canaan. The practice became especially prevalent in Judah during the seventh century B.C.E., during the reign of Manasseh, as a form of assimilation to the Assyrian-Aramaean culture of the Assyrian empire.[35]

Tigay has in mind passages like 2 Kings 21, which describes Manasseh, king of Judah: "He also bowed in worship to all the stars in the sky and served them. . . . He built altars to all the stars in the sky in both courtyards of YHWH's temple" (2 Kings 21:3, 5 CSB). Later, Josiah (Manasseh's grandson) destroyed these altars, at which point the author of the Kings narrative reported, "They had burned incense to Baal, and to the sun, moon, constellations, and all the stars in the sky" (2 Kings 23:5 CSB; cf. v. 12). At the same time that Josiah was reforming Judah's worship, Jeremiah announced punishment: "They will be exposed to the sun, the moon, and all the stars in the sky, which they have loved, served, followed, consulted, and worshiped" (Jer. 8:2 CSB). These Judeans had "burned incense to all the stars in the sky

[34] Philo, *On the Giants* 8, trans. Colson and Whitaker, 2:449.

[35] Tigay, *Deuteronomy*, 162. On worship in Canaan before the emergence of Israel, see Susnow, *Practice of Canaanite Cult*.

and poured out drink offerings to other *elohim*" (Jer. 19:13 CSB). Jeremiah's contemporary Zephaniah also criticized "those who bow in worship on the rooftops to the stars in the sky" (Zeph. 1:5 CSB). About a decade later, Ezekiel witnessed people at the entrance to the temple "bowing to the east in worship of the sun" (Ezek. 8:16 CSB).

These concepts might have influenced the way the account of creation is presented in Genesis 1. Despite the repeated representation of God naming different natural phenomena in that text (see vv. 5, 8, 10, etc.), the words "sun" and "moon" never appear in the chapter (vv. 14–19). They are just called "lights," and God establishes them for the purpose of marking time. Scholars often propose that this refusal to so much as name the great lights in the creation account stands as a polemic against worshipers of the sun and moon.[36]

All that to say: Many ancient Israelites and Judeans reflected their cultural environment in that they regarded the celestial bodies as divine beings worthy of worship (against the biblical mandate). And sometimes the Bible uses similar terminology—or, perhaps, reverses it—by describing angels or divine beings as stars. But the biblical writers promoted the idea that these other supernatural beings were subordinate to YHWH, who was/is in fact the God of these beings.

> For YHWH your *elohim* is *elohim* of *elohim* and Lord of lords,
> the great *El*, mighty and awesome. (Deut. 10:17)

CONCLUSION

What I have tried to establish in this chapter is that, according to the Bible, YHWH is not the only "god" around—not the only supernatural being, not the only *elohim*—and that ancient Jews and Christians recognized that the Bible used the term *elohim* in this manner. In the twenty-first century, Christian believers would probably refer to these other supernatural beings as angels, and the Hebrew Bible does so frequently (using the term *malak*), but it also sometimes uses the word *elohim* for these other beings. These "angels" can, in a certain sense, be considered gods. They are similar

[36] Hendel, "God and the Gods," 256. Disputing this idea is Lynch, "Mapping Monotheism," 62 n. 48.

to YHWH in some ways in which they are unlike humans (their power, immortality, heavenly dwelling, spiritual nature), but they are also similar to humans in some ways in which they are not like YHWH—they are unable to create, and they are contingent beings. Only YHWH is creator, omnipotent, noncontingent. We see references to these other *elohim* not only when that particular Hebrew term is used, but also in some passages that indicate that the heavenly bodies (sun, moon, stars) are living creatures that receive (illicit) worship.

Now that we have laid the groundwork in this chapter, we can in the next chapter explore the concept of the Divine Council, an assembly of gods. We are familiar with this concept in pagan cultures, and scholars have identified passages in the Hebrew Bible that reflect similar beliefs, with (I think) an Israelite twist.

CHAPTER TWO

THE DIVINE COUNCIL

Have you listened in the council of God?

—Job 15:8

In 1 Kings 22, the prophet Micaiah reported to King Ahab a vision. This is the only chapter in the Bible that talks about Micaiah (aside from the parallel passage in 2 Chron. 18). Ahab, king of Israel, wanted Jehoshaphat, king of Judah, to join him in battle at a place called Ramoth-gilead. Ahab had a bunch of prophets tell him that this war was a great idea, that Israel would surely win a great victory (1 Kings 22:6), but Jehoshaphat realized somehow that none of these prophets really represented YHWH, so the kings summoned Micaiah to tell them what YHWH would say about the matter (vv. 7–9). Micaiah came to "the threshing floor at the entrance to the gate of Samaria" where Ahab and Jehoshaphat sat on their thrones (v. 10), and he eventually told the kings that this battle was a terrible idea, that it would result in the death of the king of Israel (v. 17). Then Micaiah described his vision.

> Hear the word of YHWH: I saw YHWH sitting on his throne, with all the host of heaven standing beside him to the right and to the left. And YHWH said, "Who will entice Ahab, so that he

> may go up and fall at Ramoth-gilead?" Then one said one thing, and another said another, until a spirit [*ruaḥ*] came forward and stood before YHWH, saying, "I will entice him." "How?" YHWH asked him. He replied, "I will go out and be a lying spirit in the mouth of all his prophets." Then YHWH said, "You are to entice him, and you shall succeed; go out and do it." So you see, YHWH has put a lying spirit in the mouth of all these your prophets; YHWH has decreed disaster for you. (1 Kings 22:19–23)

What sort of a scene in heaven does Micaiah describe here to Ahab and Jehoshaphat? YHWH is on a throne, "with all the host of heaven standing beside him." The scene is familiar even in the twenty-first century. We can imagine the US president sitting in a room with his cabinet gathered around him, or a CEO in a boardroom with a long, rectangular table, surrounded by people. YHWH is the chairman of the board, or the president, the ruler, and his cabinet is gathered before him.

A Christian believer may ask at this point, "What does God need with a cabinet? Are they his advisers? Does God need advice?" Ancient Jewish writers sometimes struggled with the same questions. The pseudepigraphic work known as 1 Enoch, in the section called the Book of the Watchers (written probably in the third century BC), describes a similar scene this way: "Ten thousand times ten thousand stood before him, but he needed no counselor" (1 En. 14.22).[1] Well, neither does the Bible say that God *needed* a counselor, but he did ask for one. Micaiah portrayed YHWH in council with his spiritual beings, "all the host of heaven," and he asked for their suggestions. Why did he ask for suggestions? I don't know; that's just how Micaiah reported the vision. I guess we could also ask: "Why does God create angels at all?" The answer is: to send on errands. "Why does he need to send them on errands? Couldn't he just do all the errands himself?" What can I say? That's the way he wants to do it. He doesn't want to do it all by himself.

Maybe Richard Bauckham can help.

[1] Nickelsburg and VanderKam, *1 Enoch*, 35.

> Within the Hebrew canon, most "gods" besides YHWH fall into one of two categories. They are either members of YHWH's retinue, serving his rule, or they are impotent nonentities. In the former case, they are called by a variety of terms (gods, sons of gods, sons of the Most High, holy ones, watchers, the host of YHWH, the host of heaven). They accompany YHWH as warriors or attendants, and they assemble in YHWH's presence in heaven. . . . Despite the rather misleading sense suggested by the commonly used English term "divine council," the assembly around YHWH are not counsellors. He does not consult them in an open decision-making process in which they contribute advice on which he acts. [Bauckham acknowledges Job 1–2 and 1 Kings 22:19–22 as partial exceptions.] . . . YHWH's retinue are the attendants of an absolute monarch.[2]

In this sense, the divine council gathers not for discussion but to hear the decrees of YHWH. That's not exactly the scene Micaiah describes (spirits do offer suggestions; they do not merely receive orders), but Micaiah's vision is unique in that respect. Micaiah's vision is not unique, though, in describing a divine council, an assembly of spiritual beings gathered around YHWH's throne in heaven.

Think about what's happening in heaven at the beginning of the book of Job. "One day the sons of the *elohim* came to present themselves before YHWH" (1:6). The same thing happens at the start of Job 2. Could we call this a meeting of the divine council? It looks like the same sort of thing that Micaiah describes. (We will talk about Satan in these chapters, but not yet.)

Let me just quote a few more verses about a divine council:

> Have you listened in the council [סוֹד, *sōd*] of *Eloah*?
> And do you limit wisdom to yourself? (Job 15:8)

> For who has stood in the council [*sōd*] of YHWH
> So as to see and to hear his word?
> Who has given heed to his word and so as to proclaim it?
> (Jer. 23:18)

[2] Bauckham, *Jesus and the God of Israel*, 88.

> But if they had stood in my council [*sōd*],
> then they would have proclaimed my words to my people.
> (Jer. 23:22)

Now look at this scene in Daniel:

> As I watched,
> thrones were set in place,
> and an Ancient One took his throne,
> his clothing was white as snow,
> and the hair of his head like pure wool;
> his throne was firey flames,
> and its wheels were burning fire.
> A stream of fire issued
> and flowed out from his presence.
> A thousand thousands served him,
> And ten thousand times ten thousand stood attending him.
> The court sat in judgment,
> and the books were opened. (Dan. 7:9–10)

It's the same kind of scene, isn't it? The boardroom is called a "court," and it must be bigger than we'd previously imagined, since there are "ten thousand times ten thousand" (same expression as at 1 En. 14.22, quoted earlier) standing before the Ancient of Days. But other than those details, it looks like the same kind of thing as described in Job and by Micaiah.

But not all of these many thousands of spiritual beings have the same role or status. The New Testament occasionally mentions "chief angels" or "archangels" (1 Thess. 4:16; Jude 9), and some ancient (non-biblical) sources also mention these chief angels and limit their number to just a few, so that you could count them on one or two hands. Not all of the ten thousands of angels seen by Daniel are in the inner circle; they're mostly just there to glorify God and be ready to carry out his bidding. A smaller number, the archangels, would be closer to the throne. Gabriel identifies himself to Zechariah the priest (father of John the Baptist) as one "who stands in the presence of God" (Luke 1:19 CSB). According to several ancient sources (mostly outside the Protestant Bible), there are seven of these archangels. The deuterocanonical book of Tobit has one of them say, "I am Raphael, one of the seven angels who stand ready and enter before the glory of the Lord" (Tob. 12:15 NRSVCE). According to this same passage, Raphael is the one who had taken Tobit's prayer before the Lord, and he was sent to give comfort, healing, and guidance to Tobit and his family. The book of Revelation reflects the idea of seven archangels: "I saw the seven angels who stand before God, and seven trumpets were given to them" (Rev. 8:2).[3]

In other places, especially in 1 Enoch, there are only four chief angels: Michael and Gabriel (both mentioned in Daniel; see 8:16; 9:21; 10:13, 21; 12:1), along with either Suriel and Uriel (1 En. 9.1) or Raphael and Phanuel (1 En. 40; 54.6; 71.9, 13) or Raphael and Sariel (War Scroll [1QM] 9.15–16). In the work known as 4 Ezra (late first century AD), there is an archangel named Jeremiel (4 Ezra 4.36). In the Christian work Epistle of the Apostles (second century AD), the four archangels are Michael, Gabriel, Uriel, and Raphael (§13).[4]

Whether four or seven, there is a small number of archangels making up God's council. 1 Enoch describes each of these archangels as having their own particular sphere of activity, as if they are department heads in the divine government.

> These are the names of the holy angels who watch. Uriel, one of the holy angels, who is in charge of the world and Tartarus. Raphael, one of the holy angels, who is in charge of the spirits of men. Reuel, one of the holy angels, who takes vengeance on the world of the luminaries. Michael, one of the holy angels, who has been put in charge of the good ones of the people. Sariel, one of the holy angels, who is in charge of the spirits who sin against the spirit. Gabriel, one of the holy angels, who is in charge of

[3] At *Paradise Lost* 3.648, Uriel is one of the seven archangels who stand in God's presence. (Uriel appears in ancient Jewish sources, as we will see.) There are also seven chief angels at 1 Enoch 87.2–3; at 81.5, though there is a textual difficulty regarding the number.

[4] For a translation, see, e.g., Gathercole, *Apocryphal Gospels*, 266.

> paradise and the serpents and the cherubim. Remiel, one of the holy angels, whom God has put in charge of them that rise. The names of the seven archangels. (1 En. 20.1–8)[5]

This division of government business among these seven archangels has some resonance with the book of Daniel, where Michael—in the words of the angel speaking to Daniel—is described as "the great prince who stands watch over your people" (Dan. 12:1 CSB). Michael is the archangel in charge of Israel, or, in the words of 1 Enoch 20.5, Michael is "in charge of the good ones of the people." Another passage in 1 Enoch depicts four chief angels (Michael, Raphael, Gabriel, Phanuel), each one doing a specific task, whether praising God or blessing "the Chosen One" or interceding on behalf of humans or blocking accusers (*satans*) from approaching God (1 En. 40.3–10).

To summarize: We see a divine council, a council of *elohim*, in the following biblical passages: 1 Kings 22:19–22; Job 1–2, 15:8; Psalm 82; Jeremiah 23:18–22; Daniel 7:9–10; and probably also Isaiah 6 and Revelation 4.[6] Similar ideas also appear in other ancient Jewish literature. One evangelical scholar has described the divine council as "God's original family and household."[7] But the Bible also reveals that God was not always happy with all the members of his council (in which case, probably, the members of the council are not thought of as the four or seven archangels). One of the primary passages for this idea is Psalm 82, which we will study in the next chapter. For now, let me just quote the first verse: "*Elohim* has taken his place in the council [עֵדָה, *ēdah*] of *el*; in the midst of the *elohim* he holds judgment."

THE PLURALS OF GENESIS AND ISAIAH

Think about these passages:

---

[5] Nickelsburg and VanderKam, 40–41. As the translators note, the Ethiopic text omits verse 8.

[6] Still other possible representations of the divine council are in Amos 3:7, Zech. 3, and Ps. 29:1-2.

[7] Heiser, *Unseen Realm*, 39.

> *Elohim* said, "Let us make humankind in our image, according to our likeness; and let them have dominion over the fish of the sea, and over the birds of the air, and over the cattle, and over all the wild animals of the earth, and over every creeping thing that creeps upon the earth." (Gen. 1:26)

> YHWH *Elohim* said, "See, the man has become like one of us, to know good and evil; and now, he might reach out his hand and take also from the tree of life, and eat, and live forever." (Gen. 3:22)

> Come, let us go down and confuse their language there, so that they will not understand one another's speech. (Gen. 11:7)

> I heard the voice of YHWH saying, "Whom shall I send, and who will go for us?" And I said, "Here am I; Send me!" (Isa. 6:8)

What are we to make of these plural pronouns, "Let us . . ."; "Who will go for us"? The usual idea I have heard among Christians is that the plural here refers to the Trinity, as if God the Father is speaking to the Son and the Spirit.[8] This view has impressive pedigree in Christian history. The fifth-century writer Theodoret, for instance, said: "Throughout the whole of holy Scripture, one can hear God speaking in the singular. But in a few cases, he uses plural forms to bring out the distinction of number of the persons of the Trinity."[9] This interpretation of the plurals is found already in the early post-New Testament period in the Epistle of Barnabas 5.5.[10]

But it is doubtful that an ancient Israelite reader would have understood this aspect of his or her God (i.e., that God is Trinity). No matter what was in the mind of the author, we should probably not think "Trinity"

[8] As an example from someone whose biblical interpretation has profoundly influenced my own church context, see Campbell, *Familiar*, 78, 85, 90.

[9] Theodoret, Question 19 on Genesis, in Theodoret of Cyrus, *Questions on the Octateuch*, 47.

[10] See also Justin Martyr, *Dialogue with Trypho* 62, who explicitly rejects the interpretation he attributes to Jews, that God was talking to angels. See also Irenaeus, *Demonstration of the Apostolic Preaching* 55; Tertullian, *Against Praxeas* 12. For an example from Augustine, see *Confessions* 13.22.32. More discussion in Earl, *Reading Old Testament Narrative*, ch. 8.

when we consider how the text would have been understood in ancient Israel. Ancient Jewish interpretations of these plurals took different paths.[11] For Philo, the plurals show that God is talking to his collaborators whose help he needs in the single instance of the creation of humans, because humans exhibit a mixed nature (good and evil), and God needs others to contribute the evil element.[12] Josephus, on the contrary, insisted that God did not use helpers in creation, though in his retelling of Genesis 1 he ignored the plurals.[13] But another common view among ancient Jews was that God spoke to angels. This is the view articulated in the book of Jubilees, a pseudepigraphic book found among the Dead Sea Scrolls.[14] The rabbis expressed various views,[15] but one of the Targums translates Genesis 1:26 this way: "And God said to the angels who minister before him, who were created on the second day of the creation of the world, Let us make man in our image, in our likeness."[16] Theodoret calls such an idea heretical,[17] but his predecessor Origen, perhaps uniquely among early Christian authors, also interpreted these plurals in terms of God speaking to angels.[18]

Scholars these days typically interpret these plurals in terms of the divine council.[19] When God says, "Let us," the "us" includes God with his council. This explanation bears a close affinity to that found in Jubilees and among some of the rabbis, such that God was addressing his angels. The creation passage (Gen. 1) goes on to show that the council doesn't

---

[11] Reviewed in Feldman, *Flavius Josephus*, 12 n. 53.

[12] Philo, *On the Creation*, 72–76, esp. 74–75. For discussion of who these collaborators might be, see Runia, *On the Creation of the Cosmos*, 241. Plato (cf. *Timaeus* 41c–d) had articulated a similar idea, that lesser gods had contributed to the creation of humans (cited by Augustine, *City of God* 12.27).

[13] For Josephus's account of the creation of humans in his retelling of Genesis, see *Jewish Antiquities* 1.32; for his statement that God did not use helpers in creation, see *Against Apion* 2.192. Some scholars believe this latter passage may be a polemic against Philo; see Runia, *On the Creation*, 243.

[14] See Jubilees 3.4 on Gen. 1:26; Jubilees 10.22 on Gen. 11:7.

[15] See the various opinions expressed in Genesis Rabbah 8, in the translation by Freedman, *Midrash Rabbah*, 1:54–63.

[16] *Targum Pseudo-Jonathan: Genesis*, trans. Maher, 19–20. The same view is found in Genesis Rabbah 8.4.

[17] Theodoret, Question 19 on Genesis.

[18] See Haring, "Origen and the Council of YHWH," at 491, in reliance on Origen, *Commentary on John* 13.331; see also Origen's *Homilies on Numbers* 11.4.4.

[19] For a scholarly treatment of the plurals, see Garr, *In His Own Image*.

contribute anything to the creation of humans: "So *Elohim* created man in his own image," not "their own image" (Gen. 1:27 ESV). As Benjamin Sommer has written,

> In fact, God is not described as consulting them but simply as informing them of his decision. Indeed the next verse pointedly states that God created humanity—and whatever beings God addressed in 1.26 have no role. These verses do not portray any group efforts or deliberation.[20]

COMPARISON WITH DIVINE COUNCILS OUTSIDE ISRAEL

The notion of a divine council was prominent in other cultures as well. We easily think of the Greek gods sitting on Mount Olympus arguing with one another, plotting, scheming to betray certain humans and gods and to support their favorites. The same sort of thing happens in ancient Near Eastern literature.[21] In the Epic of Gilgamesh, for example, the human Enkidu (the friend of King Gilgamesh) responds to his friend's question by describing a dream he had.

> "My friend, why were the great gods in counsel?" . . .
>
> Enkidu began to speak to Gilgamesh: "My brother, this night what a dream [I had!]. The gods Anu, Enlil, Ea and celestial Shamash [held assembly], and Anu spoke unto Enlil."[22]

Enkidu continues by reporting the deliberations of this meeting of the gods. The same type of scene recurs frequently in other literature from Mesopotamia. Readers may be especially interested in texts such as Atrahasis, containing a flood story, and the Enuma Elish, an account of creation.[23] At Ugarit in modern Syria, several preserved texts from

---

[20] Sommer, *Bodies of God*, 269 n. 92; Sommer goes on to interpret Gen. 1:26–27 as an anti-polytheistic text.

[21] For a summary, see Parker, "Council," *DDD*, 204–8.

[22] George, *Epic of Gilgamesh*, 54. This episode would have been on the damaged Babylonian Tablet VII, which preserves now only the opening question; the lacuna is partially supplied from Ugaritic material.

[23] Translations of both of these stories are available in Dalley, *Myths from Mesopotamia*.

the second millennium BC contain divine council scenes. In the Baal Cycle, almost the first scene in the preserved portions of text (on Tablet 2) begins by recording the instructions of the god Sea (or Yam) to a couple of messengers.

> Leave, lads, do not delay;
> now head to the Assembly in council,
> to the midst of Mount Lalu.
> Do not fall at El's feet,
> do not prostrate yourselves before the Assembly in council;
> still standing speak your speech,
> recite your message;
> and address the Bull, my father El,
> recite to the Assembly in council.[24]

The passage continues with the report that these two messengers are supposed to present in the divine assembly.

There are some obvious similarities and some obvious differences when comparing these divine council scenes from ancient Near Eastern literature (and ancient Greek literature) with similar scenes in the Hebrew Bible. The Bible coheres with this other literature in its presentation of a Most High God flanked by other divine beings. But the differences are striking: There is no argument in the divine council scenes of the Hebrew Bible. (Does Job 1–2 count as an argument? It's the closest thing in the Bible.) There is no struggle for power in these scenes. There's not much in the way of discussion of plans or counsel being bandied about. For the most part, YHWH delivers his verdict, and the members of the council can be considered (and are sometimes called) servants of YHWH, not his rivals. When ancient Israelites heard about their God in council with other divine beings, they probably thought about it in terms of the similar scenes they had heard about from other cultures—but they also heard stark differences from those other scenes that demonstrated the uniqueness, the unparalleled wisdom and power and love, of their God.

---

[24] Coogan and Smith, *Stories from Ancient Canaan*, 111.

CONCLUSION

Scenes in the Bible representing YHWH sitting on a throne in the midst of a council of *elohim* adopted a way of describing the supernatural realm well-known in ancient literature. Given the existence of multiple *elohim* (as we saw in the previous chapter), these *elohim* are shown to be servants of YHWH. In this way, the Bible adapts the familiar notion of a divine council to the peculiar theology of the Israelite authors, which allowed for no conniving among the gods against YHWH, nor any argument with the Most High God. In this divine council, the buck always stops with YHWH.

CHAPTER THREE

THE NATIONS AND THE ELOHIM

He has separated us from the rest of the nations, over whom He appointed various angels and other gods, and given us His land, so that He—bless Him!—would be our God and we would be particularly devoted to His Name.

—Nachmanides (thirteenth-century Jewish scholar), commenting on Leviticus 18:25[1]

If there are *elohim* in the Bible that are not YHWH and some of these *elohim* form a divine council (as we have seen in previous chapters), and if nations besides Israel are represented as devoted to gods besides YHWH (as the Bible frequently depicts), is there a relationship between the *elohim* that we've been studying and the pagan gods mentioned in Scripture (Baal, Asherah, etc.)? Is that what Nachmanides (epigraph above) was thinking? The issues are complex.

DEUTERONOMY 32

We must start with a textual problem.[2] Deuteronomy 32:8–9 in the traditional (Hebrew Masoretic) text says the following:

[1] Translation in Carasik, *Commentators' Bible: Leviticus*, 141.

[2] On this textual problem, see the edition of Deuteronomy edited by McCarthy, *Deuteronomy*, Biblia Hebraica Quinta, text and apparatus on p. 93, textual commentary on pp. 140*–41*. For discussion of the passage, see Excursus 31 in Tigay, *Deuteronomy*, 513–18.

> When the Most High gave the nations their inheritance, when he separated the sons of man, he set the boundaries of the peoples according to the number of the sons of Israel. For YHWH's portion is his people; Jacob is the allotment of his inheritance. God separated the nations from one another and assigned boundaries to them all.[3]

According to the apostle,

> And he made from one man every nation of mankind to live on all the face of the earth, having determined allotted periods and the boundaries of their dwelling place, that they should seek God, and perhaps feel their way toward him and find him. Yet he is actually not far from each one of us. (Acts 17:26–27 ESV)

These ideas correspond to the division of the nations in Genesis 10, after the flood. Moreover, the passage in Deuteronomy says that out of all these nations, Israel belonged to YHWH. Easy enough.

But what does it mean that "he set the boundaries of the peoples according to the number of the sons of Israel"? Anselm of Canterbury in the eleventh century thought that it had something to do with the number of people who would inhabit heaven, but most interpreters have thought that the verse had a more mundane meaning.[4] The early-twentieth-century scholar Samuel Driver proposed this interpretation: "When Jehovah allowed the various nations of the earth gradually to settle themselves in separate localities, He so determined their boundaries as to reserve among them a home for Israel, adequate to its numbers."[5] Driver seems to be taking the preposition "according to" (the single Hebrew letter *lamed*, ל)

---

[3]Translation of the Hebrew here my own. Sometimes scholars interpret this text as if YHWH is not the "Most High" who separated the nations; against this view, see Bauckham, "The 'Most High' God and the Nature of Early Jewish Monotheism," in *Jesus and the God of Israel*, 107–26, esp. 111–14.

[4]Anselm of Canterbury, *Cur Deus Homo* 1.18. Anselm indicated that the view he mentioned was a common view of the time. Anselm was aware of the alternative readings "children of Israel" and "angels of God," and he considered both phrases to have the same meaning or compatible meanings (probably in reliance on the biblical theory elaborated by Augustine, *City of God* 18.42–44).

[5]Driver, *Deuteronomy*, 355.

in the sense "with a view to." To paraphrase: "God divided up the nations of the earth and established their boundaries in such a manner that he left a plot of ground sufficient for the full number of the sons of Israel." But the rabbis usually took the verse in a different direction, connecting the "number of the sons of Israel" to the seventy descendants of Jacob/Israel who entered Egypt (Gen. 46:27; Exod. 1:5; Deut. 10:22) and to the seventy nations listed in Genesis 10 (the table of nations),[6] or connecting the twelve sons of Jacob/Israel to the twelve descendants of Canaan (including Canaan) listed at Genesis 10:15–19.[7]

The Septuagint reads differently (thus the textual problem I mentioned earlier): not "sons of Israel" but "according to the number of the sons of God."[8] According to the editor of the critical edition of LXX Deuteronomy, "What is meant is that the Most High divided up the nations in such a way that each one had a divine protector."[9]

This idea—a divine protector (something like an angel) for each nation—might find support in other writings as well. The deuterocanonical book of Sirach (Ecclesiasticus) in the early second century BC said, "He appointed a ruler [ἡγούμενον, *hēgoumenon*] for every nation, but Israel is the Lord's own portion" (Sir. 17:17 NRSVCE).[10]

Though the rabbis were reading a Hebrew Bible that did not contain "sons of God" in Deuteronomy 32:8 but rather "sons of Israel," still they

---

[6] See the rabbinic sources cited by Tigay, *Deuteronomy*, 302, with notes on p. 402.

[7] See both views expressed by Rashi (70) or Rashbam and others (12) in Carasik, *Commentators' Bible: Deuteronomy*, 219–20.

[8] This is the text as printed in Wevers, *Deuteronomium*, 347: κατὰ ἀριθμὸν υἱῶν θεοῦ. Wevers's apparatus shows that most Greek manuscripts have the reading "angels of God." And the three later translators (Aquila, Symmachus, and Theodotion) have "sons of Israel." Only a single (but very early) LXX manuscript (Ra 848, first century BC)—along with a correction in a fourteenth-century manuscript, Ra 106—has the reading "sons of God" instead of "angels of God," and the relevant fragment of Ra 848 is tiny, but according to Wevers, "the reading [of 848] is assured"; Wevers, *Notes on the Greek Text of Deuteronomy*, 513. For a facsimile of the fragment of 848, see Aly and Koenen, *Three Rolls of the Early Septuagint*, plate 46, col. 73, frag. 177.

[9] Wevers, *Notes on the Greek Text of Deuteronomy*, 513. Moberly thinks that either reading—sons of Israel or sons of God—implies national deities; Moberly, *God of the Old Testament*, 102 n. 30. On the other hand, Walton and Walton, *Demons and Spirits*, 192–94, question this common reading of Deuteronomy 32.

[10] This verse is not attested in Hebrew.

attested the idea that each nation had its own angel. Louis Ginzberg summarizes rabbinic thought this way:

> Beside the chastisement of sin and sinners by the confounding of speech, another notable circumstance was connected with the descent of God upon earth—one of only ten such descents to occur between the creation of the world and the day of judgment. It was on this occasion that God and the seventy angels that surround His throne cast lots concerning the various nations. Each angel received a nation, and Israel fell to the lot of God. To every nation a peculiar language was assigned, Hebrew being reserved for Israel—the language made use of by God at the creation of the world.[11]

Even in the Bible, some verses indicate that there are, as it were, "national angels." This evidence comes mostly from the end of the book of Daniel. When an angel comes to Daniel in response to a prayer, the angel reports: "The prince of the kingdom of Persia opposed me twenty-one days. So Michael, one of the chief princes, came to help me, and I left him there with the prince of the kingdom of Persia" (Dan. 10:13). Later, the angel explains that he must depart: "Now I must return to fight against the prince of Persia, and when I am through with him, the prince of Greece will come" (Dan. 10:20). Here in Daniel, the impression one might get is that the national angels (the princes) of Greece and Persia are opposed to Israel, maybe even opposed to God, certainly opposed to the angel delivering this message to Daniel. Such an interpretation of Daniel resonates with the pseudepigraphic Jubilees (second century BC).

> He sanctified them and gathered (them) from all humanity. For there are many nations and many peoples and all belong to him. He made spirits rule over all in order to lead them astray from following him. But over Israel he made no angel or spirit rule because he alone is their ruler. He will guard them and require them for himself from his angels, his spirits, and everyone, and

[11] Ginzberg, *Legends of the Jews*, 1:181.

> all his powers so that he may guard them and bless them and so that they may be his and he theirs from now and forever. (Jub. 15.31–32)[12]

This passage from Jubilees coheres with the common interpretation of Daniel 10, at least to the extent that various nations seem to have national angels (or spirits or deities) and some of these national angels are opposing the will of Israel's God or leading people away from him. On the other hand, the translation and interpretation of the crucial passages in Daniel 10 are not exactly certain, and it has been proposed that the national angels in Daniel 10 are not actually hostile to one another.[13] In any case, the passage does seem to imply national angels.

The evidence of the Septuagint in Deuteronomy 32:8, in agreement with this idea of national angels, already led several scholars in the nineteenth and early twentieth centuries to posit that the Septuagint reading ("sons of God") of Deuteronomy 32:8 was more original than the reading of the Masoretic Text ("sons of Israel").[14] This supposition was strengthened by the discovery of the Dead Sea Scrolls, in which a fragment (4QDeutj)—the only Dead Sea Scroll preserving this portion of Deuteronomy—agrees with the Septuagint: "sons of *elohim*."[15]

The majority of our Greek manuscripts have the reading "angels of God," perhaps representing a pious correction (because "sons of God" here was judged to be theologically problematic), perhaps simply representing

---

[12]Translation in VanderKam, *Jubilees*, 1:507. On the interpretation of this passage, see VanderKam, 1:521–24; Stokes, *Satan*, 87, 94–98.

[13]Walton and Walton, *Demons and Spirits*, 189–92.

[14]See Moore, *Judaism in the First Centuries*, 1.226–27; Driver, *Deuteronomy*, 354–55. Driver himself preferred the Masoretic reading, but he cited several scholars who preferred the Septuagint reading. Note that both Moore and Driver translated the received Greek text κατὰ ἀριθμὸν ἀγγέλων θεοῦ, "according to the number of the sons of God," based on the Greek translations of Gen. 6:2 and Job 1:6, 2:1, and 38:7. The original reading of Deut. 32:8 was probably בני אל, "sons of *El*," though this reading is not preserved in any Hebrew manuscript and so must be reconstructed from available evidence; see Tov, *Textual Criticism* (3rd ed.), 248–49, a discussion not present in the corresponding section of the fourth edition (Fortress, 2022), 312.

[15]The official publication is DJD 14 (1995, ed. Julie Ann Duncan). Digital images of the relevant fragment are available online: https://www.deadseascrolls.org.il/explore-the-archive/image/B-359054 (color); https://www.deadseascrolls.org.il/explore-the-archive/image/B-359055 (infrared).

a clarifying reading. Philo knew the reading "angels of God," which he allegorized in reference to virtue: "then did He fix the boundaries of the offspring of virtue corresponding to the number of the angels."[16] Justin Martyr was familiar with two readings, "angels of God" and "sons of Israel," but the latter reading was the one in the Jewish manuscripts, whereas the Septuagint had the former, according to Justin (*Dialogue with Trypho* 131).

So the original reading of Deuteronomy 32:8 probably meant that God had allotted the various nations of the world to other divine beings, whether we think of those divine beings as gods or angels,[17] and this is how the text has been understood in Christian circles. We have also seen that the book of Daniel shows familiarity with the notion of "national angels." In fact, Pseudo-Dionysius (fifth century) used the evidence from Daniel to argue that even Israel was assigned a national angel, namely Michael, and all these national angels were under the authority of the Lord God (who himself made the assignments), and all of them were tasked with protecting their nations and bringing their people to salvation (*Celestial Hierarchy* 9.2, 4). Most interpreters—whether modern or ancient Jewish or ancient Christian—relate Deuteronomy 32:8 to the Tower of Babel episode in Genesis 11, when God dispersed people throughout the earth.[18] The idea of national angels continued to be found in postbiblical Jewish literature, such as the Animal Apocalypse of 1 Enoch (chs. 85–90, second century BC).[19]

---

[16] Philo, *On the Posterity and Exile of Cain* 91, trans. Colson and Whitaker, 2:379.

[17] See Origen, *On First Principles* 1.5.2; Eusebius, *Demonstration of the Gospel* 4.7. Sommer, *Bodies of God*, 164–65, interprets Mic. 4:1–5 in light of these concepts: At the eschaton, other nations will still have their own "gods," but all nations will acknowledge that ultimate authority resides in Zion; but see also his interpretation of Isa. 2:2–4 (p. 165), and his interpretation of Isa. 9:5, such that Ashur (the Assyrian god) is the instrument (even, angel) of YHWH (p. 268 n. 87). Cf. Plato, *Timaeus* 41d, describing creation: "He divided it into souls equal in number to the stars." In Plato, as in the Bible, the term "stars" sometimes stands for divine beings (see *Timaeus* 40a; and our earlier Chapter One).

[18] For a modern scholar, see, e.g., Heiser, *Unseen Realm*, ch. 14.

[19] Collins, *Apocalyptic Imagination*, 87.

PAGAN GODS

In Chapter One, we found that sometimes supernatural beings are described as stars. Such a concept may lie behind this next passage from Deuteronomy.

> And when you look up to the heavens and see the sun, the moon, and the stars, all the host of heaven, do not be led astray and bow down to them and serve them, things that YHWH your *elohim* has allotted [חלק, *ḥalaq*] to all the peoples everywhere under heaven. But YHWH has taken you and brought you out of the iron-smelter, out of Egypt, to become a people of his very own possession, as you are now. (Deut. 4:19–20)

We could understand the "sun, moon, and stars" here as references to those objects created on day four (Gen. 1:14–19) that give light to all people on the earth, including Israel.[20] Or, we could understand these terms at Deuteronomy 4:19 as a reference to divine beings (see Deut. 17:3), which belong to other nations, whereas Israel is YHWH's special possession. As the thirteenth-century Jewish scholar Nachmanides put it: "Above each of these stars is the angel on high who has been given authority over it and thus over its nation."[21] It is this second interpretation that has convinced most scholars, though the matter is not easily decided.[22] If we opt for the second interpretation, the verse ends up sounding a lot like Deuteronomy

---

[20] Some medieval Jewish commentators (not all; see Nachmanides, next note) considered it possible that the verse simply meant that God allotted the heavenly bodies (the actual sun, moon, and stars) to provide light to all nations (see Carasik, *Commentators' Bible: Deuteronomy*, ad loc.); Driver, *Deuteronomy*, 70–71, rejected this interpretation, but some (more conservative) scholars still propose it, e.g., Christopher Wright, *Deuteronomy*, NIBC, 51–52, and more confidently in *Mission of God*, 141 n. 6. Jerome (in the Latin Vulgate) translated the disputed clause in agreement with Wright and those aforementioned medieval Jewish commentators: *quae creavit Dominus Deus tuus in ministerium cunctis gentibus quae sub caelo sunt.*

[21] Nachmanides is commenting on Deut. 4:19–20 within his comment on Lev. 18:25; see Carasik, *Commentators' Bible: Leviticus*, 140. Nachmanides immediately follows the comment quoted above with the observation that Daniel 10 provides additional evidence, with its mention of "the prince of Persia" and "the prince of Greece" (Dan. 10:20).

[22] For a balanced appraisal, ultimately landing on the second interpretation, see the long footnote in MacDonald, *Deuteronomy and the Meaning*, 172–73 n. 91.

32:8–9: Israel is YHWH's special possession, whereas the other nations are "allotted" to "the sun, the moon, and the stars, all the host of heaven."[23] One way of understanding this passage is that YHWH has placed his lieutenants over other nations. And so the psalmist says, "Surely there are *Elohim* who judge [plural] on earth" (Ps. 58:11). The apostle Paul regularly calls certain angelic beings by the title "rulers" (ἄρχοντες, *archontes*),[24] and the Greek version of Daniel 10:13 uses the same term for the archangel Michael (ἄρχων, *archōn*) and the "prince" of Persia.[25]

Some early Christians interpreted the verse in this second sense.[26]

> But the angel-guardians and shepherds of the other races allowed them, inasmuch as they were not able with their mind to see the invisible, nor to ascend so high through their own weakness, to worship things seen in the heavens, the sun and moon and stars. For these, indeed, being the most wonderful of the things of the phenomenal world, invited upwards the eyes of those who see, and as near as possible to heaven, being as it were in the precincts of the King's court, manifesting the glory of him that is the Source of all by the analogy of the vastness and beauty of created visible things.[27] "For his invisible things," as the divine Apostle says, "from the creation of the world are clearly seen, being understood by the things that are made, even his eternal power and Godhead" [Rom. 1:20]. And this again the great Moses mystically says. For in exhorting the portion of the Lord to grasp with clear mind and pure soul that which is known to the mind

---

[23] For the verb "allotted," the LXX uses ἀπονέμω, Symmachus uses διακοσμέω, and Aquila uses μερίζω, all basically meaning the same as the Hebrew.

[24] Eph. 1:20–21, 2:2, 3:10, 6:12; Col. 2:15; 1 Cor. 2:6, 2:8. (Some of these passages use the Greek noun *archai* rather than *archontes*.) "Ruler" language is also applied to the devil in the New Testament: Matt. 9:34, 12:24; Mark 3:22; Luke 11:15; John 12:31, 14:30, 16:11; Eph. 2:2.

[25] This is the so-called Theodotion version of Daniel, which was more widely accepted in the ancient church (especially from the third century) than the so-called LXX version of Daniel. The LXX version uses *archōn* in reference to Michael in this same verse but not in reference to the prince of Persia.

[26] See Danielou, *Angels and Their Mission*, 14–23.

[27] See the similar statement of Glaucon in Plato, *Republic* 7.528e–529a, though Socrates immediately denies that astronomy compels the soul to look up.

> only and unembodied, he prohibits all terror of the things seen in heaven, adding that "The Lord thy God has divided them for all the nations" [Deut. 4:19]. And it is worth realizing why he says that they were divided. Since unseen by us they that bear the earthy and dæmonic nature are everywhere wanderers, flying through the air around the earth unknown and undistinguished by men, and the good spirits and powers and, indeed, the divine angels themselves are ever at variance with the worse, there was but one way for those who failed of the highest religion of the Almighty to prosper, namely to choose the best of things visible in heaven.[28]

Eusebius seems to think that even the worship of these heavenly bodies was allotted to the nations by God, on the grounds that such worship would lift up their eyes at least part of the way to the true God. Other ancient Christians and some modern scholars hold a similar view.[29] An example is Origen (third century AD) who said the worship of the heavenly bodies "was given by God to all the peoples who are under heaven, except to those whom he wished to set aside for himself as his chosen part."[30] The verse does not explicitly say that the nations worship the sun, moon, and stars, but it is easy to see from the context of the verse why so many interpreters suppose that worship is implied. Though Israel was reserved for YHWH, Deuteronomy reports that Israel was influenced by the worship practices of other nations: Israel "turned and served other *elohim*, worshiping them,

---

[28] Eusebius, *Demonstration of the Gospel* 4.8, trans. Ferrar, 1:176–77. According to Eusebius, *Demonstration of the Gospel* 4.9, it is one of Satan's schemes to obliterate the boundaries of nations and thus undo God's work of Deut. 32:8.

[29] Driver, *Deuteronomy*, 70–71, took it as evident that the worship of the heavenly bodies by these other nations was intended by YHWH, as indicated in Deuteronomy 4:19, and he could cite for this interpretation Justin, *Dialogue with Trypho* 55 (Trypho), 121; Clement of Alexandria, *Stromata* 6.14.110–11. From a perspective different from that of Driver's, Heiser, *Unseen Realm*, 114, thinks that Deut. 4:19 means that YHWH assigned "lesser *elohim*" as objects of worship for the nations as a punishment for the Tower of Babel. For another interpretation, see Schenker's view as reported in Sommer, *Bodies of God*, 268 n. 82: "by praying to their own gods, the other nations also give glory to Yhwh, who assigned those gods to them and commanded them to pray to those gods."

[30] Origin, *Against Celsus* 5.10; Chadwick, *Origen*, 270.

elohim whom they had not known and whom he had not allotted [חלק, *ḥalaq*] to them" (Deut. 29:26).

A couple of other verses perhaps can be explained by supposing that the idea of national angels/gods, which we have been exploring, generated in the minds of some ancient people the notion that YHWH himself could be served properly only in the land of Israel, the special possession of YHWH. At 1 Samuel 26:19, David complained against Saul that if people were persuading the king to expel David from "YHWH's inheritance" (= Israel), then that action would be tantamount to encouraging David to serve other *elohim*.[31] Naaman the Aramaean—once he was healed by Elisha the prophet—acknowledged that "there is no *elohim* in all the earth except in Israel" (2 Kings 5:15). Naaman took some dirt from Israel back to Aram so that he could worship YHWH there—as if YHWH were so tied to a geographical location (at least, in Naaman's mind) that he could only be worshiped properly on that bit of real estate, so he took some of that real estate with him.[32] The God of Israel was thought to be tied to the land of Israel. There are also biblical stories that push back against this supposition. (Think about Jonah.)

THE BIBLE AGAINST PAGAN GODS

Whether or not the worship of other "gods" by other nations (not Israel!) was viewed as acceptable or even determined by God in Deuteronomy 4:19, there are other passages in which the God of Israel brings judgment upon the gods of other nations. "Who is like you, YHWH, among the *elim*?" (Exod. 15:11). This verse is in the middle of the Song of the Sea, the song that Israel sang in celebration of God's victory over Egypt at the Red Sea, where God had just shown himself more powerful than all the gods of Egypt. That is exactly what God intended to do:

> I will pass through the land of Egypt that night, and I will strike down every firstborn in the land of Egypt, both human beings

[31] For this interpretation, and discussion of other examples, see Heiser, *Unseen Realm*, ch. 15.

[32] See Block, *Gods of the Nations*, 86.

> and animals; on all the *elohim* of Egypt I will execute judgments. I am YHWH. (Exod. 12:12)

Moses's father-in-law, Jethro, got the point:

> Blessed be YHWH, who has delivered you from the Egyptians and from Pharaoh. Now I know that YHWH is greater than all *elohim*, because he delivered the people from the Egyptians. (Exod. 18:10–11)

In the book of Numbers, Moses reflected back on what God had done to the Egyptians:

> On the day after the passover the Israelites went out boldly in the sight of all the Egyptians, while the Egyptians were burying all their firstborn, whom YHWH had struck down among them. YHWH executed judgments even against their *elohim*. (Num. 33:3–4)

The plague narrative is a story about YHWH, the God of Israel, bringing judgment against the *elohim* of Egypt, and it demonstrates decisively that the God of Israel is more powerful than the gods of any other nation, so that Israel exclaims in wonder, "Who is like you, YHWH, among the *elim*?"

According to the apostle Paul, there are spiritual beings, "rulers" and "powers," arrayed against God's people.

> For we do not wrestle against flesh and blood, but against the rulers [*archai*], against the authorities [*exousiai*], against the cosmic powers [*kosmokratores*] over this present darkness, against the spiritual forces [*pneumatika*] of evil in the heavenly places. (Eph. 6:12 ESV)

> For I am convinced that neither death, nor life, nor angels, nor rulers [*archai*], nor things present, nor things to come, nor powers [*dunameis*], nor height, nor depth, nor anything else in all creation, will be able to separate us from the love of God in Christ Jesus our Lord. (Rom. 8:38–39)

Christ will render to God the kingdom when he has defeated "every ruler [*archē*] and every authority [*exousia*] and power [*dunamis*]" (1 Cor. 15:24).[33]

Perhaps the crucial text in the Old Testament on the theme of judgment against gods is Psalm 82 (a psalm quoted in the New Testament; John 10:34), though the interpretation of the psalm is difficult. The psalm is not long, and it begins:

> *Elohim* has taken his place in the council [עֵדָה, *ēdah*] of *el*.
> in the midst of the *elohim* he holds judgment.

Let's pause here and consider the phrase "council of *el*." We could translate it straightforwardly as "council of God" or "divine council," but the council of Psalm 82 is sometimes understood to be a council headed by El, the Ugaritic high God (i.e., *El* as a proper name).[34] The NET Bible translates the phrase "assembly of El" and promotes this understanding in its note, such that *Elohim* (= YHWH) invades the council of *El* and takes over. In that sense, it would be like the God of Israel is crashing someone else's party and bringing judgment on them. On the other hand, Mark Smith comments: "The name El was understood in the tradition—and perhaps at the time of the text's original composition as well—to be none other than Yahweh and not a separate god called El."[35] Now, back to the psalm.

> *Elohim* has taken his place in the council of *el*;
> in the midst of the *elohim* he holds judgment:
> "How long will you judge unjustly

[33] See also Eph. 1:20–21 and 1 Pet. 3:22; on 1 Cor. 2:6–8 and Col. 2:15, see Williams, *Spirit World*, 134–37.

[34] See, e.g., Smith, *Origins of Biblical Monotheism*, 48; Thompson, "Local Manifestations of YHWH."

[35] Smith, *Origins of Biblical Monotheism*, 48. For an inscription from around 700 BC Judah (Khirbet Beit Lei) that seems to equate YHWH with El, see Keel and Uehlinger, *Gods, Goddesses, and Images*, 311–12. If the poet of Ps. 82 considered El to be another name of YHWH, it is not clear to me how this poem "preserves a tradition that casts the god of Israel in the role not of presiding god of the pantheon but as one of his sons," as Smith goes on to argue. For a lengthy discussion of the identity of El in Ps. 82:1, see Machinist, "How Gods Die," at 195–203. Machinist opts for understanding El as an epithet for YHWH in the psalm. On the topic of the Elohistic Psalter and how this theory should affect our reading of Ps. 82, see Moberly, *God of the Old Testament*, 106–10. Smith, *Origins of Biblical Monotheism*, 223 n. 62, expresses some reservations about the theory of the Elohistic Psalter.

and show partiality to the wicked? *Selah*
Give justice to the weak and the orphan;
maintain the right of the lowly and the destitute.
Rescue the weak and the needy;
deliver them from the hand of the wicked."

They[36] have neither knowledge nor understanding,
they walk around in darkness;
all the foundations of the earth are shaken.

I say,[37] "You are *elohim*,
sons of *Elyon*, all of you;
nevertheless, you shall die like mortals [*adam*],
and fall like any prince [*sar*]."

Rise up, O *Elohim*, judge the earth;
for all the nations belong to you![38]

Who are the *elohim* who are going to die? Traditionally these *elohim* in Psalm 82 have been identified with human judges, an interpretation found everywhere from Luther and Calvin to one of the standard (but older) Hebrew lexicons still used by scholars (BDB).[39] It has been thought that some verses in Exodus provide parallels to the use of *elohim* for human judges:

---

[36] They who? This question becomes crucial for Walton and Walton, *Demons and Spirits*, 199. As Moberly, *God of the Old Testament*, 114, notes, the usual interpretation is that "they" are the bad gods just condemned. But "they" can also be the wicked of verse 4 (p. 114 n. 77). Moberly (p. 114) takes the position that "they" are "the poor, the victims of these deities' malpractice."

[37] Moberly, *God of the Old Testament*, 115–16, analyzes an idiom here which suggests the translation, "I had taken you for gods . . . but you shall die like mortals."

[38] The verbs in the final two lines are all singular.

[39] See the survey of this view in Moberly, *God of the Old Testament*, 97–100. For Calvin, in addition to his Psalms commentary, see *Institutes* 1.14.5. Moberly points out that the interpretation of *elohim* at Exod. 21:6 and 22:7–8 as human judges is also traditional in Judaism, going back at least to Targum Onkelos. BDB is Brown, Driver, and Briggs, *Hebrew and English Lexicon*, see p. 43, אלהים, definition 1a, where our psalm is cited.

> But if the slave declares, "I love my master, my wife, and my children; I will not go out a free person," then his master shall bring him before the *elohim*. He shall be brought to the door or the doorpost; and his master shall pierce his ear with an awl; and he shall serve him for life. (Exod. 21:5–6)

> When someone delivers to a neighbor money or goods for safekeeping, and they are stolen from the neighbor's house, then the thief, if caught, shall pay double. If the thief is not caught, the owner of the house shall be brought before the *elohim*, to determine whether or not the owner had laid hands on the neighbor's goods. (Exod. 22:7–8)

The problem with using these verses to establish that *elohim* can mean human judges is that it is not at all clear that *elohim* in these Exodus passages signifies human judges.[40] Peter Machinist compares these passages to Exodus 18, where Jethro advises Moses to appoint more judges and tells him that Moses himself will represent the people before the *elohim* (Exod. 18:19). Here, *elohim* must mean God (not "judge"), and it provides a context for understanding the other Exodus passages: God confirms legal decisions.[41]

The more important consideration for a Christian reading of Psalm 82 is the quotation by Jesus of Psalm 82:6 at John 10:34. Readers have usually thought that Jesus interpreted the *elohim* of Psalm 82 as humans. This New Testament quotation has been decisive for the interpretation of Psalm 82 throughout much of Christian history, going back to the second century.[42]

> The Jews answered, "It is not for a good work that we are going to stone you, but for blasphemy, because you, though only a human being, are making yourself God." Jesus answered, "Is it not

---

[40] Gordon, "אלהים in Its Reputed Meaning"; David P. Wright, *Inventing God's Law*, 255–56, argues that "judges" cannot be the meaning of *elohim* in the Exodus passages.

[41] Machinist, "How Gods Die," 205–6.

[42] Both Justin Martyr, *Dialogue* 124, and Irenaeus, *Against the Heresies* 3.6.1, interpret Ps. 82:6 as referring to humans because they interpret the quotation in John 10:34 as pointing in this direction.

> written in your law, 'I said, you are gods'? If those to whom the word of God came were called 'gods'—and the scripture cannot be annulled—can you say that the one whom the Father has sanctified and sent into the world is blaspheming because I said, 'I am God's Son'?" (John 10:33–36)

Jesus interprets Psalm 82:6 in reference to "those to whom the word of God came." Usually, readers have thought that Jesus must be applying the verse to the Israelites, who received the word of God from Moses and the prophets. Such an interpretation necessitates that, for the Jesus of the Fourth Gospel, the *elohim* of Psalm 82:6 are human—or at least that Jesus expected his interlocutors to hold this view. Michael Heiser has suggested another interpretation: that the word of God mentioned by Jesus is the decree of Psalm 82:6–7, the sentence of death on the *elohim*, so that "those to whom the word of God came" are not the Israelites but the *elohim* of Psalm 82. This interpretation of John 10 would not solve the problem of the identity of the *elohim* of Psalm 82, but it would allow for a nonhuman interpretation, which is the direction Heiser takes it.

Heiser's view is not common even among evangelical scholars, I think, but still, most conservative scholars these days have abandoned the idea that the gods of Psalm 82 are humans, even if that is the view assumed in the conversation reported in John 10 between Jesus and the Jews. The idea of these conservative scholars, I think, is that Jesus doesn't really present an interpretation of Psalm 82 in John 10; he merely uses an interpretation he thinks his opponents will accept—an interpretation attested in some ancient Jewish sources (e.g., Targum Onkelos)—in order to build a different argument. This view takes Jesus's statement in John 10 as a "for the sake of argument" kind of assertion: "For the sake of argument, let's say that the Israelites, 'the ones to whom the word of God came,' are the ones called 'gods' in Psalm 82:6, an interpretation that I know a lot of you accept. Well, if you don't have a problem with the Bible calling those people 'gods,' why do you have a problem with me calling myself a son of God?"

The common interpretation of Psalm 82:6 for all scholars (conservative and otherwise) over the past several decades has been that these gods are divine beings of the sort that we have been examining in this chapter.[43] Certainly, this approach makes the most sense of the psalm. In this case, *Elohim* (= YHWH) passes judgment on lesser divine beings, the members of the divine council, due to their willful neglect of their responsibility to promote justice.[44] Who are these divine beings facing YHWH's wrath? Could the psalmist, or ancient readers, have conceptualized them as the gods of other nations, or perhaps national angels? A reader who is motivated to interpret Psalm 82 in light of Deuteronomy 4:19 and 32:8–9 might plausibly imagine that the psalm describes YHWH's judgment upon pagan gods.

It has been a traditional view among believers that the pagan gods have some reality to them (that they are not simply invented by people). The ancient Israelites—routinely criticized by the prophets for idolatry and syncretism—seem to have attributed some power to these pagan gods (at least, according to the biblical authors). Such acknowledgment from the perspective of the biblical authors is harder to find and more ambiguous, but the judge Jephthah, for one, spoke as if he believed Chemosh to be a true and powerful god of the Ammonites (Judg. 11:24). Could there be a relationship between the pagan gods and the fallen angels/gods that we have been studying? This is the view memorialized in Milton's *Paradise Lost*. Here, Milton describes Satan's band of rebel angels:

> Though of their names in heavenly records now
> Be no memorial, blotted out and razed
> By their rebellion, from the books of life.
> Nor had they yet among the sons of Eve
> Got them new names, till wandering o'er the earth,
> Through God's high sufferance for the trial of man,
> By falsities and lies the greatest part

[43] Machinist, "How Gods Die," 204, points out that the change in scholarship from viewing the gods of Psalm 82 as human to viewing them as divine occurred about the middle of the twentieth century. He attributes the change to the increased awareness of the ancient Near Eastern context for the psalm.

[44] See Machinist, "How Gods Die"; McClellan, "The Gods-Complaint." Walton and Walton, *Demons and Spirits*, 203, have argued that the psalm represents the human psalmist calling on YHWH to pass judgment on these other divine beings. According to Moberly, *God of the Old Testament*, 113, "little, however, hangs on the issue" of whether the speaking voice beginning at v. 2 is human or divine.

Of mankind they corrupted to forsake
God their creator, and the invisible
Glory of him that made them, to transform
Oft to the image of a brute, adorned
With gay religions full of pomp and gold,
And devils to adore for deities:
Then were they known to men by various names,
And various idols through the heathen world.
(1.361–75)

Milton goes on to name these fallen angels (1.392–521): Moloch, Chemos, Baalim, Ashtaroth, Astoreth, Thammuz, Dagon, Rimmon, Osiris, Isis, Orus, Belial, and various Greco-Roman gods (Saturn, Jove, etc.). Milton here reworks older ideas about the pagan gods. In the late second century AD, Tertullian (*Apology* 22–24) tried to convince his readers that the pagan gods were evil demons. Earlier still, the apostle Paul insisted that pagans worship demons (1 Cor. 10:19–21), a view he read in his Bible (Ps. 96:5; LXX 95:5). The passage from Jubilees 15.31–32, quoted earlier, interprets the spiritual beings over the nations as the pagan gods.

One way of trying to hold all these concepts together is to imagine that God placed national angels over each nation, and these national angels abused their post, thereby bringing upon themselves the judgment of God and the ire of the biblical authors. These angels became evil, became demons, as we think of them. Though Israel's ancestors had participated in the worship of these pagan gods (Josh. 24:2), the people of Israel had been elected by YHWH for a covenant relationship. Yet Israel often fell into worshiping these same gods: "They sacrificed to demons [שדים, *shēdim*], not *eloah*, to *elohim* whom they had never known" (Deut. 32:17).

Or maybe the pagan gods are not the national angels. According to Jean Daniélou, the dominant patristic view was that the angelic national rulers did not lead the pagan nations astray, but the sinfulness of those nations did in spite of the angelic national rulers.[45] Pseudo-Dionysius (fifth century AD) insisted that the angels put in charge of the various nations

[45] Daniélou, *Angels and Their Mission*, 21–23.

did their job, but the nations freely chose idolatry.[46] In the third century AD, Origen offered this interpretation:

> Angels that governed human affairs . . . were vigilant day and night. But, at some point, they were unable to bear the labor of governing the peoples who had been entrusted to them and accomplish it diligently.[47]

In Origen's mind, the national angels appointed by God were trying their best to steer their nations toward God, but they were meeting much resistance from the people themselves. He expands on this idea in the next section of his sermon, where he also brings in the notion of angels trying to steer individuals.

> [At the incarnation] the angel who administered the affairs of Egypt received a considerable advantage after the Lord came down from heaven, for the Egyptians could become Christians. It profited all who governed the various provinces, for example, the guardian of Macedonia, the guardian of Achaea, and the guardians of the other regions. It is not right to believe that wicked angels govern individual provinces, and good angels do not have the same provinces and regions entrusted to them. I think that what Scripture says about individual provinces should also be believed more generally about all people. Two angels attend each human being. One is an angel of justice, the other an angel of iniquity. If good thoughts are present in our hearts and justice springs up in our souls, the angel of the Lord is undoubtedly speaking to us. But, if evil thoughts turn over in our hearts, the devil's angel is speaking to us. Just as there are two angels for individuals, so, I believe, there are different angels in individual provinces, some good and some evil.[48]

[46] *Celestial Hierarchy* 9.3.
[47] Origen, *Homilies on Luke* 12.3 (48–51).
[48] Origen, *Homilies on Luke* 12.4.

Origen thought that God had appointed the good angels over the various provinces, not (as in the view discussed earlier) that God appointed angels who then became evil.

CONCLUSION

There is no single traditional view on the relationship between the national angels of Deuteronomy 32:8 (etc.) and the pagan gods condemned in Scripture or the gods facing God's wrath in Psalm 82. But there is a significant tradition—found in ancient Jewish literature, early Christian literature, and modern scholarly literature—that certain biblical passages (especially Deut. 32:8) envision the God of Israel assigning certain divine beings to oversee nations other than Israel. These divine beings were a part of what the Bible calls "the divine council," a concept that has illuminating parallels in other ancient Near Eastern literature, especially at Ugarit. The concern that YHWH shows for other nations by his appointment of divine overseers coheres with other themes in Scripture, such as his condemnation of non-Israelite nations for their failure to uphold justice (e.g., Nahum, Jonah, the Oracles against the Nations in Isa. 13–23; Jer. 46–51; Ezek. 25–32). These same passages further presuppose that the ultimate authority on earth is the God of Israel, the creator of the heavens and the earth, and that other nations—no matter what gods they worship—are in reality subject to YHWH.

CHAPTER FOUR

GOD'S AGENTS OF EVIL

Now the spirit of YHWH departed from Saul,
and an evil spirit sent from YHWH tormented him.

—1 Sam. 16:14

I form light and create darkness,
I make weal and create woe;
I YHWH do all these things.

—Isa. 45:7

Shall there be evil in a city,
and YHWH hath not done it?

—Amos 3:6 KJV

Maybe evil isn't the right word, either in the title of this chapter or in the first verse quoted immediately above. "Evil" usually implies something immoral, something like wickedness. It seems unlikely that Scripture is trying to attribute to YHWH actions that are morally wicked.[1] Maybe a better translation would be "bad," or even "unpleasant," in which case this would be a chapter on "God's Agents of Unpleasantness." To call

[1] For a brief discussion of this point, see Barton, *Ethics in Ancient Israel*, 257–61. Whether Jewish Scripture represents the Jewish God as evil was a point of importance for some ancient Christian groups; see Litwa, *Evil Creator*.

this spirit that torments Saul an "unpleasant spirit" makes some sense, and it relieves some of the tension of attributing such a spirit to God. But, then again, to refer to killing babies as "unpleasant" seems a gross understatement; such an action seems evil. And Scripture sometimes attributes to the God of Israel such actions, as in the tenth plague (Exod. 12:29). We might still not want to call it evil if God is doing it, but how about this? We can think of this chapter as treating "God's Agents of (What Might Seem to Us as) Evil, or at the Very Least, Unpleasant."

The passages we will be covering here usually make believers uncomfortable, and they force readers to struggle with questions about the nature of the God presented in the Bible. Many Jews and Christians don't like to think about the God of the Bible as telling lies or sending an angel to kill kids. Let's look at the examples, and then we can think about ways of handling their testimony to the divine.

We've seen that God has all kinds of agents at his disposal, angels that he puts in charge of various tasks. Christian Scripture—especially the Old Testament, but not only the Old Testament—portrays agents of God that are in charge of doing things people don't like. I am not sure whether Scripture intends to depict specific spiritual beings as having permanent authority over particular negative jobs, or whether it envisions that God randomly assigns the negative tasks to a variety of angels. The way that God's agents are named in Scripture (e.g., "the destroyer"; "the spirit of falsehood") might suggest that there are certain angels or spirits that always get the "dirty work" assignments, that every time God wants to accomplish something negative, he calls on these particular agents.

As a preview of our discussion later in this chapter, let's notice that there are plenty of times in the Bible that God does things that we would call rather negative, like destroying people. Sometimes God does such things directly, without apparently using agents. Sodom and Gomorrah is an example: "Then YHWH rained on Sodom and Gomorrah sulfur and fire from YHWH out of heaven" (Gen. 19:24). Or remember what happened to Ananias and Sapphira? They simply dropped dead, apparently by direct action of God (Acts 5:5, 10). But sometimes God uses human agents, whether the human realizes the fact or not: 2 Kings 17:1–20 justifies the destruction of Israel by the Assyrians because Israel had turned away from

God, and therefore, "YHWH was very angry with Israel and removed them out of his sight" (v. 18). God was responsible, but he used the Assyrians to accomplish his will of punishing Israel.

And sometimes God uses celestial beings to perform these tasks. Hebrews 1:14 (CSB) describes angels as "ministering spirits sent out to serve those who are going to inherit salvation"; the passages we will discuss below would perhaps compel us to offer some nuance to that description. Maybe we would want to say that Hebrews 1:14 offers a good description for how the Bible depicts God's use of angels on behalf of his children, but the Bible also shows God using them in other ways regarding people who have rejected him. Or perhaps we would want to say that the description in Hebrews applies to most but not all angels (though the word "all" is used in the text). Or maybe we would want to say that it depends on the meaning of the word "serve," since God can use bad situations to bring about his purposes for our good. Or maybe we should highlight the word "angel" in Hebrews, recognizing that God's agents of evil are called "spirits" but not "angels." At any rate, the Bible shows that God sometimes uses spirits to do things that don't seem beneficial to humans. On the other hand, the humans that suffer from these actions are not the kind that the writer of Hebrews would describe as "those who are going to inherit salvation."

OLD TESTAMENT PASSAGES

The Destroyer

Exodus 12 is the Passover chapter. The Israelites are still enslaved to the Egyptians, but nine of the ten plagues have already passed, so escape is nigh, after one last plague. The final plague will involve the death of the firstborn children of the Egyptians. The Israelites themselves will not suffer this tragedy of the death of the firstborn because they'll slaughter a lamb and slather some of its blood on their doorposts.

> When YHWH passes through to strike Egypt and sees the blood on the lintel and the two doorposts, he will pass over the door and not let the destroyer [המשחית, *ha-mashḥit*] enter your houses to strike you. (Exod. 12:23; cf. Heb. 11:28)

Wait, what's this? Who's the "destroyer"? Some evil being going around killing kids? Well, killing kids, yes, but this spiritual being is under the authority of God, acting as God's agent. We know that because it's God's plan to strike down all the firstborn of the Egyptians; that's been a part of the plan all along, since God first called Moses (Exod. 4:23). And just a few verses later, when the firstborn die, it's God who gets the credit: "At midnight YHWH struck down all the firstborn in the land of Egypt" (12:29; see also 11:4–5; 12:12–13). But judging from the earlier verse (v. 23), God did not directly kill the firstborn; he sent the "destroyer" to do so.[2]

Now, let's think about something. If we hadn't known that, according to Exodus, killing the Egyptian kids was a part of God's plan to punish Egypt and redeem Israel, we might have assumed that this action could be performed only by a wicked being. If we hadn't known that God was behind it all, we might have thought that Satan was responsible. After all, couldn't "the destroyer" be another name for Satan, like "the evil one" in the New Testament? Since Exodus 12:23 says that God would prevent the destroyer from entering the Israelite houses to strike them, we might have interpreted this to mean that God would rescue his people from the Prince of Darkness.

Some ancient Jews read the text in this way, sort of. The book of Jubilees (second century BC) tells this same story in terms of "the forces of Mastema" (the name of a harmful spirit) going around killing the kids (Jub. 49.2).[3]

---

[2]By the way, Paul seems to imply that the destroyer was active also in the wilderness stories, tasked with bringing punishment against certain rebellious Israelites (1 Cor. 10:10). The same implication is in the deuterocanonical book Wisdom of Solomon 18:20–25; the "destroyer" is mentioned at v. 25, in a passage reflecting the events of Numbers 16:41–47. Earlier in the same passage, the Wisdom of Solomon identifies the one who killed the Egyptian firstborn as God's "all-powerful word" (ὁ παντοδύναμος λόγος; 18:15).

[3]Admittedly, the portrait of Mastema in Jubilees is difficult to pin down. The Hebrew word *mastema* means "hostility," and it appears in the Hebrew Bible only at Hosea 9:7–8 (not as the name of an angel), though a verbal form of the same word appears a little more often (Gen. 27:41, 49:23, 50:15; Job 16:9, 30:21; Ps. 55:3). Possibly the word "Mastema" was not intended to be an angel's name at Jubilees 49.2. On this terminology in Jubilees, see VanderKam, *Jubilees*, 2:1172; Stokes, *Satan*, 81–82; and see below, Chapter Seven, note 6.

But that's not the impression one gets about the destroyer from the narrative in Exodus. It seems that the destroyer is not in rebellion against God, but rather he's one of God's servants. The full context assures us that God controls the destroyer, and so the destroyer is apparently doing the task assigned to him by God. Of course, God can use agents who do not acknowledge that God controls them; that's the case with Nebuchadnezzar, whose role we will explore at the end of this chapter. Possibly the destroyer plays that same role, but given all the other verses we're about to examine that more clearly indicate that God employs spiritual agents to do unpleasant things, I think it makes more sense to interpret the destroyer also as one of God's agents.[4]

The Destroying Angel

The same Hebrew word, *mashḥit*, that we saw in Exodus 12:23 appears also at 2 Samuel 24:16, in the phrase *ha-malak ha-mashḥit*, "the destroying angel." This is the chapter in which David takes a census of his soldiers, which turns out to be a sin, as David quickly realizes (v. 10). God's punishment for this sin is a plague that lasts three days (vv. 13–15), and the plague is carried out by an "angel," also called "the destroying angel" and "the angel of YHWH" (all three terms in v. 16).[5] Note that also in Exodus 12, the death of the Egyptian firstborn is caused by a plague (v. 13), apparently brought by the destroyer (v. 23). Here in 2 Samuel 24, David can see the angel, who is apparently enormous (cf. 1 Chron. 21:16), with a sword in his

---

[4] I think this interpretation of Exodus works even if Moffitt, *Rethinking the Atonement*, 16–22, 40–41, is correct that the epistle to the Hebrews (esp. Heb. 2:14–15, 11:28) alludes to an interpretation of the destroyer in the vein of Jubilees. Moffitt does not show that "the author of Hebrews understands the Destroyer of the firstborn who threatened God's people during the initial Passover to be none other than the Devil, the malevolent angelic figure who holds the power of death" (23) or that both Jesus and Moses "*faced the same opponent*" (25, italics orig.). If Moses was not truly Jesus in disguise but there was only an analogy between the two highlighted in Hebrews (note the word "analogy" several times at Moffitt, pp. 24–25), the same could be (and probably is) true for the destroyer and the devil. See again Wisd. of Sol. 18:25, mentioned above in note 2.

[5] The same story appears in 1 Chron. 21, where the phrase *ha-malak ha-mashḥit* does not appear, but 1 Chron. 21:12 does say that the "angel of YHWH" will bring the "destruction" (*mashḥit*), and the same root (related to *mashḥit*) appears 3x in v. 15.

hand. God's command to the angel to put his sword in his sheath (1 Chron. 21:27) corresponds to the end of the plague (2 Sam. 24:25).

In a somewhat similar story, 2 Kings 19:35 reports that the angel of YHWH killed 185,000 Assyrian soldiers, thus rescuing Judah from this invading army. But the word *mashḥit* does not appear in this story.

Spirits from God Doing Evil

Here we may mention a few texts.[6] Most well-known, probably, is the evil spirit (*ruaḥ rah-ah*) from God that afflicts King Saul, which we mentioned earlier (1 Sam. 16:14–16, 23; 18:10; 19:9). Again, maybe we shouldn't translate the term as "evil spirit" but something like "unpleasant spirit." Esther Hamori renders it "a harmful spirit."[7] According to Stephen Chapman, "while the narrative therefore indicates that God may chasten and punish, it does not—contrary to the implication of several modern translations (e.g., NJPS, NRSV)—attribute evil to God. This troubling of Saul is presented, moreover, as a continual occurrence, which can only be intermittently relieved by music (16:16, 23)."[8] In the words of Ryan Stokes, "That this spirit is called *rāʿâ* ['evil'] does not constitute a moral assessment of the spirit, but specifies that the spirit is one that inflicts harm."[9]

God also sends an evil spirit—or unpleasant spirit, or harmful spirit—between Abimelech and the men of Shechem (Judg. 9:23) in order to bring about the downfall of Abimelech, who had killed his seventy half brothers (see v. 5).

And then there is the spirit of falsehood (*ruaḥ sheqer*) who, according to Micaiah, volunteers to deceive Ahab in order to bring about his death (1 Kings 22:19–23 // 2 Chron. 18:18–22). We looked at this passage in Chapter Two. To punish Ahab for all his wickedness, God inspires Ahab's (false) prophets with a deceitful spirit so that these prophets tell the king what he wants to hear, that is, that victory in the upcoming battle is assured. This is all according to the (true) prophet Micaiah's report of a vision. One may wonder how effective such deception is when the messenger explains the deception. And we may wonder—at least, I wonder—how seriously

6 On these passages, see Hamori, "Spirit of Falsehood."
7 Hamori, "Spirit of Falsehood," 19.
8 Chapman, *1 Samuel as Christian Scripture*, 151.
9 Stokes, *Satan*, 55.

we're supposed to take Micaiah's report of a vision; could he just be making up a story (a parable of sorts) in order to get Ahab to see that he's being tricked by his prophets, who have no secure message from any god?

Other texts that should be considered include at least 2 Kings 19:7 (// Isa. 37:7) and Isaiah 19:13–14. In the first passage, God sends a spirit of falsehood (without the word "falsehood" being used) to the king of Assyria to get him to leave Judah alone. In the second passage, God sends a "spirit of confusion" to Egypt. Note also that God says that he deceives false prophets (Ezek. 14:9).

NEW TESTAMENT PASSAGES

The New Testament doesn't present a picture of God using "harmful" or "unpleasant" agents in order to destroy people, but there are New Testament passages that present God as bringing about the downfall of people in a way pretty similar to what we've seen in the Old Testament. It will be worth our time to notice that the idea is not limited to the Old Testament. I'll just quote a few verses.

> God sends them a powerful delusion, leading them to believe what is false. (2 Thess. 2:11)
>
> Therefore God gave them up in the lusts of their hearts to impurity, to the degrading of their bodies among themselves. (Rom. 1:24; see also vv. 26, 28)
>
> As it is written, "God gave them a sluggish spirit, eyes that would not see and ears that would not hear, down to this very day." (Rom. 11:8, quoting Isa. 29:10)
>
> In order that
> "they may indeed look, but not perceive,
> and may indeed listen, but not understand;
> so that they may not turn again and be forgiven."
> (Mark 4:12; cf. Isa 6:9–10)

WHAT SHOULD CHRISTIAN BELIEVERS DO WITH THESE PASSAGES?

I do not know the best way to account theologically for these passages, but I will mention a few points that readers might find helpful as they reflect on this aspect of Christian Scripture.

Actually, I have just one thing to say about it all: What we notice about God in these passages could be viewed as an aspect of his justice. All of the passages we've examined—in the Old Testament and in the New Testament—concern people against whom God wants to bring judgment, because they are all people who have rejected God. This is exactly how Hamori describes the spirit of falsehood: "The purpose is judgment-related, as the one afflicted with falsehood is shown to have been in the wrong already. The result is often death to a king (usually violent) or removal of political opponents, ensuring Israel's security and preserving God's plan for the elect."[10] Whether we're talking about Ahab or Pharaoh or the Assyrians or the people who receive the strong delusion in 2 Thessalonians 2:11, all of the harmful actions from God are directed against people who have already rejected God.

Christian readers are usually fine with the notion that God will punish the wicked, that God must punish the wicked because he is a just God. So, again, the passages that we have looked at in this chapter are simply an aspect of God's justice, punishing the wicked. I think the hesitation we have about it in these cases is that—in the Old Testament, at least—God uses an agent to accomplish his judgment, an agent who does rather unpleasant things.

These passages are not too distant from those other passages we mentioned at the beginning of this chapter in which God uses human agents (like the Assyrians) to accomplish his purpose of punishment. Let's think about another example along those lines. Several passages of Scripture make it clear that Nebuchadnezzar accomplished the will of God by his destruction of Judah and his exiling the Judeans to Babylon. When Zedekiah, king of Judah, sent word to Jeremiah asking if God would rescue Judah out of Nebuchadnezzar's hand (Jer. 21:1–2), God responded, "I myself will fight against you" (v. 5). God was on Nebuchadnezzar's side,

---

[10] Hamori, "Spirit of Falsehood," 18.

calling him "King Nebuchadnezzar of Babylon, my servant" (25:9, 27:6). To Zedekiah's predecessor, Jehoiachin (also known as Jeconiah or Coniah), God said, "I will hand you over to those you dread, who intend to take your life, to Nebuchadnezzar" (22:25 ESV). The same sort of thing is in Ezekiel, where God says that he is bringing Nebuchadnezzar against Tyre and Egypt (Ezek. 26:7, 29:18–19, 30:10). Nebuchadnezzar was God's agent of destruction, sort of like the destroyer in Exodus 12:23. Habakkuk does not at all like the fact that God planned on using the Chaldeans (Babylonians) to punish the Judeans (Hab. 1:1–2:1), and God's response is that "the righteous live by their faith" (Hab. 2:4).

We need to distinguish these evil spirits in the Old Testament from the evil spirits in the New Testament. The New Testament evil spirits are also called "demons," and they do afflict people who haven't necessarily rejected God, such as the Syrophoenician woman's daughter (Mark 7:25) and a young boy (Mark 9:17). These demons in the New Testament are not servants of God but are in conflict with God. We will talk about them in Chapter Ten.

But the spiritual beings we've been talking about in this chapter are God's servants. They are sent on missions by God for the purpose of harming people in some way, just as YHWH used Nebuchadnezzar to harm people—people who needed punishment for their wickedness. The difference is that Nebuchadnezzar probably did not realize he was serving the purposes of YHWH, whereas the spirits we've been talking about did realize it. When God's spiritual servants are sent on missions of harm toward people, they can even be described with a Hebrew term we have not yet met in our study: the word *satan*. In fact, the angel of the Lord is at times described as *satan*. We will examine those passages in the next chapter.

CONCLUSION

The main point of this chapter is that God has a variety of spiritual servants at his disposal. Some of those servants have the job of taking care of God's children, whereas Scripture also mentions other spiritual servants of God who have a different job: to bring harm to people. These servants are under God's control, accomplishing his purposes, and fulfilling his justice.

CHAPTER FIVE

THE HEBREW TERM SATAN

Now there was a day when the sons of God came to present themselves before YHWH, and the satan also came among them.

—Job 1:6 ESV

We don't know Satan's name. Or let me put it this way: The being we know as Satan does not have a name in the Bible. Yes, the word *satan* appears plenty in the Bible, especially in the New Testament, but it's a title or description rather than a name. The Hebrew word *satan* (pronounced saw-tawn) means . . . well, the meaning is debated (we'll get to that), but something like "adversary," and in the Hebrew Bible (the Old Testament) the word *satan* applies to more characters than just the Prince of Darkness. Indeed, some scholars argue—just as I will argue—that the word *satan* never applies to the Prince of Darkness in the Old Testament.

Now maybe you're thinking that if his name is not Satan, it must be Lucifer. Well, no, it's not. The word *lucifer* came to be associated with Satan through a particular interpretation of Isaiah 14:12, but most of our Bibles (the recent translations) do not have the word *lucifer* there, and that term was not originally intended to be the name of an evil spirit. We will discuss Isaiah 14:12 in Chapter Eight.

The Hebrew word *satan* came into Greek as *satanas* (saw-taw-naws), a transliteration rather than a translation, and this transliteration appears in the New Testament quite a bit. The Hebrew term was sometimes translated in the Septuagint with the Greek word *diabolos* (also meaning something close to "adversary"), which in English morphed into the word "devil." We know that "devil" is not a name, and that's why we put a definite article ("the") in front of the word: the devil. We should probably do the same for the word *satan* in the New Testament: We should probably say "the satan." Only one time is the word *satan* in the New Testament possibly used as a name (Luke 22:3).[1]

At any rate, whether we know his name or not, we're talking about the chief enemy of God, and we will refer to him in this study as Satan (as if it's his name, which we know it's not) and as the devil.

A CHRISTIAN CONCEPT

You'll probably be surprised to learn that ancient Judaism says barely anything about the devil or Satan. A "chief agent of evil" never comes up in Philo or Josephus, and hardly at all in the deuterocanonical literature (maybe Sir. 21:27 and Wisd. of Sol. 2:24).[2] The Dead Sea Scrolls and some other apocalyptic literature do mention sometimes an angelic opponent of God's people, but this angel is rarely or maybe never called Satan. But Satan appears all over the place in the New Testament and other early Christian literature.[3]

In the Old Testament, Christians often find Satan in several passages. English Bibles usually print "Satan" as a personal name in the first two chapters of Job, as well as in Zechariah 3 and 1 Chronicles 21. I have already indicated that very likely we should not consider these passages as talking about the Prince of Darkness, the chief opponent of God. I mean that the use of "Satan" as a personal name in English Bibles in these passages is a

[1] See Farrar, "New Testament Satanology," 60 n. 241.

[2] Cf. Farrar, "New Testament Satanology," 34–39. It is common to interpret Sir. 21:27 in reference to a human rather than a supernatural being (see Chapter Six, note 5). It is also possible (preferable, I think) to interpret Wisd. of Sol. 2:24 in reference to a human, as I show in Chapter Eight.

[3] See the studies of Farrar and Williams, "Diabolical Data"; Farrar and Williams, "Talk of the Devil"; Farrar, "Intimate and Ultimate Adversary."

mistake. It would be better to have "the *satan*" maybe, or "the adversary" or some such. We'll talk about translation possibilities in a moment.

It is often the case that Christians also find the Prince of Darkness in the Old Testament where the term *satan* does not appear, such as in the snake in Genesis 3, and the descriptions of rulers in Isaiah 14 and Ezekiel 28. We'll get to these passages in Chapter Eight. For now, let's look at the passages in the Old Testament where the word *satan* appears.

THE TERM SATAN IN THE HEBREW BIBLE

The Hebrew noun *satan* (שָׂטָן) appears twenty-seven times in the Hebrew Bible (see Chart 5.1). Let's go through the verses one by one. I'm going to leave the word *satan* untranslated so that you can see it, and I'm going to put in a footnote the way the Septuagint (LXX) translates the term,[4] because that will be useful when we get to the New Testament in the next chapter.

Chart 5.1. The Word *Satan* in the Hebrew Bible (27 appearances)

Verse	Referent	Greek Translation (LXX)
Numbers 22:22	angel of the Lord	ἐνδιαβάλλειν
Numbers 22:32	angel of the Lord	εἰς διαβολήν
1 Samuel 29:4	David	ἐπίβουλος
2 Samuel 19:22	sons of Zeruiah	εἰς ἐπίβουλον
1 Kings 5:4	no adversary for Solomon	ἐπίβουλος
1 Kings 11:14	an adversary for Solomon	σαταν (twice)

[4]Aside from the times that Greek *diabolos* translates Hebrew *satan*, the term *diabolos* appears in the LXX in the following passages, including deuterocanonical books: Esther 7:4, describing Haman (the Hebrew has צר *ṣar*, "enemy"); 8:1, also describing Haman (Hebrew: צרר *ṣōrēr*, "enemy"); Wisd. of Sol. 2:24, a passage to be discussed in Chapter Eight; and 1 Macc. 1:36, in reference to the citadel in Jerusalem. Moreover, the Greek transliteration *satanas* (with a Greek ending), which appears frequently in the New Testament, appears only once in the LXX, at Sir. 21:27, and it has the definite article, i.e., "the adversary." The Common English Bible translates: "When the ungodly curse their enemies [= the *satan*], they curse themselves." But for another form of the Greek transliteration of *satan* (without a Greek ending) in the LXX, see 1 Kings 11:14, 23.

Verse	Referent	Greek Translation (LXX)
1 Kings 11:23	an adversary for Solomon	σαταν (cf. 1 Kings 11:14)
1 Kings 11:25	an adversary for Solomon	--
Zechariah 3:1	celestial being	ὁ διάβολος
Zechariah 3:2 (twice)	celestial being	ὁ διάβολος (second time in the vocative without the article)
Psalm 109:6	human	διάβολος
Job 1:6	celestial being	ὁ διάβολος
Job 1:7 (twice)	celestial being	ὁ διάβολος
Job 1:8	celestial being	--
Job 1:9	celestial being	ὁ διάβολος
Job 1:12 (twice)	celestial being	ὁ διάβολος
Job 2:1	celestial being	ὁ διάβολος
Job 2:2 (twice)	celestial being	ὁ διάβολος
Job 2:3	celestial being	ὁ διάβολος
Job 2:4	celestial being	ὁ διάβολος
Job 2:6	celestial being	ὁ διάβολος
Job 2:7	celestial being	ὁ διάβολος
1 Chronicles 21:1	???	διάβολος

Human Adversary

Sometimes the word *satan* refers to a human being. There are seven clear examples.

First, the Philistine commanders worry that David—who is currently living among them because King Saul of Israel has driven him from his homeland—might become their enemy when they are most vulnerable.

> But the commanders of the Philistines were angry with him; and the commanders of the Philistines said to him, "Send the man back, so that he may return to the place that you have assigned to him; he shall not go down with us to battle, or else he may become a *satan*[5] to us in the battle. For how could this fellow reconcile himself to his lord? Would it not be with the heads of the men here?" (1 Sam. 29:4)

In another passage, David gets angry with Abishai, son of Zeruiah, for suggesting that he kill Shimei for cursing King David.

> But David said, "What have I to do with you, you sons of Zeruiah, that you should today become a *satan*[6] to me? Shall anyone be put to death in Israel this day? For do I not know that I am this day king over Israel?" (2 Sam. 19:22)[7]

Next, Solomon reflects on the prosperity granted him by God.

> But now YHWH my God has given me rest on every side; there is neither *satan*[8] nor misfortune. (1 Kings 5:4)

But, at the end of his life, Solomon no longer enjoys God's blessing, and God raises up opponents for the king.

> And YHWH raised up a *satan*[9] against Solomon, Hadad the Edomite; he was of the royal house in Edom. (1 Kings 11:14)

> God raised up another *satan*[10] against Solomon, Rezon son of Eliada, who had fled from his master, King Hadadezer of Zobah. (1 Kings 11:23)

---

[5]LXX: ἐπίβουλος, *epiboulos*, "one who makes schemes or plots." I take definitions for Greek terms appearing in the LXX from Muraoka, *Greek-English Lexicon*.

[6]LXX: same as in 1 Sam. 29:4.

[7]This is verse 23 in the Hebrew text. We will talk about the interpretation of this verse near the end of this chapter.

[8]LXX: same as in 1 Sam. 29:4.

[9]LXX: σαταν, *satan*. That is, the LXX does not translate the word but transliterates it. This move implies that the Hebrew word had already come into Greek as a recognizable term.

[10]LXX: σαταν, *satan*. The LXX has a different arrangement for the passage, so that the content of this verse is in v. 14.

> He was a *satan*[11] of Israel all the days of Solomon, making trouble as Hadad did; he despised Israel and reigned over Aram. (1 Kings 11:25)

In Psalm 109, the psalmist is pretty upset with some people that have been doing him wrong. So he asks God for a whole string of punishments on his enemies, one of which is as follows.

> Appoint a wicked man against him; let a *satan*[12] stand on his right. (Ps. 109:6)

Good Angelic Adversary

Sometimes a good angel is an adversary to someone. There are two clear examples, both used in the story of Balaam in Numbers 22. You remember that God didn't like what Balaam was up to, so he sent his angel to oppose him. Balaam couldn't see the angel, but his donkey could.

> God's anger was kindled because he was going, and the angel of YHWH took his stand in the road as his *satan*.[13] (Num. 22:22)

> The angel of YHWH said to him, "Why have you struck your donkey these three times? I have come out as your *satan*[14] because your way is perverse before me." (Num. 22:32)

An Unclear Example: Chronicles

Some appearances of *satan* in the Bible might leave the reader uncertain as to the type of being we're talking about. There is one clear example of unclarity, a known unknown, as Donald Rumsfeld might have labeled it. In truth, it's only an unknown in Hebrew; in English Bibles, the text is usually very clear, because the translators have made the interpretation for you.

---

[11] The LXX omits this verse.

[12] LXX: διάβολος, *diabolos*, "he who is intent on harming [somebody] else's well-being and interests." This Greek term is often associated with evil speech, such as slander; see below, note 21. As mentioned earlier, this Greek word eventually morphed into the English word "devil."

[13] LXX: ἐνδιαβάλλειν, *endiaballein*, "to calumniate, speak ill of." This provides an interesting interpretation of the mission of the angel. NETS translates: "to oppose him" and puts the alternative meaning "to accuse him" in a note.

[14] διαβολή, *diabolē*, "false, malicious accusation."

(That is, English translations have eliminated the unclarity that exists in the Hebrew Bible; as often, by clarifying the text, they have obscured the text.)

> A *satan*[15] stood up against Israel, and incited David to count the people of Israel. (1 Chron. 21:1)

This verse is usually translated in English with a capital *s* "Satan" so that there is no doubt readers will think of the Prince of Darkness. But the Hebrew text is not clear; it just says "an adversary" incited David. I prefer that translation because it leaves the matter of interpretation up to the reader instead of having the translators do that work for you.[16]

If our text says that an adversary incited David to number Israel, who might this adversary be? As in the first set of examples above, it could be a human being, maybe a foreign king who challenged David's strength.[17] Or, like in the second set of examples above, it could be an angelic adversary sent by God, perhaps the angel of YHWH, as in the case of Balaam. Or maybe it's Satan. The text is not clear, and I don't know what the right answer is, although I strongly prefer the first two options.

Let's remember the parallel passage in 2 Samuel 24, where the text does not use the word *satan* but rather says, "Again the anger of YHWH was kindled against Israel, and he incited David against them, saying, 'Go, count the people of Israel and Judah'" (v. 1). According to 2 Samuel, it is YHWH who orchestrated the census, resulting ultimately in punishment on David and Israel. As we saw in the previous chapter, sometimes God uses agents to accomplish his purposes, even purposes that are in some ways harmful to humans. It seems unlikely that the Chronicler was attempting to correct the theology of 2 Samuel by attributing David's census to Satan rather than to YHWH; more plausibly, the Chronicler was specifying the agent (a *satan*) that God used to accomplish his harmful purposes. In my view,

---

[15] LXX: διάβολος, *diabolos*. See earlier on Ps. 109:6.

[16] See also Stokes, "Satan, YHWH's Executioner," 269.

[17] Japhet, *I & II Chronicles*, 375, argues that the word refers to a human, against the common view that Satan is a proper name here, as, for example, in Bell, "Demon, Devil, Satan," 193; see also Clines, *Dictionary of Classical Hebrew*, 8:123, which says that *satan* is apparently a personal name here.

this *satan* in 1 Chronicles 21 was one of YHWH's angelic agents.[18] I do acknowledge, however, that Christian theology has room for God's use of even Satan himself to accomplish divine purposes.[19]

The Remaining Examples: Zechariah and Job

We've gone through ten examples of *satan* in the Hebrew Bible. There are seventeen more, and they're all concentrated in two books: Job (14x) and Zechariah (3x). In both books, the word *satan* refers to a celestial being. If Satan appears anywhere in the Old Testament under that name (i.e., actually called "Satan"), it is in one of these books, or both. The word *satan* in these two books always has the definite article in Hebrew, "the" *satan* (Heb.: *ha-satan*), and the Septuagint always translates in these two books with the phrase *ho diabolos* (ὁ διάβολος),[20] a word often interpreted with reference to slander (a "slanderer" or a "gossip"), though it could bear a more general meaning, "opponent."[21] In any case, English Bibles often render the Greek term as "devil" in the New Testament.

In the book of Job, the scene with the *satan* takes place in heaven, God's throne room, and the same seems to be true for the scene in Zechariah. Let's start with the passage in Zechariah, just because it's shorter.

In this passage, the postexilic prophet Zechariah has a vision of Joshua, the high priest.

---

[18]According to Laato, "Devil in the Old Testament," the agent in 2 Samuel 24 // 1 Chronicles 21 cannot be human, because the "anger of YHWH" in 2 Samuel 24 is itself a celestial being. Stokes, *Satan*, 17–26, also argues strongly (and largely convincingly) that the *satan* of 1 Chronicles 21 is a celestial being in the employ of YHWH, perhaps even the angel of YHWH, on analogy with the Balaam narrative. On the other hand, Archie T. Wright, *Satan*, 26, believes that "the most likely scenario in the case of 1 Chronicles 21 is that this is not a heavenly being at all but rather is a military adversary of David and Israel."

[19]For an example of how the apparently wicked spiritual being called the Prince of Mastema in Jubilees unwittingly accomplished God's purposes in the exodus at Jubilees 48.15–19, see the discussion in Stokes, *Satan*, 108–9.

[20]Exceptions: *satan* is not translated at Job 1:8; and at Zech. 3:2, in the speech of God, the LXX does not use the definite article (the Hebrew does) because *diabolos* is in the vocative case.

[21]For the translation "slanderer" or similar, see Liddell et al., *Greek-English Lexicon*, 390; Danker, *Greek-English Lexicon*, 226–27; Montanari, *Brill Dictionary of Ancient Greek*, 481; Diggle, *Cambridge Greek Lexicon*, 1:341. For the more general definition, see Muraoka, *Greek-English Lexicon*, 149; Chadwick, *Lexicographica Graeca*, 87–94, discussing the verbal form (διαβάλλω).

> Then he showed me Joshua the high priest standing before the angel of YHWH, and the *satan* standing at his right hand to accuse [or "oppose" or "attack"] him. And YHWH said to the *satan*, "YHWH rebuke you, the *satan*! YHWH who has chosen Jerusalem rebuke you! Is not this man a brand plucked from the fire?" (Zech. 3:1–2)

What is happening in this scene? If you keep reading, you learn that Joshua is wearing dirty clothes—an offense that brings guilt on him and, according to Exodus 28:43, might result in his death—but he gets to remove those clothes, and he is told: "I have taken your guilt away from you, and I will clothe you with festal apparel" (Zech. 3:4). Then God tells Joshua, "If you will walk in my ways and keep my requirements, then you shall rule my house and have charge of my courts, and I will give you the right of access among those who are standing here" (v. 7). Immediately thereafter, we read a prophecy about the coming "branch" (v. 8), a messianic title (cf. Jer. 23:5).

So, what's going on? God is commissioning Joshua as "his man," his priest for the current time. Joshua needs to step up and be a leader for God's people. The change of clothes symbolizes the purification (from dirty to clean) of Joshua for his task, with the promise he will have a place "among those who are standing here" (Zech. 3:7). That must be a reference to heavenly beings and confirms that this scene does take place in heaven, with angels serving as witnesses.

Now for the part of the passage quoted above: The *satan* is doing what to Joshua? The Hebrew verb that appears at the end of verse 1 is a verbal form of *satan*, so the meaning of this verb is bound up with the meaning of the noun, which we have already noted is in dispute.[22] It means something like "oppose," but scholars often give a more precise meaning, usually "accuse," which is how the NRSV translates the verb at Zechariah 3:1. Ryan Stokes has argued that the translation "accuse" is off base and that the verb really means "attack."[23] For the moment, let's go with the usual interpretation, that the *satan* is accusing Joshua of something. What's the accusation?

---

[22] For the meaning of the verb and the noun, see the end of this chapter.

[23] Stokes, "Satan, YHWH's Executioner." Moberly also pushes back against the translation "accuse"; see Moberly, *Old Testament Theology*, 248 n. 11.

Most likely he's accusing him of wearing dirty clothes, that is, of being impure, of not being a worthy recipient of God's trust. But even though the accusation is in some ways true—Joshua is, in fact, wearing dirty clothes; he is impure—God has plans for Joshua, and so God will purify him. But if Stokes is right and the verb *satan* means "attack," then the *satan* here would be "attacking" Joshua and poised to kill him if permitted to do so by the angel of YHWH.

Here's the big question for our study: Who is the *satan* here? Is the *satan* a creature under God's authority, or is he in rebellion against God? What are the *satan*'s ultimate motives? There's going to be disagreement about this, but I think it's completely possible (and many scholars do, also) that the *satan*'s motives in this passage are to serve God. The role of the *satan* here is often compared to a prosecuting attorney, and, while that analogy might not be exactly right,[24] it does help us to think through the possibilities. Consider the different officers of the court in the legal system. There's the prosecutor; there's the defense attorney; there's the judge; there are others. Which one is the good guy, and which one is the bad guy? Well, none of them are "the bad guy." They all have their role to play, even though the prosecutor and the defense attorney are opposed to each other. But they are not opposed regarding the ultimate goal, which is that justice be done. No prosecutor wants to send an innocent person to prison. No defense attorney wants a criminal to get away with murder. But they play their respective roles, offering vigorous arguments for "their side," with the confidence that everyone working together in this way will result in justice.[25]

---

[24]Sometimes scholars note that there was no spiritual prosecutor in conceptions of the divine council in the ancient Near East; on the other hand, that meaning is precisely the role played by Satan in the late antique rabbinic work *Pesikta Rabbati* 45.2, for which see Reeg, "Devil in Rabbinic Literature," 73–74 (but others also bring accusations before God; "Devil in Rabbinic Literature," 77). This same passage from *Pesikta Rabbati* also comes into focus in Anderson, *Sin*, 107–8. The notion that the *satan* is a type of supernatural prosecuting attorney is tied to the translation of *satan* as "accuser," which might not be right, as we have seen. See the end of this chapter for a discussion.

[25]I recognize that this characterization of the criminal justice system in most countries, certainly in my own, is so idealistic as to be naïve. See Martens, *Reforming Criminal Justice*. The fact that in practice the system does not work as well as in theory does not obviate the point I am trying to make.

What we've got in Zechariah 3 looks like a courtroom scene. God on his throne is the judge. (Or maybe it's God's representative, called here the "angel of YHWH.") The *satan* plays his part, making sure that Joshua's unworthiness is fully exposed.[26] The Lord knows full well about Joshua's impurity, but he doesn't accept the *satan*'s accusation because he has plans for Joshua. So the Lord tells the *satan* to shut up. (Or, as I keep saying, maybe the *satan* is not accusing Joshua but standing ready to attack or execute him for his impurity in the presence of God.)

Could the *satan* be Satan here, the Prince of Darkness, the enemy of God? I suppose we could follow that interpretation, and certainly many Christian readers have assumed the truthfulness of that interpretation, helped along by their English translations that refer to "Satan" (unhelpfully, in my view). But let's notice what the *satan* is not doing here. We usually think about Satan as lying (John 8:44) and tempting people (Matt. 4:1–11) to get them to sin. This picture of Satan is based on the New Testament, which we'll consider in the next chapter. But the *satan* in Zechariah 3 is not doing these things. He is not lying to Joshua or about Joshua—Joshua really is wearing dirty clothes; he really is impure; he really is unworthy of God's confidence. If the *satan* is accusing Joshua of wearing dirty clothes (or standing ready to execute him for the same), it's an accurate accusation. And the *satan* is not trying to get Joshua to sin; he is not tempting Joshua. If the *satan* is accusing Joshua, he is doing something connected with Satan in the New Testament, at least in one passage (Rev. 12:10). But, of course, others also accuse, such as Moses (John 5:45), so it's not necessarily a bad thing to do. But if this *satan* in Zechariah is Satan, it's an unusually tame Satan, standing before God's throne, explaining the truth about one of God's servants.

I prefer the other interpretation, that this *satan* is not God's enemy but God's servant, doing the job assigned him by God. Mostly the reason I lean this way is because we haven't found a being called *satan* in the Old

[26]This idea is pretty common in biblical scholarship. See, e.g., Heiser, *Unseen Realm*, 57: "The *satan* described in these passages is not the devil. Rather, he's an anonymous prosecutor, as it were, fulfilling a role in Yahweh's council—bringing an accusatory report." See also Laato, "Devil in the Old Testament," 4: "a certain office in the divine council" (though Laato apparently thinks this is the devil himself).

Testament that is God's enemy, and since our passage can be read as if this adversary is in God's service, I think that's how ancient Jews would have interpreted the vision. (Remember our previous chapter, where we saw that God employs spiritual beings who do things negative toward humans.)

The biggest roadblock to this reading is the statement in verse 2: "YHWH rebuke you, *satan*!" Farrar sees in this divine rebuke of the *satan* some tension in the relationship, as if God and the *satan* are not exactly on the same side (though neither does Farrar think Zechariah 3 contains the Satan of the New Testament).[27] I wonder if the same sort of tension can be found when a judge overrules a prosecutor's objection or holds the prosecutor in contempt of court. Despite such judgments against the prosecutor, both parties are still officers of the same court, ultimately sharing the same goals. They are not enemies. Ryan Stokes compares this to 2 Samuel 19:22, where David rebukes his buddy Abishai for wanting to carry out an execution of the traitor Shimei; such a rebuke did not mean that David and Abishai were enemies.[28] For me, this interpretation provides a better scenario for making sense of Zechariah 3 than positing that the *satan* is God's enemy.

Now for the book of Job, containing the most well-known appearance of Satan in the Old Testament. In Job, Satan appears only in the first two chapters. Let's look at the relevant verses with the name "Satan" removed and the Hebrew noun *satan* inserted.

> Now there was a day when the sons of the *elohim* came to present themselves before YHWH, and the *satan* also came among them. YHWH said to the *satan*, "From where have you come?" The *satan* answered YHWH and said, "From going to and fro on the earth, and from walking up and down on it." And YHWH said to the *satan*, "Have you considered my servant Job, that there is none like him on the earth, a blameless and upright man, who fears God and turns away from evil?" Then the *satan* answered YHWH and said, "Does Job fear God for no

[27] Farrar, "New Testament Satanology," 33.

[28] Stokes, *Satan*, 15. Stokes also points to Isaiah 6, where Isaiah stands guilty (v. 7) in God's presence, deserving (by his own admission) death but receiving pardon and a commission.

> reason? Have you not put a hedge around him and his house and all that he has, on every side? You have blessed the work of his hands, and his possessions have increased in the land. But stretch out your hand and touch all that he has, and he will curse you to your face." And YHWH said to the *satan*, "Behold, all that he has is in your hand. Only against him do not stretch out your hand." So the *satan* went out from the presence of YHWH. (Job 1:6–12 ESV)

And after killing most of the people Job loves and destroying most of his possessions, the *satan* engages in another conversation with God.

> Again there was a day when the sons of the *elohim* came to present themselves before YHWH, and the *satan* also came among them to present himself before YHWH. And YHWH said to the *satan*, "From where have you come?" The *satan* answered YHWH and said, "From going to and fro on the earth, and from walking up and down on it." And YHWH said to the *satan*, "Have you considered my servant Job, that there is none like him on the earth, a blameless and upright man, who fears God and turns away from evil? He still holds fast his integrity, although you incited me against him to destroy him without reason." Then the *satan* answered YHWH and said, "Skin for skin! All that a man has he will give for his life. But stretch out your hand and touch his bone and his flesh, and he will curse you to your face." And YHWH said to the *satan*, "Behold, he is in your hand; only spare his life."
>
> So the *satan* went out from the presence of YHWH and struck Job with loathsome sores from the sole of his foot to the crown of his head. (Job 2:1–7 ESV)

Given how the discussion has proceeded so far, you probably won't be surprised that I'd like to explore the possibility that the *satan* in Job is not truly God's enemy, not the Satan of the New Testament, but a being in God's service. If that kind of a reading for the *satan* is possible for Zechariah 3, I think the same could be done with the story in Job. How would such a reading proceed? If the *satan* is God's servant—one of the "sons of God" who has come to God's throne room to report on his recent activities, how he's faring in carrying out his duties—then the *satan*'s assignment from the Lord would apparently be to examine people's lives to make sure they were being obedient, and to inform the Lord when he suspects something fishy. Like in Zechariah, here the *satan* would be like a prosecuting attorney, or—maybe better—a police officer, patrolling the earth, looking for people to "arrest" and bring before the judge (God). He's on the lookout for people committing crimes.[29] According to Stokes, "he was authorized to dispense corporal or capital punishment on behalf of God."[30] There's a similar type of passage at Zechariah 6, where four "winds" or "spirits" are sent out by God to patrol the earth (Zech. 6:7). At Zephaniah 1:12, God speaks as if he himself is doing the patrolling.

Notice that it is the Lord who mentions Job as someone beyond reproach, someone about whom the *satan* could find nothing worthy of reporting in the divine council. But the *satan* suspects that Job is serving God only to get all the perks that come with piety. According to this reading strategy, it's not that the *satan* is Job's enemy, certainly not God's enemy, but that the *satan* suspects that Job is just a little too perfect, and there must be something he's hiding. One of the points that the book of Job makes is that the *satan*'s suspicions turn out to be baseless, but the type of suspicion he voices is perfectly legitimate, and one that we often share. Walter Moberly asks:

> Is it not legitimate to want to know whether a person really is what he appears to be? Especially when someone is held up as exemplary, is it not appropriate to seek assurance that this person is genuine? To raise such a question may not leave the questioner sounding "nice," but that is beside the point.[31]

---

[29] For an interpretation of the *satan* similar to the one I present here, see Pope, *Job*, 10. Other commentators think that the *satan* is not a rightful member of the divine council but an intruder; see Andersen, *Job*, 82.

[30] Stokes, *Satan*, 41.

[31] Moberly, *Old Testament Theology*, 250.

Let's imagine a similar case. What if you ran a day care, and someone you've known all your life applied for a job at the day care. You have no concern about this person being around kids. You know this person is a faithful churchgoer, has a good family, has raised a good set of kids. Would you ask this person, as a part of the application process, to submit to a background check? Of course you would. First of all, it's the law; but second, there are too many cases we've heard about of exactly this kind of thing—that is, someone hiring a trusted friend who ends up abusing people. Imagine if you're shopping around for day cares for your own children, and one of the day cares tells you that they haven't done background checks on their employees. Is there any chance your kids would be going to that day care? What if they said they'd done background checks on most of the employees, but not the janitor, and anyway he's a very sweet guy who loves being around kids? I would say, "Good luck with that," and find a different day care.

Or let's go a different direction. What are some of the questions that a potential campaign manager is going to ask a political candidate before signing on to run a campaign? It's going to get pretty personal, pretty invasive, pretty fast. "Tell me about any extramarital affair, or anytime you've kissed someone besides your spouse, even if you just kissed the back of the person's head. Tell me about anyone besides your spouse whose shoulders you have rubbed, or whom you've touched in any way that someone else might interpret as sexual. Tell me about your finances—yours, and the finances of your whole extended family. Tell me about any addictions you've ever had or anyone in your extended family. Tell me about any police records in your family."

I'm not saying that God needs to run a background check on Job before he knows whether Job is really who he seems to be. It's more like God needs to run a background check on Job so that God can show everyone (including Job?) that Job is really who he seems to be, that there are people in the world who serve God not for the perks but because they love God. I think we can even imagine that there is some suspicion among God's heavenly servants that God is not administering justice fairly, that he's giving Job special treatment. Everyone else has to endure various hardships, but Job lives a cushy life, protected by God. Perhaps the *satan* is just voicing the concern of other "sons of God" who are not brave enough to accuse God of playing favorites. The *satan* is not brave enough, either, not brave enough to bring up the matter. But since God asked, the *satan* takes his chance and tells God what everyone's been thinking. God plays along, allows Job to endure incredible hardship, to make it clear that Job's piety is not basically selfish but arises from genuine faith. The result is to the glory of God.

If we think about the book of Job after chapter 2, who is to blame for all of Job's sufferings? The *satan* is never mentioned in the book again, and all the characters (even God! see Job 42:7) agree that it was God who brought suffering on Job; he's the one responsible. Now, that fact in itself does not prove that the *satan* is not Satan, since God can use even Satan for his own purposes (e.g., the crucifixion). As Augustine said, God "knows how to make good use of good and evil alike."[32] And you might read the Lord's comment to the *satan* at Job 2:3—"you incited me against him, to destroy him for no reason"—as indicating a strain in the relationship between God and the *satan*, maybe because the *satan* is Satan.[33] I think that interpretation would be pushing God's comment too far. Given the lack of a Satan figure in the Old Testament, I am inclined to think of this character labeled "the *satan*" as one of the sons of God giving his regular report to the Lord, not someone intending to bring pain to God, nor intending to entice Job to sin, just intending to show that Job is not so perfect, after all.[34]

One more point: This reading perspective answers the common question from readers of Job "How can Satan be in heaven?" The answer is: He's not.

WHAT DOES "SATAN" MEAN?

Now that we've looked at all the appearances of the noun *satan* in the Hebrew Bible, and we've been introduced to the cognate verb *satan* (which

---

[32] *City of God* 14.27.

[33] On this verse, see also the Babylonian Talmud, tractate Bava Batra 16a §§5–7, where Satan persuades God to harm Job. (The section numbers for the Talmud refer to the divisions in the online presentation of the Talmud at sefaria.org.)

[34] I understand the circularity in this argument: The *satan* in Job can't be Satan because Satan doesn't appear in the Old Testament.

appears six times in the Hebrew Bible),[35] let's think about what the words mean. Just like the noun, the verb is translated into English with words like "oppose" or "accuse." Let's notice that "oppose" (like adversary) is a more general word, and "accuse" is more specific, a particular type of opposition. Does "accuse" work as the meaning of *satan*?

If you look through all the verses we have examined in this chapter, "accuse" and "accuser" don't always work. The angel of the Lord in Numbers 22 wasn't about to accuse Balaam of anything; he was about to smite him with the sword in his hand (vv. 23, 31). The angel tells Balaam that if Balaam's donkey hadn't turned aside, "I would have killed you" (v. 33). So also the opponents of Solomon in 1 Kings 11 weren't accusing the king, and the Philistines didn't fear that David would accuse them of anything (1 Sam. 29:4).[36] The word "accuse" does make sense in Zechariah 3 and, maybe, Job 1–2, but based on the fact that *satan* cannot mean accuse in the other passages, we might suggest that even in Zechariah and Job we should translate the term with the more general "oppose" (for the verb) and "opponent/adversary" (for the noun).[37]

But this translation might not work either—at least, in a passage like 2 Samuel 19:22 (v. 23 in Hebrew), where David rejects Abishai's offer to slay Shimei: "What have I to do with you, you sons of Zeruiah, that you should today become a *satan* to/for me? Shall anyone be put to death in Israel this day?" It is unclear how Abishai's killing Shimei would make him an adversary to David, as English translations often render this verse. What Abishai wants to do is kill the traitor Shimei on David's behalf. Abishai wants to be an executioner for David. And that is the translation favored by Ryan Stokes: ". . . that you should today become an executioner for me? Shall anyone be put to death in Israel this day?"[38] Most of the verses fit with the idea that the *satan* is going to physically attack someone: the angel of

[35] Zech. 3:1; Ps. 38:20, 71:13, 109:4, 109:20, 109:29. Clines, *Dictionary of Classical Hebrew*, 8:122, says that the verbal form means "to be an adversary" and "perh[aps] specif[ically] accuse," citing Zechariah.

[36] Stokes, "Satan, YHWH's Executioner," 253.

[37] This is the suggestion of Moberly, *Old Testament Theology*, 248.

[38] Stokes, *Satan*, 8–9. See also Stokes, "Satan, YHWH's Executioner," 253–61, where Stokes examines all the appearances of *satan* (noun and verb) in the Bible, aside from Job and Zechariah, and convincingly argues that the notion of "attack" fits the context much better than the notion of "accusation."

the Lord versus Balaam, the *satan* versus Job, David versus the Philistines. When the psalmist prays that God appoint a *satan* for his enemy (Ps. 109:6), the following verses make it clear that the psalmist wants this *satan* to kill his enemy. Stokes translates Zechariah 3:1 this way: "Then he showed me the high priest Joshua standing before the angel of YHWH, and the Executioner standing on his right to execute him."[39]

CONCLUSION

I know there's going to be disagreement, especially about Zechariah and Job, but what I have tried to show is that every single appearance of the word *satan* in the Hebrew Bible can be interpreted without reference to Satan, and many of them must be interpreted without reference to Satan because they refer to a human being or the angel of the Lord. If Job and Zechariah do not contain appearances of Satan, then the *satan* in these books must be interpreted as a member of the divine council—one of the "sons of God," as Job puts it—whose assignment is to accuse or, probably better, to attack or execute. In carrying out this divine assignment, the *satan* would be something like the destroyer of Exodus 12:23 or the "evil spirit" that afflicted Saul, discussed in the previous chapter. No matter what interpretation one prefers, though, I (alongside others) would argue that there is no instance in which the Hebrew word *satan* is used as a proper name, and therefore there is no Old Testament passage in which we ought to read in our English Bibles about Satan with a capital *s*. It would be much better if translations would talk about "the Adversary" or "the Opponent" or "the Executioner"; that translation choice would leave the matter open enough that readers of the English Bible could make their own decisions about the identity of this character.

[39] Stokes, "Satan, YHWH's Executioner," 264. See also the discussion of this passage in Stokes, *Satan*, 12–17.

"Have you forgotten the Deep Magic?" asked the Witch.

"Let us say I have forgotten it," answered Aslan gravely. "Tell us of this Deep Magic."

"Tell you?" said the Witch, her voice growing suddenly shriller. "Tell you what is written on that very Table of Stone which stands beside us? Tell you what is written in letters deep as a spear is long on the fire-stones on the Secret Hill? Tell you what is engraved on the scepter of the Emperor-beyond-the-Sea? You at least know the Magic which the Emperor put into Narnia at the very beginning. You know that every traitor belongs to me as my lawful prey and that for every treachery I have a right to a kill."

"Oh," said Mr. Beaver. "So *that's* how you came to imagine yourself a queen—because you were the Emperor's hangman. I see."[40]

[40] Lewis, *Lion, the Witch and the Wardrobe*, ch. 13. Mr. Beaver's description of the White Witch is reminiscent of the description of the devil in James, *Daemonologie* (1597), preface, "God's hangman." See also Orr, "'God's Hangman.'"

CHAPTER SIX

SATAN IN THE NEW TESTAMENT

The God of peace will shortly crush the satan under your feet.

—Rom. 16:20

The reason the Son of God appeared was to destroy the works of the devil.

—1 John 3:8 ESV

In the New Testament, the situation is altogether different from that of the Old Testament.[1] Here the terms "devil" and "Satan" are used many times in reference to a spiritual being that is opposed to God and his purposes in the world. He is "the evil one" (Matt. 13:19, 13:38; John 17:15), "the tempter" (Matt. 4:3), "the ruler of the demons" (Matt. 9:34, 12:24), and "the enemy" (Matt. 13:39; Luke 10:19). Satan has his own kingdom (see Mark 3:24–27) that stands opposed to God's kingdom, and so Satan removes the seed of God's kingdom from people's hearts (Mark 4:15 // Matt. 13:19 // Luke 8:12), or he sows weeds among God's wheat (Matt. 13:25, 28; cf. v. 39).

---

[1] Or is it? For an attempt to see the New Testament Satan as equivalent to the *satan* of the Hebrew Bible (i.e., a willing servant of YHWH), see Kelly, *Satan*. I am open to this interpretation, but I find that it fails in the face of New Testament passages depicting Satan with his own kingdom opposed to that of God (e.g., Mark 3:22–30) and as destined for punishment (e.g., Matt. 25:41).

Punishment in eternal fire awaits the devil and his angels (Matt. 25:41; cf. Rev. 20:10).

TERMINOLOGY

Satan

The New Testament, written in Greek, adopts the Hebrew word *satan* and gives it a Greek ending, so that we often read in the New Testament about *ho satanas* (ὁ σατανᾶς). That *ho* before *satanas* is the definite article in Greek, so we could translate the expression, "the satan," just as in the Hebrew Bible, as we saw in the previous chapter.[2] Although *satanas* in the New Testament is usually understood as a name, it could be a title.[3] The word *satanas*, with (30x) or without (6x) the definite article, appears thirty-six times in the New Testament (Chart 6.1). The third-century Greek Christian author Origen provides a helpful introduction to the term.

> The word Satan in Hebrew, which some spell in a more Hellenic fashion as *Satanas*, means adversary [ἀντικείμενος, *antikeimenos*] when translated into Greek. Every man who has chosen evil and to live an evil life so that he does everything contrary to virtue is a Satan, that is, an adversary to the Son of God who is righteousness, truth, and wisdom. But speaking more strictly, the Adversary is the first of all beings that were in peace and lived in blessedness who lost his wings and fell from the blessed state.[4]

Origen tells us what the word *satan* means and explains that it has a general use—whoever is opposed to God—and a particular use in reference to the great Adversary. But we will see that the New Testament does

[2] On the other hand, Greek can use the definite article with proper names (unlike Hebrew and English); see Siebenthal, *Ancient Greek Grammar*, §134.

[3] Stokes, *Satan*, 198.

[4] Origen, *Against Celsus* 6.44, trans. Chadwick, 361. Origen immediately quotes Ezekiel 28, a passage that will occupy us in Chapter Eight. For the Greek text, I have used Origenes, *Contra Celsum libri viii*, ed. Marcovich, 422. The Greek term ὁ ἀντικείμενος was a common designation for the chief agent of evil in early Christian literature after the New Testament, as documented by Farrar, "Intimate and Ultimate Adversary," 521–33. For another early Christian definition of the term *satan*—or, actually, the Greek term *satanas*—see Justin, *Dialogue with Trypho* 103.5, who (incorrectly) divides the word: *sata*, "apostate," *nas* "serpent."

not explain his origins, so that Origen's statement that this adversary fell from his original blessed state—no matter how common it is in Christian tradition—is not directly substantiated in Scripture.

Before the New Testament, the Greek word *satanas* (with the Greek ending) or *satan* (without a Greek ending) appears in the Greek Old Testament only three times, twice in 1 Kings 11:14 and once in the deutero-canonical book of Sirach (or Ecclesiasticus) 21:27, and each of these three appearances refers to a human *satan*, a human adversary.[5] There is also at least one instance when *satanas* is used in the New Testament in reference to a human being, when Jesus told Peter, "Get behind me, *satan*!" (Mark 8:33 // Matt. 16:23). This use of the Greek word in reference to humans, both in the Septuagint and in the New Testament, suggests that perhaps the word is not to be understood as a proper name. Neither was it a proper name in first-century Jewish literature outside the New Testament, such as the Dead Sea Scrolls.[6]

Chart 6.1. Satan in the New Testament (36x)

Verse	Speaker and Greek Grammar	Context
Matt. 4:10	Jesus: vocative, anarthrous	Jesus rebukes Satan after tempting
Matt. 12:26 (// Mark 3:23)	Jesus: articular	Satan can't cast out Satan
Matt. 16:23 (// Mark 8:33)	Jesus: vocative, anarthrous	rebuking Peter
Mark 1:13	Narrator: articular	Jesus tempted by Satan
Mark 3:23 (// Matt. 12:26)	Jesus: anarthrous	Satan can't cast out Satan

[5]The one in Sirach is debatable, but the major translations (such as the NRSVCE and the NAB) render the word as "adversary"; see also Skehan and Di Lella, *Wisdom of Ben Sira*, 311–12. The Hebrew text of this verse is not extant, but presumably it had *ha-satan*. Farrar, "New Testament Satanology," 35–38, argues that Sir. 21:27 refers to a supernatural *satan*, since the verse warns against cursing the *satan* and the Dead Sea Scrolls attest the practice of cursing Belial or Melki-reša (1QM 13.4; 4Q280 2.2; 4Q286 7 ii). The Greek translator of Sirach possibly understood the term *satan* differently from the original Hebrew author; see Lange, "Satanic Verses," 42–43.

[6]Lange, "Satanic Verses."

Verse	Speaker and Greek Grammar	Context
Mark 3:26 (// Luke 11:18)	Jesus: articular	Satan divided against himself
Mark 4:15	Jesus: articular	parable of the sower
Mark 8:33 (// Matt. 16:23)	Jesus: vocative, anarthrous	rebuking Peter
Luke 10:18	Jesus: articular	watching Satan fall
Luke 11:18 (// Mark 3:26)	Jesus: articular	Satan divided against himself
Luke 13:16	Jesus: articular	woman bound by Satan
Luke 22:3	Narrator: anarthrous	Satan entered Judas
Luke 22:31	Jesus: articular	Satan asked to sift Peter
John 13:27	Narrator: articular	Satan entered Judas
Acts 5:3	Peter: articular	Satan filled Ananias's heart
Acts 26:18	Jesus (quoted by Paul): articular	the dominion of Satan
Rom. 16:20	Narrator: articular	God will crush Satan
1 Cor. 5:5	Narrator: articular	deliver such a one to Satan
1 Cor. 7:5	Narrator: articular	Satan will not tempt you
2 Cor. 2:11	Narrator: Narrator: articular	advantage taken by Satan
2 Cor. 11:14	Narrator: articular	Satan disguises himself as an angel of light
2 Cor. 12:7	Narrator: anarthrous	angel of Satan
1 Thess. 2:18	Narrator: articular	Satan hindered Paul from going to the Thessalonians
2 Thess. 2:9	Narrator: articular	man of lawlessness in accord with Satan
1 Tim. 1:20	Narrator: articular	Paul handed Hymenaeus and Alexander over to Satan
1 Tim. 5:15	Narrator: articular	some are following Satan
Rev. 2:9	Jesus (quoted by John): articular	synagogue of Satan
Rev. 2:13	Jesus (quoted by John): 2x, both articular	Satan's throne; where Satan dwells
Rev. 2:24	Jesus (quoted by John): articular	Satan's "deep secrets"

Verse	Speaker and Greek Grammar	Context
Rev. 3:9	Jesus (quoted by John): articular	synagogue of Satan
Rev. 12:9	Narrator: articular	the great dragon
Rev. 20:2	Narrator: articular	Satan bound for a millennium
Rev. 20:7	Narrator: articular	Satan released

On the other hand, the New Testament use of the term *satanas* is distinctive, at least in terms of the prevalence of this term for the chief agent of evil. We will see in the next chapter that *satan*, or *satanas*, was not at all a popular term in contemporary Jewish literature. There were all sorts of terms for the chief agent of evil in ancient Jewish literature, including Mastema, Asael, Melkiresha, and Belial. This last term (or, actually, the similar Beliar, βελιάρ) does appear once in the New Testament (2 Cor. 6:15), but the others are absent. In the New Testament, along with the word *satan*, we also find the word *diabolos* (διάβολος), often rendered in English as "devil" and, as we saw in the previous chapter, usually interpreted as a "slanderer."[7] While these two terms, *satan* and *diabolos*, were not prominent in ancient Jewish literature at the time of the New Testament, they are very prominent in the New Testament. As Thomas J. Farrar has said, the New Testament consolidates Satanological terminology; outside the New Testament, a variety of terms refer to the chief agent of evil, but the New Testament usually uses only two terms.[8] The word Beelzebul also appears seven times (as we will see in a moment), but as Farrar points out, it is the Pharisees who use that term, and Jesus prefers to speak about the *satan* (Mark 3:22–30).[9]

Is the term *satan* a proper name in the New Testament (Satan)? Here, again, Farrar is helpful. He says that before the New Testament there is no clear instance of *satan* being used as a proper name, though there

[7] See Chapter Five, note 21.

[8] Farrar, "New Testament Satanology," 57–62.

[9] Farrar, "New Testament Satanology," 57. The other six appearances of *Beelzebul* are Matt. 10:25, 12:24, 12:27; Luke 11:15, 11:18–19. Even when Jesus does use the term (Matt. 10:25, 12:27; Luke 11:18–19), he seems to be merely adopting the language of his opponents.

are some possibilities (Jub. 10.11; 1 En. 53.3; etc.).[10] In the New Testament, *satan* can almost always be interpreted as a term describing a function ("adversary," "executioner," etc., as in the Hebrew Bible) rather than as a name. Remember, even in the New Testament, the word *satan* is usually preceded by a definite article, so we could render it "the *satan*" (again, just like in the Hebrew Bible).[11] It may be that Luke 22:3—"then Satan entered into Judas," without a definite article—represents the first appearance of Satan as a name. But even later, in early second-century Christian literature (the apostolic fathers), the term is still probably not a name. The mid-second-century author Justin Martyr is the first one who certainly uses Satan as a name, in his *Dialogue with Trypho* 103.5. In non-Christian Jewish literature, apparently the Hebrew term *satan* is first attested as a proper name in the third-century rabbinic work called the Tosefta (tractate *Shabbat* 17.23).[12]

Christian literature of the early second century resembles early Jewish literature in its use of a variety of terms for the chief agent of evil, with the name Satan or the descriptor "the *satan*" featuring surprisingly rarely. "The *satan*" appears in the apostolic fathers only three times,[13] and a few more times in Justin Martyr and in early Christian apocryphal texts.[14] Against the background of ancient Jewish literature and the foreground of second-century Christian literature, the prominence of the term *satan* in the New Testament is striking.

Devil (Diabolos)

The term *diabolos* ("devil," maybe "slanderer") appears more often in the Septuagint (22x) and more often even in the New Testament (37x) than the term *satanas*. In the New Testament, it almost always has the definite

[10] Farrar, "New Testament Satanology," 58. The possible exceptions are listed in note 237.

[11] Farrar, "New Testament Satanology," 60 n. 41, where he also discusses the anarthrous occurrences of the term *satan* and explains why these do not militate against interpreting the term as a function word rather than a name. On 2 Cor. 12:7, see also Stokes, *Satan*, 200 n. 16.

[12] Most of this paragraph relies on the same footnote in Farrar cited previously: "New Testament Satanology," 60 n. 41.

[13] Ignatius, *Epistle to the Ephesians* 13.1; Polycarp's *Letter to the Philippians* 7.1; Epistle of Barnabas 18.1.

[14] See the chart in Farrar, "Intimate and Ultimate Adversary," 521–33.

article, and it hardly ever refers to anything other than the chief agent of evil, so we naturally translate it as "the devil" (Chart 6.2). But three times it is plural and refers to people in an indefinite way, "slanderers" (1 Tim. 3:11; 2 Tim. 3:3; Titus 2:3), and once it refers to Judas (John 6:70).

The word *diabolos* in the Septuagint is usually the translation of the Hebrew *satan* (see Chart 5.1).[15] Given that the term *diabolos* in Greek is often interpreted in terms of wicked speech ("slanderer"),[16] this translation coheres with the view that the *satan* accuses people, as at Revelation 12:10, where the word *katēgor* (κατήγωρ, "accuser") is used, its only appearance in the New Testament.[17]

Chart 6.2. *Diabolos* in the New Testament (37x)

Verse	Speaker and Greek Grammar	Context
Matt. 4:1	Narrator: articular	tempted by the devil
Matt. 4:5	Narrator: articular	tempted by the devil
Matt. 4:8	Narrator: articular	tempted by the devil
Matt. 4:11	Narrator: articular	tempted by the devil
Matt. 13:39	Jesus: articular	sowing tares among wheat
Matt. 25:41	Jesus: articular	fire prepared for the devil and his angels
Luke 4:2	Narrator: articular	tempted by the devil
Luke 4:3	Narrator: articular	tempted by the devil
Luke 4:6	Narrator: articular	tempted by the devil
Luke 4:13	Narrator: articular	tempted by the devil

15 Wieger, "'Celui qu'on appelle διάβολος.'"

16 As mentioned in Chapter Five (note 21), some lexical resources also propose a looser definition of the term: "opponent."

17 Stokes, "Satan, YHWH's Executioner," 269 n. 42. See also Farrar, "New Testament Satanology," 35, who considers this translation to serve as "a bridge between the Hebrew Bible's heavenly accuser and the later Devil." But, of course, Farrar is assuming that Hebrew *satan* means "accuse" rather than Stokes's proposed "attack." On the meaning of the term see Chapter Five, and see later in this chapter on whether accusation is a part of the activities of the New Testament Satan.

Verse	Speaker and Greek Grammar	Context
Luke 8:12	Jesus: articular	the devil removes the word of God from people's hearts (parable of the sower)
John 6:70	Jesus: anarthrous	one of Jesus's disciples is a *diabolos*
John 8:44	Jesus: articular	descendants of the devil
John 13:2	Narrator: articular	the devil prompted Judas
Acts 10:38	Peter: articular	sick people were oppressed by the devil
Acts 13:10	Paul: anarthrous	son of a devil
Eph. 4:27	Narrator: articular	do not give place to the devil
Eph. 6:11	Narrator: articular	resist the schemes of the devil
1 Tim. 3:6	Narrator: articular	condemnation of the devil
1 Tim. 3:7	Narrator: articular	snare of the devil
1 Tim. 3:11	Narrator: anarthrous, plural	"not slanderers"
2 Tim. 2:26	Narrator: articular	snare of the devil
2 Tim. 3:3	Narrator: anarthrous, plural	"slanderers"
Titus 2:3	Narrator: anarthrous, plural	"not slanderers"
Heb. 2:14	Narrator: articular	holds the power of death
James 4:7	Narrator: articular	resist the devil
1 Pet. 5:8	Narrator: anarthrous	your adversary the devil
1 John 3:8	Narrator: 3x, always articular	destroying the works of the devil
1 John 3:10	Narrator: articular	children of the devil
Jude 9	Narrator: articular	Michael contended with the devil
Rev. 2:10	Jesus (quoted by John): articular	the devil persecutes Christians
Rev. 12:9	Narrator: articular	the so-called devil
Rev. 12:12	Narrator: articular	the devil has come down to earth
Rev. 20:2	Narrator: anarthrous	the devil is the *satan*
Rev. 20:10	Narrator: articular	the devil deceives

Other Terms

Aside from these two most common designations for the chief agent of evil, the New Testament employs an array of other terms. Farrar and Williams count 137 references to Satan in the New Testament, counting all his titles.[18] Some of these other titles include the following:

- the evil one (*ponēros*)[19]: Matt. 5:37 (?), 6:13 // Luke 11:4 (?); Matt. 13:19, 13:38; John 17:15; Eph. 6:16; 2 Thess. 3:2; 1 John 2:13, 2:14, 3:12, 5:18–19
- the tempter: Matt. 4:3; 1 Thess. 3:5
- the enemy: Matt. 13:39; Luke 10:19
- Beelzebul: Matt. 10:25, 12:24, 12:27; Mark 3:22; Luke 11:15, 11:18–19
- Beliar/Belial: 2 Cor. 6:15
- the ruler of this world: John 12:31, 14:30, 16:11; cf. 2 Cor. 4:4 ("god of this world")[20]
- the prince of demons: Matt. 9:34, 12:24 // Mark 3:22 // Luke 11:15

Most of these terms are straightforward, but two of them could use some discussion.

---

[18] Farrar and Williams, "Diabolical Data." But seven New Testament books do not mention a chief agent of evil (Gal.; Phil.; Titus; Philem.; 2 Pet.; 2–3 John).

[19] Two caveats: First, it is not clear that all of these examples are referring to a spiritual being rather than to the abstract concept of "evil." This ambiguity, reflected in the English translations, is indicated here by parenthetical question marks. Second, perhaps we should translate the Greek word πονηρός (*ponēros*) not as "evil" or "wicked" but some other way. It is the word used in the LXX for the "evil spirit" sent from YHWH in 1 Sam. 16:14 (discussed in Chapter Four). Kelly, *Satan*, 90–91, does not bring up this passage from the LXX but does insist that *ponēros* could just mean "harmful." The standard dictionary for New Testament Greek does propose different meanings: not only morally wicked but also "of poor quality" (see Matt. 7:17) and "unhealthy" (see Matt. 6:23); Danker, *Greek-English Lexicon*, 851–52. The premier dictionary of the LXX also lists several definitions, the second of which is "harmful and injurious"; Muraoka, *Greek-English Lexicon*, 575–76.

[20] While it is by no means unusual to interpret Paul's phrase "the god of this world" in 2 Cor. 4:4 as a reference to Satan, the interpretation of this title has been debated from very early times and continues to provoke disagreement; see Litwa, *Evil Creator*, 90–108. For an interpretation that sees 2 Cor. 4:4 as a reference to Satan, see Brown, *God of This Age*. For an interpretation seeing in Paul's phrase "the god of this world" a reference to the God worshiped by Paul, see Poobalan, "Who Is the 'God of This Age'?"

Beelzebul[21]

This name combines two elements, *baal* and *zevul*. The second element, *zevul*, means something like prince, and the combination, *Baal Zevul*, meaning "Prince Baal," is attested as early as the fourteenth or fifteenth century BC at Ugarit. While the two elements appear in the Hebrew Bible separately—*baal* many times and *zevul* a few times[22]—the combination *Baal Zevul* does not appear. Instead, we find *Baal Zevuv* (or *Zebub*) four times (2 Kings 1:2, 3, 6, 16), where the name is associated with a Philistine god ("the god of Ekron"). The name means "lord [*baal*] of the flies [*zevuv*]." The Septuagint translates it as Βααλ μυῖα, "Fly Lord," or perhaps "Baal the Fly." The form in the New Testament, Beelzebul ("Prince Baal"), corresponds more closely to the form probably used by this god's worshipers.[23] The term in the New Testament is associated with "the ruler of the demons" (Mark 3:22). This term, *Baal Zevul*, "is not attested in the period between the Ugarit tablets and the Synoptic gospels."[24] Outside the New Testament, the term is used in ancient sources for the chief agent of evil only in the Testament of Solomon.[25]

Belial

The Hebrew word *belial* means "wickedness" and appears twenty-seven times in the Hebrew Bible (e.g., Deut. 13:13; Judg. 19:22, 20:13), never in reference to a supernatural being. The term is often used in postbiblical Jewish literature (the Pseudepigrapha and the Dead Sea Scrolls) to describe a chief agent of evil.[26]

Interchangeable Terms

Sometimes parallel passages in the Gospels use different terms, probably indicating that the terms were considered to refer to the same being.

---

[21] Fornberg, "Baal-Zevul."

[22] For *zevul*, see 1 Kings 8:13; Isa. 63:15; Hab. 3:11; Ps. 49:14; 2 Chron. 6:2. In most of these verses, *zevul* means "exalted."

[23] Herrmann, "Baal Zebub," *DDD*, 154–56.

[24] Fornberg, "Baal-Zevul," 98.

[25] See, e.g., Testament of Solomon 3:6, 6:1. A reconstructed Aramaic form of the word is found in the Dead Sea Scrolls (4Q560).

[26] Sperling, "Belial," *DDD*, 169–71.

> These are the ones on the path where the word is sown: when they hear, the *satan* immediately comes and takes away the word that is sown in them. (Mark 4:15)

> When anyone hears the word of the kingdom and does not understand it, the evil one comes and snatches away what is sown in the heart; this is what was sown on the path. (Matt. 13:19)

> The ones on the path are those who have heard; then the *diabolos* comes and takes away the word from their hearts, so that they may not believe and be saved. (Luke 8:12)

In these three parallel passages, the chief agent of evil is referred to as the *satanas* (Mark) or the evil one (Matthew) or the *diabolos* (Luke). We can also find an example within a single Gospel pericope: Matthew's account of the temptation of Jesus in the wilderness first mentions "the tempter" (Matt. 4:3), then the *diabolos* (4:5, 8, 11), and finally (in Jesus's mouth) the *satanas* (4:10).

ACTIVITIES

What does the devil do, according to the New Testament? He is a leader of angels (see Rev. 12:7, 12:9; 2 Cor. 12:7) who will be condemned to hell, or the lake of fire (Matt. 25:41; Rev. 20:10). The Bible does not say that the devil reigns in hell, or that he is "the torturer of the damned in hell."[27] The lake of fire is a punishment for Satan, not (like Brer Rabbit being thrown into the briar patch) his preferred residence. The New Testament gives no credence to the notion that Satan might think "Better to reign in hell, than serve in heaven."[28]

Temptation

The devil tempts Jesus (Matt. 4:1–11; Luke 4:1–13), and he can be designated simply "the tempter" (Matt. 4:3; 1 Thess. 3:5). The devil lies (John 8:44), and probably this lying has something to do with temptation. The better to deceive, he disguises himself as an angel of light (2 Cor. 11:14). He influenced Ananias to lie about the money he received for the property he sold

[27] Collins in Stokes, *Satan*, ix.
[28] *Paradise Lost* 1.263.

(Acts 5:3). The devil ensnares people (2 Tim. 2:26) and wants to devour people (1 Pet. 5:8). He tempts people in regard to sex (1 Cor. 7:5). People need to resist the devil so that he will flee (James 4:7). They need the armor of God to protect them from the devil's schemes (Eph. 6:11). They must avoid making room for the devil (Eph. 4:27).

Mischief

Sometimes Satan seems to be not so much tempting people to sin but annoying or oppressing them. This is apparently his role as the ruler of the demons (Matt. 12:22–37). Sometimes the devil (rather than his demons) is directly implicated in causing some physical harm to people (Luke 13:16; Acts 10:38). Paul describes his thorn in the flesh as "a messenger [or angel] of Satan" (2 Cor. 12:7). Jesus reveals to Peter that Satan has "demanded to sift all of you like wheat" (Luke 22:31). I'm not sure exactly what Satan wanted to do to Peter, or what the implications of "sifting" are. Maybe it involves temptation, but it seems equally or more plausible that Satan wanted to physically attack Peter. But notice that the implication of Luke 22:31 is that Satan can accomplish this sifting only if God allows him such power over Peter.

Ruling the Air

Ephesians 2 begins:

> You were dead through the trespasses and sins in which you once lived, following the course of this world, following the ruler of the power of the air, the spirit that is now at work among those who are disobedient.

This passage refers to someone—apparently, Satan—as "the ruler of the power of the air" (τὸν ἄρχοντα τῆς ἐξουσίας τοῦ ἀέρος). What is this supposed to mean? What does Satan have to do with the "air"? It's really not very mysterious: Satan is the ruler of the demons, and demons fly around in the air—or, at least, so the ancients thought. Philo defined demons (δαίμονες) as "souls flying in the air" (ψυχαὶ . . . κατὰ τὸν ἀέρα πετόμεναι).[29]

---

[29] Philo, *On the Giants* 6. Philo goes on to insist that the invisible demons inhabit the invisible air. See also Augustine's report (*City of God* 7.6) of the opinion of Varro, a first-century BC Roman writer, who talked about souls inhabiting the air.

A work known as 2 Enoch describes the fall of Satan (or Satanail) from heaven, after which: "And he was flying around in the air, ceaselessly, above the Bottomless."[30] According to Testament of Levi 3.2, the lowest heaven is the abode of the spirits assigned the task of punishing the wicked. From another angle, Eusebius (the fourth-century church historian) reports Greek opinion that "the parts about the moon and the atmosphere [belong] to daemons."[31]

That Eusebius is correctly reporting pagan opinion on the matter is confirmed by writers such as Apuleius, a second-century AD Latin author.

> Now there are certain intermediate, godlike powers [*quaedam divinae mediae potestates*], who are placed between the highest level, the ether, and the lowest, the earth, in this region of air, and they carry both our desires and our good deeds to the gods. These the Greeks call "demons," who traveling between those on the earth and those in heaven convey prayers from here and gifts from there, and go back and forth carrying requests from here and help from there, as it were ambassadors and goodwill messengers for both.[32]

In the third century, Origen complained about people making pagan sacrifices, which provide sustenance to the demons and keep them in the air around the earth, whereas if people would stop feeding them, the demons would get thin and float away further from earth.[33]Even in modern times, Pearl S. Buck described the early twentieth-century conception of a typical Chinese farmer: "The air and the earth were filled with malignant spirits who could not endure the happiness of mortals."[34]

---

[30] 2 Enoch 29.5 (*OTP* 1:148).

[31] Eusebius, *Preparation for the Gospel* 4.5, trans. Gifford, 154, or (in another reference scheme) 141c.

[32] *On the God of Socrates* 6.2–3, in Apuleius, *Apologia; Florida; De Deo Socratis*, trans. Jones, 359–61.

[33] Origen, *Exhortation to Martyrdom* 45; see also Origen, *Against Celsus* 7.5, where he does not use the term "demon" but talks about the souls of dead people weighed down by sin and hovering in the air close to earth, being fed by sacrifices.

[34] Buck, *Good Earth*, ch. 4. The idea comes up again in the next chapter, where Buck mentions "any evil spirit passing by chance through the air."

It was a well-established opinion among Jews and pagans that the air around the earth was inhabited by beings called in Greek "demons." In Ephesians 2:2, Paul apparently refers to Satan as the ruler of these demons.

Ruling the Nations

In Luke's version of the temptation narrative, the second temptation goes like this:

> Then the devil led him up and showed him in an instant all the kingdoms of the world. And the devil said to him, "To you I will give their glory and all this authority; for it has been given over to me, and I give it to anyone I please. If you, then, will worship me, it will all be yours." (Luke 4:5–7; cf. Matt. 4:8–9)

Does the devil control all the kingdoms of the world? That is the claim he makes here. The New Testament tells us in no uncertain terms that the devil is not to be trusted (John 8:44), so we might conclude that he is simply lying about his power over earthly kingdoms.[35] But his statement does stand in some harmony with other passages in Scripture. We saw in Chapter Three that there is a strong tradition of interpreting certain Old Testament passages as indicating that angels—maybe even fallen angels or wicked angels—have charge of particular nations. That is presumably the meaning of the "princes" (rulers) in Daniel 10 (see verses 13, 20–21). Remember also that a few times in the New Testament we encounter a phrase such as "the ruler of this world" or "the god of this world" (John 12:31, 14:30, 16:11; 2 Cor. 4:4), apparently in reference to Satan. Moreover, Revelation 13 clearly represents Satan as the power behind the Roman Empire. So there is some reason to think that Luke expects readers to regard the devil as sincere when he claims authority over the kingdoms of the world.

If we connect those passages discussed earlier in Chapter Three to this statement from the devil in Luke 4, then we might have an answer to another curiosity in the devil's speech: "It has been given over to me"—by whom? Who gave the devil authority over the nations? Well, the obvious answer is "God," since he is the one who has all authority, but also some

[35] Irenaeus, *Against the Heresies* 5.24.3, argued that Satan was lying here.

Old Testament passages seem to say as much (e.g., Deut. 4:19, 32:8). And if we conclude that the New Testament, at least sometimes, indicates that the kingdoms of the world are under the control of Satan, we might also relate this concept to the depiction of human kingdoms in Daniel 7 as fundamentally beast-like (remember Rev. 13) and opposed to the kingdom of God.[36]

Working against God

We have seen that Satan is God's enemy (Matt. 13:39; Luke 10:19), and as his enemy he tempts people and causes people physical harm. The devil also tries to thwart God's plans in general. He sows tares among God's wheat (Matt. 13:39). He removes the word of God from people's hearts (Luke 8:12). He worked against Paul's missionizing activity (1 Thess. 2:18). He has the power of death (Heb. 2:14). Most importantly, the devil worked to bring about the death of Jesus, particularly by motivating Judas to betray his master (Luke 22:3; John 13:2, 13:27). But, of course, it was this very action by the devil that ensured the devil's ultimate defeat (John 12:31–32, 14:30; cf. 1 Cor. 2:8)—for which purpose the Son of God appeared (1 John 3:8).

Working for God?

We saw in previous chapters that the Hebrew Bible does not really mention a spiritual being that opposes God's will in the manner of the devil of the New Testament. The word *satan* is used in the Hebrew Bible in reference to God's servants, particularly supernatural beings who sometimes do rather negative things to people, like attack them. Sometimes these negative actions align with God's will, when God wants to punish people or some such. Does the New Testament ever use the word *satanas* in this same way, referring to a being who is accomplishing God's will?

Well, in a way, even the New Testament devil, the enemy of God, cannot help unwittingly accomplishing God's will. If the Son of man came into the world to "give his life a ransom for many" (Mark 10:45), then to the extent that the devil helped to bring about the crucifixion, he participated in

[36] To situate these ideas within the broader context of other New Testament evaluations of empire, see Carter, *Roman Empire*, ch. 2. The notion that the devil rules the kingdoms of the world was essential to the political vision of Lipscomb, *Civil Government*.

accomplishing God's will—but only in an unintentional way.[37] Presumably the devil would not have worked toward bringing about the crucifixion had he known that he was ensuring his own defeat by doing so (see 1 Cor. 2:8). The Old Testament *satan* is different; he intentionally works for God, subject to the divine will, wanting to accomplish God's purposes. Can we see anything like that in regard to a being labeled in the New Testament *satanas* or *diabolos*?

The short answer is that it depends on how you interpret certain texts. Take a look at these passages.

> You are to hand this man over to the *satanas* for the destruction of the flesh, so that his spirit may be saved in the day of the Lord. (1 Cor. 5:5)
>
> Therefore, to keep me from being too elated, a thorn was given me in the flesh, a messenger of *satanas* to torment me, to keep me from being too elated. (2 Cor. 12:7)
>
> Among them are Hymenaeus and Alexander, whom I have turned over to the *satanas*, so that they may learn not to blaspheme. (1 Tim. 1:20)

Ryan Stokes proposes that the being called *satanas* in these texts could be working for God. "These texts give no indication that the Satan is being manipulated and only unwittingly serves God's beneficent purposes. They presuppose that the Satan is God's agent of attack for the purpose of punishing or disciplining errant humans, much as the Satan of earlier literature."[38] Is this the right way to interpret these passages? I am not sure. It does make some sense to say that the character called *satan* in the Hebrew Bible—who (I have argued, along with many others) willingly submitted to YHWH—would make an appearance or two in the later Jewish literature gathered into the New Testament. On the other hand, it seems to me that

[37] See the similar thoughts of Lipscomb, *Civil Government*, 38, 50–51.

[38] Stokes, *Satan*, 209. Stokes also sees this "good" *satan* (or, let us say, a *satan* that is submissive to God) at Luke 22:31; Matt. 6:13; and Rev. 12:10. For a much more thoroughgoing argument that the "good" *satan* of the Old Testament is the only *satan* familiar to the New Testament authors, see Kelly, *Satan*.

the character of the *satanas*, or the *diabolos*, is so consistently negative in the New Testament, so consistently an enemy of God and of everything that is good, that it is hard for me to imagine that Paul didn't have this negative character in mind in the quoted texts. In the New Testament, we do not see God assigning tasks to the *satanas*, for instance. It's true that Paul could use the term *satanas* in his own way,[39] and if the cited passages appeared in the Old Testament, I would probably interpret them along the lines proposed by Stokes, but since they appear in the New Testament, I am inclined to think of the term *satanas* even in these instances as referring to a wicked being.

Accusation?

Is accusation a part of the devil's work? Is he "the accuser"? Our previous chapter showed that there is debate about what exactly the word *satan* means in Hebrew. It has often been translated as "accuse," but maybe that translation is off base: Maybe it should be more general, "oppose," or maybe it should just be different, "attack." But there is one New Testament verse that takes away the ambiguity.

> Then I heard a loud voice in heaven, proclaiming, "Now have come the salvation and the power and the kingdom of our God and the authority of his Messiah, for the accuser [ὁ κατήγωρ, *ho katēgōr*] of our comrades has been thrown down, who accuses [ὁ κατηγορῶν, *ho katēgorōn*] them day and night before our God." (Rev. 12:10)

Here the devil, Satan (Rev. 12:9), participates in the activity of accusation against God's people—or, at least, he used to, but now he cannot. The verse uses a different word, not *satan* but *katēgōr*, so there is no debate about the translation; it definitely means "accuse." But it's the book of Revelation, so we might wonder how far to press the details, whether the book intends for us to take such a description of Satan in a literal or concrete way, or whether the description is symbolic like the rest of the book. I wonder, for instance, whether Revelation is borrowing imagery from the book of Job, where the character called the *satan* suggests that Job is

[39] Williams, *Spirit World*, 92.

not all he's cracked up to be. If the book of Job associates the *satan* with accusation (not the meaning of the word *satan*, but the character *satan*) in heaven, perhaps Revelation is merely borrowing that imagery, applying it to the evil character Satan, or the devil, in order to point out the impotence of Satan, who is no longer allowed to bring accusations against God's people. He has been thrown down. The reality signaled by these symbols is that God's people need worry about no accusation (whether in heaven or on earth); their status with God is secure.

WHAT THE NEW TESTAMENT DOES NOT SAY ABOUT SATAN

In the first decades of the third century, Origen recognized that preachers often gave more information about the devil than did the Scriptures.

> Regarding the devil and his angels and the opposing powers, the ecclesiastical preaching has taught that they indeed exist, but what they are, or how they exist, it has not explained sufficiently clearly. This opinion, however, is held by most, that this devil was an angel, but having become an apostate he persuaded as many angels as possible to fall away with himself, and even until now these are called his angels.[40]

Origen is right: That opinion is held by most—or, if not most people, at least most Christians I know believe that the devil "was an angel, but having become an apostate he persuaded as many angels as possible to fall away with himself." That's the view enshrined in *Paradise Lost*, and it obviously goes back long before Milton if Origen can already report it as the common opinion. Indeed, we've already seen the same view or something like it in the statement from Origen's *Against Celsus* that we quoted earlier in this chapter. Before Origen, we find something like this view in Irenaeus at the end of the second century, for whom the devil is a rebel angel.[41]

In pre-Christian Jewish literature, we find a story about a rebellion of angels that has different motivations and consequences from the tale in *Paradise Lost*. Actually, there are two rebellions: One group of angels

[40] Origen, *On First Principles* preface 6, trans. Behr, 8.

[41] *Haer.* 5.24.4. See Unger's translation in Irenaeus of Lyons, *Against the Heresies: Books 4 and 5*, 177–78.

lusts after human women and thereby falls into sin, and another group of angels teach humans the dark arts (such as sorcery and cosmetics). That's the story in the Book of the Watchers (the first part of 1 En.) from the third century BC, and it's a story that became influential in Christianity. We'll talk more about it in the coming chapters. For now we simply note that it is not a story that is found in Scripture—even if it is based on the strange account at the beginning of Genesis 6. And it's not a story that is usually told in Jewish literature in terms of "the devil" or "Satan" as the leader of these rebellious angels. It seems that the identification of the devil/Satan as an apostate angel did not long precede Origen.

Origen knew Scripture well enough to realize that the New Testament never makes this same identification. That is, the New Testament never refers to the devil as an angel (he *appears* as an angel of light at 2 Cor. 11:14), and it never refers to his origins at all, certainly not in terms of an apostasy that precipitated a rebellion of angels. Yes, Revelation 12 does describe a war in heaven, in which "Michael and his angels fought against the dragon. The dragon and his angels fought back" (Rev. 12:7). John next tells us that the dragon is Satan (Rev. 12:9), but this heavenly battle does not mark Satan's first rebellion against God, on the order of *Paradise Lost*, because the dragon has already, before the war, tried (unsuccessfully) to eat the messiah child (Rev. 12:4).[42] The New Testament does not describe the origins or being of Satan. We best listen to Origen: "The ecclesiastical preaching has taught that [the evil powers] indeed exist, but what they are, or how they exist, it has not explained sufficiently clearly."

Unsurprisingly, C. S. Lewis provides a nice summary of what we can know or infer about the devil from Scripture.

> One of the things that surprised me when I first read the New Testament seriously was that it talked so much about a Dark Power in the universe—a mighty evil spirit who was held to be the Power behind death and disease, and sin. The difference is that Christianity thinks this Dark Power was created by God, and was good when he was created, and went wrong.

---

[42] For more on this passage, see Chapter Eight.

Just a brief comment to point out the care with which Lewis wrote that last sentence. Notice that "Christianity thinks" this about the Dark Power; Lewis is careful not to claim that the Bible says as much. The idea itself—that the Dark Power was created good by God and then veered off course—is implicit in essential Christian doctrines and in biblical teaching that nothing exists that was not created by God (including the Dark Power) and that everything created by God was good. The Bible does not say that the Dark Power was created by God or that the Dark Power started out good; those are necessary inferences from clear biblical teaching.

Now, back to Lewis.

> Christianity agrees with Dualism that this universe is at war. But it does not think this is a war between independent powers. It thinks it is a civil war, a rebellion, and that we are living in a part of the universe occupied by the rebel.
>
> Enemy-occupied territory—that is what this world is. Christianity is the story of how the rightful king has landed, you might say landed in disguise, and is calling us all to take part in a great campaign of sabotage. When you go to church you are really listening-in to the secret wireless from our friends: that is why the enemy is so anxious to prevent us from going. He does it by playing on our conceit and laziness and intellectual snobbery. I know someone will ask me, "Do you really mean, at this time of day, to re-introduce our old friend the devil—hoofs and horns and all?" Well, what the time of day has to do with it I do not know. And I am not particular about the hoofs and horns. But in other respects my answer is "Yes, I do." I do not claim to know anything about his personal appearance. If anybody really wants to know him better I would say to that person, "Don't worry. If you really want to, you will. Whether you'll like it when you do is another question."[43]

All of that is good and helpful, an accurate depiction of a major element of the Christian story. But in a section on "what the New Testament does

[43] Lewis, *Mere Christianity*, 36. The quoted section is the conclusion of ch. 2 in book 2.

not say about Satan," we also need to take note of what Lewis says later (in the subsequent chapter).

> How did the Dark Power go wrong? Here, no doubt, we ask a question to which human beings cannot give an answer with any certainty.[44]

As much as we sometimes think we can answer that question, we who care about reading Scripture closely can only agree with Lewis, because Scripture has not revealed to us the origins of the Dark Power. Nevertheless, people have taken guesses—the subject of our next chapter.

[44] Lewis, *Mere Christianity*, book 2, ch. 3.

CHAPTER SEVEN

THE ORIGINS OF SATAN

It is perilous to study too deeply the arts of the Enemy, for good or for ill.

—Elrond

Elrond's advice is wise, but it's hard to be brief with this topic.[1] Most of what we know about Satan we don't really know. The Bible says so little about the things we want to know that people have filled in the gaps. The legend has grown. As we saw in the introduction, John Milton provided in *Paradise Lost* (1674) perhaps the most developed form of the Satan legend, certainly a very prominent form that has proven influential and entertaining. In this chapter we survey Milton's predecessors.

The previous two chapters have attempted to demonstrate how little the Bible says about the nature and origins of Satan—at least, how little it says on these topics in an explicit and straightforward way. The Old Testament, I have argued, never even mentions Satan with a capital *s*, the

[1] Elrond is referring to Saruman's study of Sauron, near the end of the chapter called "The Council of Elrond," in Tolkien, *Lord of the Rings*, book 2. Karl Barth said much the same thing about the study of demons, insisting that the theologian "must not linger or become too deeply engrossed" in such study; *Church Dogmatics*, vol. 3, pt. 3, 519 (§51.3). Compare also the advice of Socrates on not "imitating" vices while telling a story (Plato, *Republic* 392c–398b).

chief agent of evil. The New Testament does mention Satan—or, perhaps still, *the satan*, a title rather than a name, though now referring to an opponent of God rather than a servant—but the New Testament does not really cover his motivations (except very bluntly, to tempt people to sin, to cause mischief, etc.) or reveal what kind of being he is (except that he's the ruler of the demons) or explain where he came from. The Satan legend familiar to many modern Christians covers all of these issues and more, and the answers to the questions are based on peculiar (not, I think, straightforward) interpretations of biblical texts. Of course, non-straightforward interpretations of biblical texts might, indeed, be correct or helpful—or maybe not. Regardless, we should at least recognize that they are not straightforward.

This chapter investigates the origin of several of the elements of the developed Satan legend. We will survey what ancient Jewish literature outside the Bible has to say about Satan. Then we will trace the biblical data and ancient thought regarding the Satan legend, such as whether he's a fallen angel and how his fall came about. In the next chapter, we will explore three biblical passages that have been perhaps most influential to an understanding of Satan, though none of them use the term *Satan* or *devil*: Genesis 3, Ezekiel 28, and Isaiah 14. This is all territory that has been covered many times before—though I think it's worthwhile covering it again, and from the angle employed here.[2]

CHIEF AGENTS OF EVIL IN SECOND TEMPLE JUDAISM[3]

Let's start by getting a lay of the land in regard to Jewish ideas contemporary with the New Testament concerning *satan* figures. There is no unified Satan legend in Second Temple Judaism. There are several versions of a chief agent of evil, none of them given the name Satan or Lucifer but instead using several other names. Let's look at some of the relevant literature.

---

[2] For much more, see the series by Russell, *The Devil*; *Satan*; *Lucifer*; *Mephistopheles*. See also Stokes, *Satan*; Archie T. Wright, *Satan*.

[3] This territory has been much covered in recent scholarship. If I were you, I'd start with Stokes, *Satan*. If you want more, try these: Fröhlich and Koskenniemi, *Evil and the Devil*; Keith and Stuckenbruck, *Evil in Second Temple Judaism*; Tilly et al., *L'adversaire de Dieu—Der Widersacher Gottes*.

I mentioned in Chapter Five that neither Josephus nor Philo ever mentions a chief agent of evil. Another (unknown) author from the first century retold the stories of the Bible in a work called the Book of Biblical Antiquities (or its Latin title: *Liber antiquitatum biblicarum*, abbreviated LAB), which was formerly transmitted among the works of Philo, so that now the author is known as Pseudo-Philo (or Ps-Philo). The work was probably originally written in Hebrew, but the original is lost and we have only a Latin text that was probably translated from Greek. This author mentions (something like) a chief agent of evil only one time (LAB 45:6). In response to the atrocities narrated in Judges 19 (regarding the Levite's concubine) and the prior idolatry of Israel as prompted by Micah (Judg. 17–18), God condemns Israel, and he does so while talking to a character named "the adversary"—otherwise unmentioned in Pseudo-Philo's entire book. The Latin term for "adversary" here is *anteciminum*, which probably translates the Greek term τὸν ἀντικείμενον (*ton antikeimenon*), which in turn is likely a translation of Hebrew *ha-satan*. There is no reason to think that the *satan* here is Satan, an opponent of God; rather, as in the Hebrew Bible, the *satan* in the Book of Biblical Antiquities seems to be a servant of God, perhaps assigned the task of punishing Israel, though the *satan* doesn't do anything except listen to God.[4]

Not every ancient Jewish text cared to talk about a chief agent of evil, but several did, under various names. In what follows, we will briefly survey two parts of 1 Enoch—the Book of the Watchers (1 En. 1–36) and the Similitudes of Enoch (1 En. 37–71)—as well as Jubilees and the Dead Sea Scrolls.

Book of the Watchers, Third Century BC

Chief Agents of Evil: Shemihazah, Asael (Azazel)

The Book of the Watchers is the opening section of 1 Enoch (chapters 1–36). Fragments in Aramaic were found among the Dead Sea Scrolls, and most of the Book of the Watchers is available in Greek, but the entirety is known only in the Ethiopian Bible. In the Book of the Watchers, we read about the sin of angels, but there are two sets of angels that sin and two angelic

[4] Ps-Philo does mention sinful angels a couple times: LAB 32.1–2, 34.3.

leaders of the sinful angels. On the one hand, the angel Shemihazah leads some angels to mate with human women (an interpretation of Gen. 6:1–4). On the other hand, the angel Asael (or Azazel) leads some angels to sin by revealing secret knowledge, such as cosmetics and sorcery (similar in some ways to the Prometheus legend).[5]

Jubilees, Second Century BC

Chief Agent of Evil: Mastema

The book of Jubilees is (like 1 En.) known in full only in its Ethiopian version, though fragments of the original Hebrew were discovered among the Dead Sea Scrolls. The Ethiopic version presents the chief agent of evil as Mastema (מַשְׂטֵמָה) or Prince Mastema, whose name means "hostility."[6] At one point, the term *satan* is applied to Mastema (Jub. 10.11), though not as a name but rather a description ("adversary" or "attacker"); the term also appears a few other times, but not in reference to Mastema.[7] Jubilees describes some evil spirits, but it is not clear whether Mastema is himself one of them; in one passage he seems to be distinguished from them (Jub. 10). He is never identified as an angel. The origins of Mastema are not described, nor his ultimate end. There are times in Jubilees when Mastema appears as a servant of God carrying out the divine will to bring torment on wicked humans. Other times, Mastema works against God's will. These two aspects of Mastema's character in Jubilees perhaps arise from two different authors whose work has been combined in the present form of Jubilees.[8]

---

[5] On the link between Asael and Prometheus, see the discussion in Archie T. Wright, *Origin of Evil Spirits*, 116–19.

[6] The word appears twice in the Bible (Hos. 9:7–8). At Qumran (outside of Jubilees), it appears ten times, sometimes connected to Belial, e.g., the War Scroll 13.11, where Belial is called "a hostile angel" (*malak mastema*). Jubilees is cited and "the angel Mastema" is mentioned at Damascus Document 16.1-5. The original Hebrew of Jubilees might have used *mastema* not as a name but a common noun, "hostility," or "prince of hostility." On the term *mastema*, also also Chapter Four above, note 3.

[7] The word *satan* is used only as a common noun (Jub. 23.29, 40.9, 46.2, 50.5, and one debatable instance—common noun or name?—at 10.11; see Stokes, *Satan*, 82–84). Stokes thinks that most of these could refer to a human (not the one in ch. 23), but VanderKam seems to think that they all refer to a supernatural being, because the context is eschatological; VanderKam, *Jubilees*.

[8] See the discussion in Stokes, *Satan*, chs. 4–5; VanderKam, *Jubilees*, 1.50–52.

Mastema's first appearance in Jubilees is in chapter 10, when he gains permission from God to have some evil spirits under his command. He asks for and is granted a tenth of the evil spirits who are about to be imprisoned. As summarized by Thomas J. Farrar, in Jubilees Mastema "sends birds to devour the seed sown in the land, only to be thwarted by young Abram (Jub. 11.11–24). . . . Later Mastema provokes God to test Abraham by ordering him to sacrifice Isaac (Jub. 17.15–16; cp. Gen. 22:1), tries to kill Moses on his way to Egypt (Jub. 48.2–3; cp. Exod. 4:24), enables Pharaoh's magicians to perform wonders (Jub. 48.9; cp. Exod. 7:11) and is identified with the destroyer of Exod. 12:23 (Jub. 49.2)."[9]

Mastema is an accuser (Jub. 48.15–19; 1.20), at least in the Ethiopic version if not in the Hebrew.[10] He deceives people and he leads a host of demons—both new features of any depiction of the chief agent of evil. Whereas in the Hebrew Bible the term *satan* seems to refer to a function that a variety of angels could fulfill, in Jubilees Mastema is clearly an individual and not an office.

Similitudes of Enoch, First Century BC or AD

Chief Agent of Evil: Azazel

The Similitudes of Enoch is a middle section in 1 Enoch (chs. 37–71), and it is known only in its Ethiopian version. The chief agent of evil is named Azazel (cf. Lev. 16:8–10), who will be punished in a burning furnace (1 En. 54.5–6). The word *satan* appears four times, twice in the plural (40.7, 65.6), twice in the singular (53.3, 54.6), each time describing a celestial being, once (54.6) apparently referring to Azazel. This chief agent of evil seems to be a rebel, not in subjection to God but working against the divine will and therefore deserving of punishment. For Azazel, see also the Apocalypse of Abraham 13, 23; Jubilees 10.1–11.

---

[9] Farrar, "New Testament Satanology," 41.

[10] Stokes, *Satan*, 112–14.

Dead Sea Scrolls, Third Century BC through the First Century AD

Chief Agents of Evil: Melkiresha, Belial, Angel of Darkness

In the entirety of the Scrolls, the noun *satan* appears six times (other than in copies of the Bible), never with the definite article, never "the *satan*" but always "a *satan*."[11]

- Words of the Luminaries (4Q504): "there is neither adversary nor misfortune" (4.12–13; cf. 1 Kings 5:18)[12]
- Hodayot (1QH[a])[13]
    - "you rebuke every adversary who ruins . . ." (22.25)
    - "every adversary and destroyer" (24.19)
- Aramaic Levi Document (4Q213a): "Let no demonic adversary have power over me." (1.17)[14]
- 1QSb (1Q28b): "to *satan* . . . holy . . ." (1.8).[15] The line is very fragmentary, but the word *satan* is preserved.
- Prayer of Deliverance in 11QPsalms[a] (11Q5): "Let Satan not rule over me, nor an unclean spirit." (19.15)[16]

Only in this final instance can the word *satan* possibly be a proper name, as it is translated above. Still, it could well be a common noun: "Let an adversary not rule over me," or even "let a *satan* not rule over me."[17]

What title or name is usually applied to the chief agent of evil in the Dead Sea Scrolls? There are several terms.

Angel of Darkness. In the Rule of the Community (1QS), a section (3.13–4.26) concerns the righteous and the wicked, and the two spirits that rule

[11] On all of these passages, see Archie T. Wright, *Satan*, 51–60.

[12] See the translation in Wise et al., *Dead Sea Scrolls*, 523.

[13] Translation in Wise et al., *Dead Sea Scrolls*, 170–205.

[14] Translation in Wise et al., *Dead Sea Scrolls*, 304–14, at 305.

[15] Wise et al., *Dead Sea Scrolls*, 141, have not included the relevant line, for which see Qimron and Charlesworth, *Rule of the Community*, 123. While the line is also included in the commentary of Collins and Nati, *Rule of the Association*, 160–62, they make no comment on the term *satan* (but they translate it "adversary").

[16] I have used the English translation and Hebrew text printed by the scroll's first editor in Sanders, *Dead Sea Psalms Scroll*, 120–21. A similar translation is in Wise et al., *Dead Sea Scrolls*, 575.

[17] For the idea that *satan* is a common noun (not a proper name) in 11Q5, see Stokes, *Satan*, 147–48; Archie T. Wright, *Satan*, 54–57.

over both groups.[18] The section is called "The Treatise on the Two Spirits," and it begins this way:

> He created humankind to rule over the world, appointing for them two spirits in which to walk until the time ordained for His visitation. These are the spirits of truth and falsehood. Upright character and fate originate with the Habitation of Light; perverse, with the Fountain of Darkness. The authority of the Prince of Light extends to the governance of all righteous people; therefore, they walk in the paths of light. Correspondingly, the authority of the Angel of Darkness embraces the governance of all wicked people, so they walk in the paths of darkness. (3.17–21)[19]

The text goes on for a while, describing these two spirits. The Angel of Darkness tries to corrupt the righteous people (3.21–23), and he joins with other spirits in his work. "All the spirits allied with him share but a single resolve: to cause the Sons of Light to stumble" (3.24). To the Angel of Darkness is attributed *mastema*, "hostility" (3.23).

Melkiresha. The scroll known as 4QCurses (4Q280) consists in its preserved state almost entirely of a curse on an evil being called Melkiresha ("king of wickedness"). "Cursed are you, O Melkiresha, for all the schemes of your sinful desires. May God appoint you as an object of terror in the hands of those who wreak vengeance. May God not be gracious to you when you call out . . ." and so on.[20] The same name for the chief agent of evil is used in a work called the Visions of Amram, found in several copies of Cave 4 at Qumran (4Q543–548).[21] Amram is the father of Moses (Exod. 6:20). In his vision, he saw two angels arguing with each other for authority over Amram. After Amram chose to follow the angel of light, he was told by this angel that the other angel was named Melkiresha.

[18] See the commentary of Collins and Nati, *Rule of the Association*, 21–22.
[19] Translation in Wise et al., *Dead Sea Scrolls*, 120.
[20] Wise et al., *Dead Sea Scrolls*, 372.
[21] Wise et al., *Dead Sea Scrolls*, 547–50.

Belial. The word *belial* (בליעל) means "worthlessness" or "wickedness" and appears with this meaning in the Bible (e.g., Deut. 13:14; 2 Sam. 22:5 // Ps. 18:4), in Jubilees (1:20, 15:33), and sometimes in the Dead Sea Scrolls (e.g., 1QH[a] 11.30, 33).[22] But in ancient Judaism, Belial also became the name for a wicked being, as it is frequently in the Dead Sea Scrolls. In the War Scroll, depicting a battle between the forces of good and the forces of evil, the wicked angels are led by Belial.[23] The scroll begins: "The first attack of the Sons of Light shall be launched against the lot of the Sons of Darkness, against the army of Belial."[24] According to the War Scroll, Belial was made by God and remains under his control (1QM 13.11–12), though he is hostile to God's purposes (13.4).[25]

Belial also appears several times in the Damascus Document, a work found in several copies among the Dead Sea Scrolls but also in the Cairo Genizah, so that it is abbreviated CD (Cairo Damascus [Document]).[26] CD 12.2 mentions "the spirits of Belial," apparently indicating that Belial rules a band of wicked spirits.[27] Belial promotes sin in Israel, such as unchastity, arrogance, and defilement of the sanctuary (CD 4.13–18). It was Belial who empowered the Egyptian magicians to imitate some of the signs that Moses performed (CD 5.18–19; cf. Exod 7:8–13, 22; 8:3, 15)—an action attributed to Mastema in Jubilees 48.9, as we have seen. The wicked in Israel "will be visited unto destruction by the hand of Belial" (CD 8.2, 19.14).

In 4QBerakhot (i.e., 4QBlessings, 4Q286–289), a curse is pronounced on Belial. "Cursed is Belial because of his malevolent purposes, and he is damned for his guilty dominion. Cursed are all the spirits of his lot for their wicked purpose, and they are damned for their filthy unclean purposes. For they are the lot of darkness and their punishment is the eternal pit. Amen. Amen" (4Q287 2.1–5).[28]

---

[22] Daoust, "Belial in the Dead Sea Scrolls, 217–33.

[23] On Belial in the War Scroll, see Stokes, *Satan*, 181–90.

[24] Translation by Jean Duhaime and Hebrew text available in Charlesworth, *Damascus Document*, 97.

[25] See the description of Belial by Duhaime at Charlesworth, *Damascus Document*, 86.

[26] On Belial in the *Damascus Document*, see Stokes, *Satan*, 158–60. See also the commentary by Fraade, *Damascus Document*.

[27] For Hebrew text and English translation, see Charlesworth, *Damascus Document*, 51.

[28] Translation in Wise et al., *Dead Sea Scrolls*, 373.

Belial is mentioned in several other scrolls, such as the Rule of the Community (1QS 1.18, 23–24; 2.5, 19), and the Melchizedek Scroll (11Q13), where Belial has a band of wicked spirits under his control and together they are in rebellion against God.[29] Outside the Dead Sea Scrolls, Belial (or Beliar) is used as a name for the chief agent of evil in the Testaments of the Twelve Patriarchs, the Sibylline Oracles, and other texts, including the New Testament (2 Cor 6:15).[30]

Second Temple Jewish literature evidences quite a bit of diversity when it comes to the name, character, and origins of the chief agent of evil, or whether there even is such a being. The trends continue into rabbinic literature, where the early rabbinic (tannaitic) texts largely ignore a chief agent of evil, while later on he becomes only somewhat more prominent.[31] This diversity in some ways highlights the strangeness of the New Testament within its environment, because the diverse authors of the twenty-seven books of the New Testament collectively are so uniform in their use of the terms *satanas* and *diabolos*, which are basically interchangeable, as we saw in the previous chapter. This unity in the New Testament is strange because, as Farrar notes, "Approaches to Satanology were diverse in Second Temple Judaism and there does not seem to have been a *communis opinio*. There was no standard Jewish LSO [Leading Suprahuman Opponent] concept that the early church simply inherited, no linear development from Hebrew Bible to New Testament."[32]

On the other hand, there are some ways in which the appearance of a chief agent of evil in Second Temple Judaism, as opposed to the Hebrew Bible, does have much in common with the New Testament. Ryan Stokes has helpfully highlighted what some of the ancient Jewish literature has in common.

[29] For a translation of the Melchizedek Scroll, see Wise et al., *Dead Sea Scrolls*, 590–93. For a translation of the Rule of the Community, see pp. 112–36. For comments on Belial in the Rule of the Community, see Stokes, *Satan*, 163–65.

[30] On Beliar in the Pseudepigrapha, see Archie T. Wright, *Satan*, 122–39.

[31] Reeg, "Devil in Rabbinic Literature," 71–83.

[32] Farrar, "New Testament Satanology," 56.

> While Jewish literature from this period retains the notion of numerous heavenly beings who rule over the nations, whether spirits or angels, works such as Jubilees, the War Rule, and other writings from Qumran differ from Daniel and earlier biblical literature in that they have subordinated all of these beings to a single satanic ruler (cf. Luke 4:5–6). Beliefs about national gods and about the opposition between the Satan and the angel of Yahweh have been combined. In the War Rule Israel is led by Michael, and all the other nations of the world have Belial as their leader.[33]

The Gospel of Mark—to take as an example what most scholars consider to be the earliest of the four Gospels—presupposes that its readers know about Satan, or the *satanas*, the chief agent of evil (see, e.g., Mark 1:13). Second Temple Jewish literature, despite its diversity, helps to explain how Mark could assume familiarity with this being (though not necessarily familiarity with Satan as a name).

What are the characteristics of the chief agent of evil in ancient Judaism? Often he is in rebellion against God. Sometimes he is identified as an angel of some sort. He is a leader of angels or of demons. Such characteristics provide useful background for the New Testament. Out of all the pre-Christian Jewish literature, it is the character Mastema in Jubilees that is probably the closest thing we find to the Satan of the New Testament.[34]

IS SATAN A FALLEN ANGEL?

According to perhaps the most important theologian of the twentieth century, "The devil was never an angel."[35] Is Karl Barth right? It's hard to know. The Bible does not say whether Satan was at one time an angel of God. Much of the postbiblical tradition about Satan—or the chief agent of evil under whatever name—identifies him as an angel. Inference comes into play here: If he's not an angel, what is he? Either we admit our ignorance and refuse to answer the question, or we insist that Satan must be a type

[33] Stokes, *Satan*, 188.
[34] Williams, *Spirit World*, 91.
[35] Barth, *Church Dogmatics*, vol. 3, pt. 3, 531.

of being mentioned in Scripture, and if we go that second route, there are few options for spiritual beings that are not God. "Angel" is the obvious candidate here. Barth still denies that the devil was an angel because of the way Jesus describes him in John 8:44. "He was a murderer ἀπ' ἀρχῆς [from the beginning]. He never stood in the truth. No truth was ever in him. He speaks falsehood, and he does so ἐκ τῶν ἰδίων [from his own], because he is a liar and the father of lies. This is how he is described in John 8[44], and it agrees with everything else that we are told in the New Testament concerning him and demons."[36]

Besides angels, there are, in fact, other spiritual beings mentioned in Scripture, about which we know very little. There are demons, and there are spirits, such as the spirit that afflicted King Saul (1 Sam. 16:14) and the spirits mentioned in Micaiah's vision report (1 Kings 22:19–23). Oftentimes modern readers assume that these spirits are related to or are just another name for angels. The origins of demons is a contested issue that will concern us in Chapter Ten. For now, we can simply say that Satan is definitely in the New Testament related in some way to demons, since he is their ruler (Mark 3:22). Are demons also angels? Maybe.

As far as I can tell, it was Irenaeus, bishop of Lyon in the late second century, who first labeled Satan an angel—unless the nearly contemporary Theophilus of Antioch was first.[37] That statement discounts the Second Temple Jewish texts that do sometimes label the chief agent of evil an angel without naming that angel *Satan*; this being is instead the Angel of Darkness at Qumran, or Shemihazah and Asael in the Book of the

---

[36] Barth, *Church Dogmatics*, vol. 3, pt. 3, 531.

[37] Irenaeus, *Against the Heresies* 4.41.1, 5.21.2–3, 5.24.3–4; Theophilus, *To Autolycus* 2.28. If I have read closely enough, it seems that Justin Martyr (a couple decades before Irenaeus) never calls the devil a fallen angel, but he probably believed it (cf. *Dialogue with Trypho* 45). He certainly believed that some angels had sinned and fallen, and that these angels were under the authority of the devil (*Dialogue* 79). See also the reference to a wicked angel at Epistle of Barnabas 9.4 (possibly referring to Satan), references to the angel of wickedness several times in the Shepherd of Hermas (see Farrar, "Intimate and Ultimate Adversary," 527, who regards this as probably referring to Satan), the angel of lawlessness at Ascension of Isaiah 2.4, and the great angel at Ascension of Isaiah 4.2.

Watchers. The first person to say that an evil being named Satan is an angel was Irenaeus or Theophilus.[38]

For now, let's assume for the sake of argument that Satan is/was an angel. Let's concentrate on the word *fallen*: Is he a fallen angel? The other option is that Satan was created evil. This is the idea, or something similar, that Barth seems to have been driving at, since John 8:44 says that the devil's deceit arises from his very nature and that from the beginning he has been a murderer. Some people have thought that maybe the chief agent of evil was created by God for the purpose of harming people and misleading whoever would allow themselves to fall for his schemes. See, for instance, the Angel of Darkness at Qumran, mentioned earlier. Some Christian groups advocated the view that the creator of the world was evil, and perhaps he was the father of the devil,[39] but these groups—whether associated with the second-century teacher Marcion or with the groups commonly falling under the designation "gnostic"—are generally recognized by Christians today (and even in their own time) as heretical. But most accounts of Satan's origins have not been willing to attribute an evil creation to God. After all, "God saw everything that he had made, and indeed, it was very good" (Gen. 1:31). Assuming that, whatever Satan is, he had already been created by the end of creation week, it seems that Satan is included in the "very good" in the beginning. (And not many orthodox Jews or Christians have been willing to entertain the notion that Satan was not created by God—an idea explicitly denied by Irenaeus.)[40] If he was created "very good," and he is not now "very good," then he must have fallen at some point. As I mentioned at the end of the previous chapter, it's all inference, but for most believers over the past few millennia, it has seemed like a necessary inference.

[38] One further qualification for this claim: There is a work known as 2 Enoch that uses the name Satanail for the chief agent of evil (2 En. 31.4–6) and says that this being had been an archangel (2 En. 29.4–5). The dating of 2 Enoch is very much debated, but possibly it goes back to the first century. On the problems associated with this text, see Orlov and Boccaccini, *New Perspectives on 2 Enoch*.

[39] See, for example, the Secret Book of John, one of the Nag Hammadi writings. For scholarly analysis of the idea as found in certain gnostic groups and in Marcion, see Litwa, *Evil Creator*. As Litwa shows (ch. 2), the idea that the Creator is the father of the devil (or even his grandfather) is related to an interpretation of John 8:44.

[40] Irenaeus, *Against the Heresies* 4.41.1.

In the early third century, the Greek-speaking Christian Origen considered these questions. He wondered whether God made three classes of being: (1) some that were totally blessed and incapable of falling, (2) other creatures blessed but capable of falling, and (3) still other creatures incapable of goodness.[41] He came to the conclusion that such reasoning was absurd and that one must imagine that angels are good or evil based on their own free will, not because God made them that way. (He then goes on to attempt to substantiate his inference by means of a figurative interpretation of Ezekiel 28 and Isaiah 14, two passages that will occupy our attention in the next chapter.)[42] Origen's view, that Satan was created as a good angel and freely chose to sin, became standard Christian doctrine.[43]

Perceptive Bible students have sometimes recognized the inferential nature of the usual reconstruction of Satan's history. For a medieval example, we can cite the ninth-century monk Remigius of Auxerre (a hundred miles southeast of Paris), who acknowledged that the book of Genesis did not explain the origins of Satan, but then he continued by making further guesses about what had happened.

> Moses is also silent about the fall of the first angel that had been created, when God established him and the others, long before God made the earth. Then, as soon as the first angel was established, he was arrogant, and due to his arrogance he fell before tasting the divine sweetness. If he had tasted even a little bit of the divine sweetness, he would never have been able to be arrogant or fall.[44]

In the sixteenth century, John Calvin—ever a meticulous student of Scripture—noticed the lack of biblical information on the origins of Satan.

> Some persons grumble that Scripture does not in numerous passages set forth systematically and clearly that fall of the devils, its cause, manner, time, and character. But because this has nothing

---

41 *On First Principles* 1.5.3.

42 *On First Principles* 1.5.4–5.

43 Among fourth- and fifth-century authors, see, e.g., Cyril of Jerusalem, *Catechetical Lectures* 2.3–4; Ambrose, *On Paradise* 2.9; Theodoret, *Commentary on Ezekiel* 28.15.

44 Commenting on Gen. 1:2; translation in Schroeder, *Book of Genesis*, 44.

> to do with us, it was better not to say anything, or at least to touch upon it lightly, because it did not befit the Holy Spirit to feed our curiosity with empty histories to no effect. And we see that the Lord's purpose was to teach nothing in his sacred oracles except what we should learn to our edification. Therefore, lest we ourselves linger over superfluous matters, let us be content with this brief summary of the nature of devils: They were when first created angels of God, but by degeneration they ruined themselves, and were made the instruments of ruin for others. Because this is profitable to know, it is plainly taught in Peter and Jude. God did not spare those angels who sinned [2 Pet. 2:4] and kept not their original nature, but left their abode [Jude 6]. And Paul, in speaking of the "elect angels" [1 Tim. 5:21], is no doubt tacitly contrasting them with the reprobate angels.[45]

We conclude this section by returning to Origen, and to a passage quoted in the previous chapter, which presents very clearly what the Bible says about Satan and what is often guessed about Satan.

> Regarding the devil and his angels and the opposing powers, the ecclesiastical preaching has taught that they indeed exist, but what they are, or how they exist, it has not explained sufficiently clearly. This opinion, however, is held by most, that this devil was an angel, but having become an apostate he persuaded as many angels as possible to fall away with himself, and even until now these are called his angels.[46]

THE FALL OF SATAN

There is nothing explicit in Scripture on the fall of Satan. Readers may recall a couple of biblical passages that mention something like a fall of Satan, but I think it is fairly obvious that neither of them refers to a primordial fall of Satan. The first is when Jesus tells his disciples, "I watched

[45] *Institutes of the Christian Religion* 1.14.16, trans. Battles and McNeil, 1:175. In the section of the *Institutes* that deals with devils (1.14.13–19), Calvin does not mention Isaiah 14 or Ezekiel 28.

[46] Origen, *On First Principles* preface 6, trans. Behr, 8.

Satan fall from heaven like a flash of lightning" (Luke 10:18). In Luke 10, Jesus has sent out the seventy disciples to preach (10:1–12), and they have now returned, reporting, "even the demons submit to us" (10:17). That is the immediate context for Jesus's pronouncement about Satan falling from heaven. What does Jesus mean? Is he referring to some time in the distant past when Satan was kicked out of heaven? It would be a little weird for Jesus to respond to the disciples' breathless excitement with the note that millennia (or whatever) earlier he had witnessed the expulsion of Satan. Why bring that up in this context? To my mind, it makes much more sense to interpret Jesus's statement as explaining the significance of the ministry of the seventy. The seventy went around casting out demons, and Jesus tells them that their work of exorcism contributes to the downfall of Satan's kingdom. In other words, the fall of Satan was being accomplished by means of the ministry of the seventy. The kingdom of God was being established through the ministry of the seventy—and through the work of all of Jesus's followers—and the kingdom of Satan was on the ropes.[47]

The other verse that mentions a fall of Satan is Revelation 12:9, which says that Satan "was thrown down to the earth." As I mentioned in the previous chapter, I don't think Revelation 12 can be describing something that happened before creation or near to the time of creation, because the expulsion of Satan from heaven in Revelation 12 occurs after the birth of the messiah child (Rev. 12:5).[48] There is a common interpretation of this passage of Revelation such that it narrates the primordial fall of Satan, but this interpretation goes back (probably) no further than the sixth-century Greek commentator Oecumenius, who interpreted Revelation 12 in this way only because he read into the text the patristic doctrine of the expulsion of Satan from heaven, a doctrine developed in reliance on Isaiah 14 and Ezekiel 28 rather than Revelation.[49]

[47] For this interpretation of Luke 10:18, see Evans, *Saint Luke*, 454–55; Archie T. Wright, *Satan*, 163–66. For the early Christian use of Luke 10:18 to describe the primordial fall of Satan, see Cardozo Mindiola, "Fabricating the Fall of Satan," 254–55.

[48] On the possible interpretations of Rev. 12:7–9, see Coblentz Bautch, "Fall and Fate," 75–82.

[49] This point is established by Cardozo Mindiola, "Fabricating the Fall of Satan," 262: "Oecumenius' reading of Rev. 12:7–9 is completely dependent on the patristic doctrine of the origin of Satan." The Latin contemporary of Oecumenius, Cassiodorus, seems to have read Rev. 12:7–9 similarly; see Cardozo Mindiola, 246 n. 15.

So, no, the Bible does not discuss the primordial fall of Satan, at least not in those terms (using the words *fall* and *Satan*). There are some biblical passages that have often been interpreted as concerning the fall of Satan—especially Genesis 3, Isaiah 14, and Ezekiel 28—but none of them actually mention Satan. Still, they have been influential in how the fall of Satan has been understood, and we will consider them in the next chapter. In the current discussion, we concentrate on postbiblical sources, tracing the growth of the tradition of Satan's fall, including especially looking at how the tradition represents the timing of the fall and its cause.

The cause is often jealousy, as in *Paradise Lost*, but not envy of the Son of God—or, at least, not *that* Son of God, the second person of the Trinity. We will see that ancient sources are not uniform in their depiction of the devil's fall, but one prominent way in which the ancients explained it was through Satan's jealousy of Adam, who was made in the image of God and given much glory by God, such glory that even the angels were supposed to serve him.[50] The devil, originally a glorious archangel, considered humans inferior to himself and refused to condescend when commanded by God to bow before Adam. Thus Satan's fall happened not before creation (as in *Paradise Lost*) but very early in world history, after the creation of people.

All of the accounts of Satan's fall that we will examine (except that of Athenagoras of Athens) take for granted that the devil was the snake in the garden of Eden that tempted Eve. Genesis 3 does not claim that the snake is anything other than a snake, but most readers (not all; see, e.g., Josephus) seem to have thought that Satan "possessed" the snake or perhaps took on the form of a snake in order to talk to Eve. In the next chapter, we will examine how far back we can trace this line of interpretation of Genesis 3, but the sources we are about to examine all presuppose the identity of the snake as Satan.

It's hard to know which source is the earliest one for the account of Satan's fall. We have some second-century Christian sources that tell the story, such as Athenagoras of Athens and Irenaeus of Lyon. We also have some pseudepigraphic sources that give fuller versions of the story but are

[50] Daniélou, *Angels and Their Mission*, 45–48.

hard to date, just as it is hard to know whether these particular pseudepigrapha are basically Jewish or basically Christian compositions.[51]

Let's take the Pseudepigrapha first. Perhaps the fullest ancient form of the legend of Satan's fall is found in some versions of a work known as the Life of Adam and Eve. Now, this work, the Life of Adam and Eve, exists in several forms in different languages (Greek, Latin, Armenian, Georgian, Slavonic), and the different versions do not all include the same episodes. Tales of Spiderman provide a helpful modern analogy.[52] If you mention Spiderman, everyone knows what you're talking about, but everyone also knows that there are different versions of the story of Spiderman—the live-action trilogy with Toby Maguire, and the inferior live-action movies starring other actors, not to mention the comic books with their own various iterations of the character and different storylines, and the television shows, etc. Gwen Stacy is a character in many of these Spiderman versions, but not all of them, and when she does appear, her storylines are often very different in the different versions. Sometimes the alter-ego of Spiderman is not even Peter Parker, but Miles Morales, such as in the Spider-Verse franchise that has produced the greatest Spiderman movies.

The ancient text known as the Life of Adam and Eve exists in a variety of forms reminiscent of these different Spiderman properties. The basic storyline and characters are more or less the same across the different versions of the Life of Adam and Eve, but there are also major differences between the Greek version and the Latin version (and other versions). For example, the episode that interests us right now (and is quoted below), in which the devil explains his fall from grace, is not contained in the Greek version of the Life of Adam and Eve, but it is contained in the Latin and Armenian and Georgian versions.[53] Usually scholars argue (or assume) that the Greek form of the story preserves the earliest form of the text, and that the earliest form of the text may date as early as 100 BC—though everything about the origins of the Life of Adam and Eve is debated, even

[51] This question is discussed for pseudepigrapha in general by Davila, *Provenance of the Pseudepigrapha*.

[52] Thanks to my wife, Jodi, for help with this analogy.

[53] This comparison is facilitated by Anderson and Stone, *Synopsis of the Books of Adam and Eve*, where the episode narrating Satan's fall is labeled "pericope 5." See also Frey et al., *Synopsis Vitae Adae et Evae*.

whether its author was Jewish or Christian. The earliest Greek manuscripts date to the eleventh century AD.[54] The major commentary on the Greek Life of Adam and Eve by Levison contains a lengthy discussion of the origins of the text that does not even consider a date before the Common Era.[55] Since the Greek text (presumably the earliest) does not include the story of Satan's fall, that story was apparently added to (some versions of) the Life of Adam and Eve sometime in the early Christian era.

At any rate, the story of Satan's fall in the Life of Adam and Eve (when it is included) represents the devil as jealous of the first humans.[56] When God created Adam in his own image, he commanded all the angels to bow before Adam. The devil and some other angels refused (chs. 11–17). He is called here the devil and Beliar (17.2). He describes his pre-fall nature: "My wings were more numerous than those of the cherubim, and I concealed myself under them" (12.1). Then the devil describes his rebellion, speaking to Adam:

> The very day when you were created, on that day I fell from before the face of God, because when God breathed a spirit onto your face, you had the image and likeness of Divinity. And Michael came; he presented you and made you bow down before God. And God told Michael, "I have created Adam according to (my) image and my Divinity." Then Michael came; he summoned all the troops of angels and told them, "Bow down before the likeness and the image of Divinity." And then, when Michael summoned them and all had bowed down to you, he summoned me also. And I told him, "Go away from me, for I shall not bow down to him who is younger than I; indeed, I was master before

[54] On the manuscripts of the Greek Life of Adam and Eve, see Levison, *Greek Life of Adam and Eve*, 31–38.

[55] For this discussion, see Levison, *Greek Life of Adam and Eve*, 85–154.

[56] My description of Satan's fall in the Life of Adam and Eve is based on Anderson and Stone's English translation (of the French translation by J. P. Mahé of the Georgian text) in Anderson, "Life of Adam and Eve," 2:1339–40. An English translation of the Greek text (probably earlier, but without the relevant episode) is provided by Levison, "Life of Adam and Eve," 1:445–61. For another translation of the Greek text alongside a translation of the Latin text (by M. D. Johnson), see *OTP* 2:249–95. For a full commentary on the Greek version, see Levison, *Greek Life of Adam and Eve*.

> him and it is proper for him to bow down to me." When the six classes of other angels heard that, then my speech pleased them and they did not bow down to you. Then God became angry with us and ordered us, them and me, to be cast down from our dwellings to the earth. As for you, he ordered you to dwell in the Garden. When I had realized that I had fallen by your power, that I was in distress and you were in rest, then I aimed at hunting you so that I might alienate you from the garden of delights, just as I had been alienated because of you.[57]

This story explains most of what we would want to know about the origins of Satan. He was created good and became evil by his own choice due to his jealousy of Adam. This all happened immediately after the creation of Adam. The devil wants to bring pain on Adam and pain on God in order to exact revenge for his own fall from grace. As I mentioned, this story does not appear in the preserved Greek text, but only in the Latin, Armenian, and Georgian, complicating the dating of the pericope in a work otherwise difficult to date.[58] It seems unwise to assume that this account of Satan's fall should be dated before the second century AD, when we have patristic authors, more easily datable, providing similar accounts.

For such patristic authors, we turn first to Irenaeus. In the last quarter of the second century, the bishop of Lyon explains that Adam was

> misled by the angel who, because of the many gifts of God, which He gave to the man, became jealous and looked on him with envy, and [so] ruined himself and made the man a sinner, persuading him to disobey the commandment of God. So, the angel becoming, by falsehood, the head and originator of sin, was himself struck, having offended God, and caused the man to be cast out of the Paradise. And, because he apostatized from God through his own disposition, he was called Satan in the

[57] Anderson, "Life of Adam and Eve," 13.2–16.3.

[58] For an argument that the Latin, Armenian, and Georgian versions may attest in broad strokes original features of the Life of Adam and Eve absent in Greek, see Anderson, "Original Form," 215–31. Anderson also argues that the work is a Christian composition.

> Hebrew tongue, which is, Apostate—the same one is also called the Devil.[59]

Elsewhere, Irenaeus says that "this angel and enemy has been a rebel since the day on which he envied God's handiwork and attempted to make him God's enemy."[60] Later again:

> The Devil . . . is one of the angels who has been put over the spirit of the air, as the Apostle Paul revealed in his Letter to the Ephesians [2:2]. He became envious of man, and so he became a rebel from the divine law; for envy is foreign to God. And since his rebellion was exposed by man, and since man became the test of his sentiments, he set himself more and more in opposition to man, envying his life, and he wished to include him in his own rebel power.[61]

Irenaeus shares the major features of the story with the Life of Adam and Eve: The cause of the devil's fall was jealousy of Adam; the time was shortly after Adam's creation; and the envy the devil feels for Adam explains his current desire to tempt and torment humans. Other second-century sources have similar, but sometimes slightly different, accounts of Satan's fall.

Essentially the same account is found in the writings of the Latin author Tertullian, at the very beginning of the third century.[62]

> Now, I find the origin of impatience in the Devil himself. Even when the Lord God subjected to His own image, that is, to man, all the works He had made, the Devil bore it with impatience. For, he would not have grieved, had he endured it, nor would he have envied man, had he not grieved; he deceived man because he envied him; he envied him because he grieved; he grieved because he certainly had not borne it with patience. What the angel of perdition was first—I mean, whether he was first evil or

[59] Irenaeus, *On the Apostolic Preaching* 16, trans. Behr, 49–50. For further comments on the devil from Irenaeus, see *Against the Heresies* 4.40–41, 5.23–24.

[60] Irenaeus, *Against the Heresies* 4.40.3, trans. Unger, 121.

[61] Irenaeus, *Against the Heresies* 5.24.4, trans. Unger.

[62] For further treatment of Tertullian's scattered comments on the devil, see Archie T. Wright, *Satan*, 231–34, who does not, however, consider this passage from *On Patience*.

> impatient—I do not bother to inquire; it is clear that, whether impatience had its beginning in evil or evil in impatience, they entered into combination and grew as one in the bosom of one father. For, as soon as he perceived that it was through his impatience that he had committed the first sin, having learned from his own experience what would assist in wrong-doing, he availed himself of this same impatience to lead men into sin.[63]

Both Irenaeus and Tertullian know a story of the devil's fall similar to the one we read in some versions of the Life of Adam and Eve: The devil envied humans because they were made in God's image and thus were rulers of the world, and this envy led the devil to deceive the first human pair. According to Tertullian, it was the devil's own impatience or malice that was the first sin, soon to be augmented when the devil tempted the humans. What we lack here in both Irenaeus and Tertullian is the command of God for all the angels to revere Adam, a detail found in the Life of Adam and Eve and—much later, and in reference to God's divine Son rather than Adam—in *Paradise Lost*.

One work that does contain this detail about the angels bowing before Adam is the Qur'an, which several times offers a brief account of the familiar story, calling the devil *Iblis* in Arabic. Here God speaks to Adam:

> And certainly We created you, then We fashioned you, then We said to the angels: Make obeisance to Adam. So they did obeisance except Iblis; he was not of those who did obeisance. He said: What hindered you so that you did not make obeisance when I commanded you? He said: I am better than he; Thou hast created me of fire, while him Thou didst create of dust. He said: Then get forth from this (state), for it does not befit you to behave proudly therein. Go forth, therefore, surely you are of the abject ones. (Q Araf 7.11–13)[64]

---

[63] Tertullian, *On Patience* 5.5–8, trans. Daly, 200.

[64] *The Qur'an*, trans. Shakir; see similar accounts at Q Hijir 15.28–35; Q Suad 38.71–77.

The presence of this account in the scripture of Islam demonstrates its widespread nature in the early Christian centuries.

Some ancient sources link the devil's fall to his jealousy of humans, but not jealousy at the superior status of humans. An example is Josephus, the Greek-writing Jewish historian at the end of the first century. In fact, Josephus describes the events of Genesis 3 not in terms of Satan or the devil (or any evil spirit by whatever name); rather, adhering closely to the wording of the biblical text, Josephus mentions only a snake—but, whereas the Bible attributes to the snake a motivation of sneakiness (Gen 3:1), Josephus says the snake was jealous of the humans.

> A serpent, living together with Adam and his wife, felt jealous at the happiness that he thought would be theirs if they obeyed the instructions of God; and thinking that they would fall upon misfortune if they were disobedient, he maliciously induced the woman to taste of the plant of wisdom, saying that in it was the means of distinguishing good and evil, through that, if it were theirs, they would live a blessed life not at all inferior to the divine.[65]

Another ancient account of the devil's fall is in the pseudepigraphic work known as 2 Enoch, preserved in Christian manuscripts mainly in a language called Church Slavonic, but 2 Enoch "is generally thought to be a Jewish work that may date as early as the first century CE."[66] As in the case of the Life of Adam and Eve, scholars continue to debate the origins of 2 Enoch (Jewish or Christian?), and there are different versions of the text, a long version and a short version. References to Satan (or Satanail) appear only in the long version, which some scholars regard as a later version of

---

[65] Josephus, *Jewish Antiquities* 1.41–42. Translation slightly adapted from Feldman, *Flavius Josephus*, 16. Feldman's commentary points to the rabbinic parallel in the Babylonian Talmud, tractate Sanhedrin 59b §22, in which the snake was jealous of the ease of Adam's life in the garden.

[66] Gurtner, *Introducing the Pseudepigrapha*, 145.

the text.[67] When the long version of 2 Enoch narrates the creation of the world, it says that angels were created on day two. Here God explains how one of the angels rebelled.

> But one from the order of the archangels deviated, together with the division that was under his authority. He thought up the impossible idea, that he might place his throne higher than the clouds which are above the earth, and that he might become equal to my power. And I hurled him out from the height, together with his angels. And he was flying around in the air, ceaselessly, above the Bottomless. (2 En. 29.4–5; *OTP* 1:148)

This is not a story about how the devil became envious of Adam and Eve; rather, this story sounds like Isaiah 14:13–15 (a text we will examine in the next chapter). Perhaps we would not say that 2 Enoch's rebellious archangel suffered from the sin of envy so much as from the related sin of pride—or if it is envy, it is envy of God. But later this evil archangel, now labeled the devil (among other names), tempted Eve.

> And the devil understood how I wished to create another world, so that everything could be subjected to Adam on the earth, to rule and reign over it. The devil is of the lowest places. And he will become a demon, because he fled from heaven; Sotona, because his name was Satanail. In this way he became different from the angels. His nature did not change, [but] his thought did, since his consciousness of righteous and sinful things changed. And he became aware of his condemnation and of the sin which he sinned previously. And that is why he thought up the scheme against Adam. In such a form he entered paradise, and corrupted Eve. But Adam he did not contact. (2 En. 31.3–6; *OTP* 1:154)

[67] On the Satan material in 2 Enoch with reference to whether this material is original to 2 Enoch or a later addition, see Macaskill, "2 Enoch," esp. 93–94, who suggests that some of the Satan material in the longer recension of 2 Enoch may have been interpolated after the translation into Slavonic. Both versions (short and long) are translated and presented synoptically in *OTP* 1:91–213. For a detailed discussion of the issues pertaining to dating the material in 2 Enoch, see Macaskill, *Entangled Enoch*, 41–89.

What was the devil's motivation for causing the downfall of Adam and Eve? Apparently he wanted to exact revenge against God for bringing about his own downfall. Again, it wasn't so much envy of Adam as anger at God that incited the devil to tempt the humans (similar to Milton).[68]

Three other Christian authors in the second century also mention Satan as an apostate angel, but they do not relate the story known from Irenaeus and Tertullian about the devil's jealousy of Adam and Eve. Theophilus of Antioch describes the devil as at first an angel who revolted against God, but Theophilus offers no reason for the devil's rebellion.[69] Satan inhabited the snake in order to tempt Eve but failed to bring about immediate physical death of the human couple. Again, Theophilus does not say what motivated Satan to desire the death of the humans. Reflecting on Genesis 4, Theophilus writes: "When Satan saw that Adam and his wife not only were alive but had produced offspring, he was overcome by envy because he was not strong enough to put them to death; and because he saw Abel pleasing God, he worked upon his brother called Cain and made him kill his brother Abel."[70] It is hard to tell what Theophilus is thinking, whether he is assuming a story like the one told by Irenaeus, or whether he's influenced by Josephus or Wisdom of Solomon 2:24 (on which, see the next chapter), or all of them together. He provides too few details for clarity.

Athenagoras of Athens, also from the late second century, is also a bit vague. He describes an adversarial spirit but does not report a name for this opponent of God.

> So also we have recognized that there are other powers which are concerned with matter and operate through it. One of them is opposed to God, . . . because the spirit which is concerned with matter is opposed to God's goodness. . . . The spirit opposed to him was in fact created by God just as the rest of the angels were

---

[68] Another account that sounds like Milton, with a primordial fall of the devil before the creation of the world, is that of John Chrysostom in the fourth century (*Hom. Gen.* 22.7).

[69] Theophilus of Antioch, *To Autolycus* 2.28.

[70] Theophilus of Antioch, *To Autolycus* 2.29, trans. Grant, 73.

> also created by him, and he was entrusted with the administration of matter and material things.[71]

Athenagoras immediately explains that angels were set in charge of various affairs by their creator, God (compare 1 En. 20, quoted in Chapter Two), and that some of these angels were not faithful in their assignments.[72] Regarding these unfaithful angels:

> These include the prince [ἄρχων, *archon*] over matter [τῆς ὕλης, *tēs hylēs*] and material things and others who are of those stationed at the first firmament (do realize that we say nothing unsupported by evidence but that we are exponents of what the prophets uttered); the latter are the angels who fell to lusting after maidens and let themselves be conquered by the flesh, the former failed his responsibility and operated wickedly in the administration of what had been entrusted to him.[73]

These angels "who fell to lusting after maidens" will concern us in Chapter Nine. Athenagoras continues: "The prince of matter, as may be seen from what happens, directs and administers things in a manner opposed to God's goodness" (25.1), and he quotes the ancient Greek playwright Euripides in support.

Athenagoras never names this prince of matter, this opposing power. Apparently he does not think that this prince of matter lusted after women, and maybe he doesn't think this prince was even involved in that sin. It's hard to tell from 24.5. He might think that he was the snake in the garden, though he never brings that up. At 25.3–4, he talks about the activities of these evil angels, but he seems merely to emphasize that they affect different people in different ways: "But to the extent that it depends on the reason peculiar to each individual and the activity of the ruling prince and his attendant demons, one man is swept along one way, another man another way, even though all have the same rationality within" (25.4).

---

[71] Athenagoras, *Plea for Christians* 24.3–4, in *Legatio and De Resurrectione*, trans. Schoedel, 59.

[72] Athenagoras, *Plea for Christians* 24.3–4.

[73] Athenagoras, *Plea for Christians* 24.5.

Finally—but perhaps earliest of all—Justin Martyr in the mid-second century seems to have a different account of Satan's origins in mind. In his three works—two *Apologies* and the *Dialogue with Trypho*—he mentions the devil several times but does not go into detail about where the devil came from. Justin says that demons are in the world, sometimes worshiped as gods, compelling people to do all kinds of evil.[74] Justin reports the story that we will examine in Chapter Nine, known most fully from 1 Enoch, regarding the angels that sinned with women (based on Gen. 6:1–4), a story that explains (according to Justin) the origin of demons.[75] Justin also says: "As you may learn by examining our writings, the chief of the wicked demons we call the serpent, Satan, the devil, and Christ foretold that he with his army of demons, and the men who follow him, will be cast into the fire [of hell] to be punished for endless ages."[76] So Justin seems to be thinking of a different origin for Satan than the one we encounter in Irenaeus; Justin apparently has adopted the story from 1 Enoch and made Satan the leader of the rebel angels in that narrative. In that sense, Satan did not fall because of envy of Adam, or because he wanted to exalt himself. Like everyone else in the second century, Justin thought that the snake in Genesis 3 was possessed by the devil, but he seems to think that the moment of the snake tempting Eve was the very moment of Satan's fall. After quoting Psalm 82:7 ("you shall die like mortals, and fall like any prince"), Justin comments that the verse points to "the disobedience of men, that is, of Adam and Eve, and the fall of one of the princes, namely, the serpent who fell with a great fall because he deceived Eve."[77]

In ancient Christianity, there were various accounts of the origins and motivations of Satan, but the most popular theory was that the devil was jealous of Adam and Eve, perhaps even disobeying a divine command to revere these humans, the image of God. What is the earliest account of the devil's fall in these terms? The candidates we have surveyed here include several patristic writers easily datable to the second or early third century—Justin, Irenaeus, Athenagoras, Theophilus, Tertullian—and two

---

[74] Justin Martyr, *First Apology* 5.

[75] Justin Martyr, *Second Apology* 5.

[76] Justin Martyr, *First Apology* 28, trans. Falls, 64.

[77] Justin Martyr, *Dialogue with Trypho* 124, trans. Falls, 341.

pseudepigrapha (the Life of Adam and Eve and 2 En.) that are both rather difficult to date, and for both of which the Satan material appears in a version of the text usually thought to be a later form.[78] Among these candidates, Justin's version is the earliest, unless that title should go to the Life of Adam and Eve or 2 Enoch, which seems unlikely in view of our current evidence for the origins of these pseudepigrapha.

CAN THE DEVIL REPENT?

We have one last question for this chapter on the origins of Satan: Is the devil's fall permanent? Humans are offered the opportunity to repent; what about Satan and his band of rebellious angels? The Bible does not address this question, just as it does not address the origins of the devil. On the other hand, one does not get the impression that there is any possibility of a reconciliation between God and the forces of wickedness. The rebel angels will not be converted but rather defeated. There is an eternal fire prepared for the devil and his angels (Matt. 25:41), and in the lake of fire the devil "will be tormented day and night forever and ever" (Rev. 20:10). The epistle to the Hebrews speaks about the salvation provided by Jesus in these terms: "It is clear that he did not come to help angels, but the descendants of Abraham" (Heb. 2:16).

Readers of the Bible have wondered whether Satan can repent. John Milton represented Satan as reflecting on the possibility:

> But say I could repent and could obtain
> By act of grace my former state; how soon
> Would height recall high thoughts, how soon unsay
> What feigned submission swore: ease would recant
> Vows made in pain, as violent and void.[79]

It is not clear to me if Milton's Satan thinks that he could repent if he wanted to, but he seems self-aware enough to understand that any repentance on his part would only be counterfeit, "feigned submission," and

[78] I exclude from consideration both Josephus and the Qur'an. The latter, which contains an account of Satan's fall, is much too late to be a candidate for the earliest record of this tradition, and the former does not contain an account of Satan's fall.

[79] *Paradise Lost* 4.93–97.

would soon enough be undone by further rebellion. Then he would be in a never-ending cycle of rebellion, feigned repentance, rebellion, feigned repentance. Among Jewish texts, the topic is broached in the first section of 1 Enoch, the Book of the Watchers—though not in terms of Satan or the devil. When the rebellious angels hear about their imminent punishment, they write up a petition for Enoch to deliver to God, asking for an opportunity for repentance. The request is denied (1 En. 13–14). Sinful angels cannot repent, according to this Jewish pseudepigraphon and traditional Christian theology.

The official position of the Roman Catholic Church is that the devil cannot repent, that his rebellion was an unchangeable choice on his part. The *Catechism of the Catholic Church* contains the following paragraph (quoted also earlier in the introduction).

> (393) It is the irrevocable character of their choice, and not a defect in the infinite divine mercy, that makes the angels' sin unforgivable. "There is no repentance for the angels after their fall, just as there is no repentance for men after death."

The *Catechism* quotes the seventh-century Greek writer John of Damascus. His work *On the Orthodox Faith* contains a bit more on the question.[80] In §17, he writes: "An angel is incapable of repentance because it is incorporeal, for a human being has the possibility of repentance on account of the weakness of the body." I take that to mean that humans are less blameworthy than sinful angels because the human body contributes to human sinfulness, but angels do not have such an excuse. Therefore, repentance is an option for humans but not for angels. The next section of John's work includes the passage quoted in the *Catechism*: "One also needs to know that what death is for human beings, the fall is for the angels. For after the fall there is no repentance for them, just as there is no repentance for human beings after death" (§18). According to Augustine, Satan was "so condemned, and made so obdurate in his evil, that he could no longer have a good will."[81]

[80] John of Damascus, *On the Orthodox Faith* 2.4 (§18). For Greek text and English translation, see John of Damascus, *On the Orthodox Faith*, trans. Russell.

[81] *City of God* 14.27.

In the eleventh century, Anselm of Canterbury devised several reasons for considering it "impossible for the devil to receive reconciliation."[82] First of all, angels would need an "angel-God" for their salvation, just as human salvation required a "human-God" (i.e., Jesus, the God-man). Second, humans are all descended from Adam and therefore they could all be saved through the agency of someone descended from Adam, but angels do not all have a common progenitor but are all specially created by God. Third, humans sinned through the agency of another (the devil), but angels sinned through their own agency. "Consequently, if anyone advances the opinion that our Saviour's redemption ought at some time to be extended to them, it is proved by logic that he is being deceived contrary to logic. I do not say this on the supposition that the value of the death of Christ does not outweigh in its magnitude all the sins of mankind and of the angels, but because unalterable logic opposes the granting of relief to the fallen angels."

The person who most famously suggested that the devil would repent and ultimately enjoy salvation never explicitly said such a thing. The third-century author Origen has a reputation for saying that the devil would repent, and he was condemned by a church council centuries after his death in part because it was believed that he had taught the devil's salvation.[83] The idea is "implied in at least some passages of his works" (such as *On First Principles* 1.6.2, 3.6.5), but elsewhere he explicitly denied it.[84] Origen did say that the devil is not irreparably evil, in the sense that he has free choice and has responsibility for the choices he makes. Rufinus preserved a letter written by Origen to some friends in Alexandria claiming

---

[82] This is the title of chapter 21 of book 2 of Anselm's most famous work, *Cur Deus Homo*. I am using the translation of Janet Fairweather in Anselm of Canterbury, *The Major Works*, 354–55. The quotations later in the paragraph also come from this section.

[83] On this controversy in the late fourth century, see Clark, *Origenist Controversy*, 282 in the index under "devil, restoration of."

[84] The quotation is from Daley, *Hope of the Early Church*, 58–59. See also Heine, *Origen*, 128, 255–56. For an extensive and nuanced discussion, see McClymond, *Devil's Redemption*, 231–320.

that his writings had been corrupted and misinterpreted. In the letter, he denied that he thought the devil would be saved.[85]

CONCLUSION

Where did the devil come from? What are his motivations? As far as I can tell, Christian Scripture has no interest in these questions, but Christians have had a great deal of interest in them. In Second Temple Judaism, there is not a unified account of Satan's origins and character. Indeed, in the sources from that period, he is almost never even called Satan, and sometimes this chief agent of evil is not in rebellion against the God of Israel but rather is one of his servants, carrying out his will of bringing harm to certain people or testing them. There was no coherent biography of Satan that the church received from earlier Judaism. The account of Satan's origins, his fall, and his motivations that has become familiar to many Christians can be traced back confidently to the second century AD. But those early Christian writers describing the devil's fall quote particular passages of Scripture (Gen. 3; Isa. 14; Ezek. 28) as offering such an account. Do these Old Testament passages narrate the fall of Satan, after all? That is the subject of the next chapter.

[85] The Latin text of the letter is preserved in Rufinus, *On the Falsification of the Works of Origen* 7. For an English translation, see Pamphilus and Rufinus, *Apology; On the Falsification*, trans. Scheck, 128–30. Jerome also translated and commented on parts of the letter in his *Apology against Rufinus* 2.18. See also Crouzel, "A Letter from Origen," 135–50.

CHAPTER EIGHT

SATAN INCOGNITO IN THE HEBREW BIBLE?

How art thou fallen from heaven,
O Lucifer, son of the morning!
—Isa. 14:12 KJV

I have made the argument in previous chapters that Satan does not appear at all in the Old Testament, not under the name "Satan," at any rate. The Hebrew word *satan*, meaning perhaps "adversary" or, probably better, "attacker," refers in the Old Testament to a variety of beings (sometimes a human being, sometimes the angel of the Lord, sometimes some other being), but never to the chief agent of evil, an enemy of God. But since the chief agent of evil, an enemy of God, does appear in the New Testament under the titles *satanas* and *diabolos*, it has long been tempting to try to find his influence in the Old Testament as well.

Christians have been pretty successful at this exercise of finding Satan in the Old Testament. In the mid-second century, Justin Martyr identified Satan in several Old Testament passages.

- Genesis 3, the snake that tempted Eve (*Dialogue with Trypho* 45.4, 70.5, 79.4, 88.4, 94.2, 100.4–5, 102.3, 103.5, 112.2, 124.3)
- Genesis 6:1–4, the sons of God who mated with the daughters of men (*Dialogue* 45.4; cf. 100.6)
- Exodus 7–8, the Egyptian magicians (*Dialogue* 69.1)
- 1 Kings 18, the prophets of Baal (*Dialogue* 69.1)
- Numbers 21:8–9, the bronze serpent (*Dialogue* 91.4, 94.1)
- Isaiah 27:1, Leviathan (*Dialogue* 91.4, 112.2)
- Psalm 22:13, the lion (*Dialogue* 103.5)

I think Christians today could probably also find the influence of the devil in each of these passages, though the devil is mentioned in none of them. Still, Justin does not discover in any of these passages an explanation for the origins of the devil, except perhaps for Genesis 3 and Genesis 6. Christians today would often agree that Genesis 3 is relevant, and they would often raise an eyebrow regarding the relevance of Genesis 6. We will save Genesis 6 for our next chapter, and we will examine Genesis 3 in a moment.

There are two other Old Testament passages that have often been used to explain the origins of the devil, but neither of them are cited by Justin. About a century after Justin, Origen provided a similar list of Old Testament passages in which the devil features, and he not only included Genesis 3 but also the other two prominent passages for explaining Satan's origins: Ezekiel 28 and Isaiah 14.[1] Origen, moreover, thought that Satan appears as the destroyer (Exod. 12:23), as Azazel in Leviticus 16, as the evil men (i.e., the sons of Belial) in Judges 20:13, and in the first two chapters of Job.

In none of these Old Testament passages is the devil mentioned overtly, but his influence can perhaps be seen in them. In only three have interpreters unearthed accounts of the devil's origins. We now turn to a consideration of how far back we can trace such an interpretation of Genesis 3, Ezekiel 28, and Isaiah 14.

[1] Origen, *Against Celsus* 6.43.

THE SNAKE OF GENESIS 3?

Thus the orb he [Satan] roamed
With narrow search and with inspection deep
Considered every creature: which of all
Most opportune might serve his wiles and found
The serpent subtlest beast of all the field.
(*Paradise Lost* 9.82–86)

By Milton's time, the idea that Satan inhabited the snake in the garden of Eden was established by centuries of Christian tradition. In the previous chapter we noted that Christians already in the second century (Justin, Irenaeus, etc.) understood the snake of Genesis 3 to be the embodiment of Satan. How far back does such an idea go? It is not explicitly stated in Genesis 3 that the snake is anything more than a snake, and outside of the early chapters of Genesis, the Hebrew Bible contains no references to the events of Genesis 3. We will examine these events at the end of this section, but first let's try to find the earliest explicit interpretation of the snake in Genesis 3 as an evil spirit—or as the embodiment of an evil spirit, something along the lines of what appears in *Paradise Lost*. We are not going to find it in the Hebrew Bible, but the New Testament does contain a few relevant verses that demand our attention, which we will probe in a moment.

The Earliest Interpretation in Terms of Satan

In the Jewish literature before the New Testament, there are some passages often cited in this regard.[2] For example, the deuterocanonical book Wisdom of Solomon, written in Greek probably in the first century BC, contains the following statement:

---

[2]One relevant passage blaming all evil on the serpent is found in the fourth-century *Panarion* 64.29.6 by Epiphanius, but he is quoting metrical lines, the source of which have sometimes in the modern period been identified with Ezekiel the Tragedian in the second century BC. The lines (in Greek and English) are therefore included in Holladay, *Fragments*, vol. 2, *Poets*, 404–5 (labeled fragment 18), though the attribution of the passage to Ezekiel is cast into doubt by Holladay (pp. 526–29 n. 253). See also Jacobson, "Ezekiel the Tragedian," who argues strongly against the attribution of the passage to Ezekiel, preferring to understand the verses as original to Methodius of Olympus. Since these lines likely derive from a third-century Christian source rather than a pre-Christian Jewish source, they form no part of our discussion here.

> But through the devil's envy [φθόνῳ διαβόλου] death entered the world, and those who belong to his company experience it. (Wisd. of Sol. 2:24 NRSVCE)

Is this verse about Satan? The NRSV translation clearly points in that direction. The obvious way to interpret the English verse is that in the garden of Eden, death entered the world (similarly: Rom. 5:12–21) because of the sin with the forbidden fruit, a sin committed as the result of the promptings of the snake, which was the embodiment of the devil, who himself was motivated to tempt Adam and Eve because of his envy of their lofty position (a common ancient view of the motivations of Satan, as we saw in the previous chapter). Scholars often understand the verse in this way, or at least as a reference to Satan in Genesis 3.[3]

If this is the correct way of interpreting Wisdom 2:24, then the Book of Wisdom in the first century BC is the earliest surviving text that identifies the serpent in the garden of Eden as the devil.[4] It would also be the first time an author attributed the motive of "envy" to the snake—not stated in the text of Genesis itself. Of course, somebody has to be the first to develop these interpretations, but since no one had done it earlier than Wisdom, we might ask whether we are interpreting Wisdom correctly. We should especially ask this question since the Book of Wisdom never elsewhere refers to the devil or Satan.[5]

The word at issue is *diabolos*, often rendered "devil" and meaning "slanderer" or "adversary."[6] There is no definite article in front of the word in Greek, so it should probably not be translated "the devil" but rather "a devil" or, maybe better, "an adversary." Let's try out that translation:

> But through the envy of an adversary, death entered the world, and those who belong to his company experience it. (Wisd. of Sol. 2:24)

---

[3] See Muraoka, *Greek-English Lexicon*, 149, διάβολος, under fourth definition: "w[ith] ref[erence] to the tempter in the Garden of Eden," and then a citation of our verse from Wisd. of Sol.

[4] Zurawski, "Separating the Devil from the *Diabolos*," who cites scholars making this claim at p. 371.

[5] Zurawski, "Separating the Devil from the *Diabolos*," 368–76.

[6] See Chapter Five, note 21.

Assuming our author is referring to a story in the Bible, we might ask ourselves where death first appears in the Bible. It is not in Genesis 3 but in Genesis 4, when Cain kills Abel (a point recognized also by the second-century Christian author Theophilus in *To Autolycus* 2.29). Cain was certainly an adversary to Abel, and he killed his brother out of envy, thus ushering death into the world. As for the second half of the verse, "those who belong to his company" could be similar to those who "go the way of Cain," as Jude says (v. 11). Could Cain be the "adversary" (*diabolos*) mentioned by the author of Wisdom?[7] This interpretation in reference to Cain seems to be preferred in the first Christian comment on the passage, 1 Clement 3:4–4:7, at the end of the first century AD.[8]

Other interpretations are possible and perhaps to be preferred,[9] but the point I want to make is that the language of Wisdom 2:24 does not at all point obviously to Genesis 3 or to Satan. If we are looking for our earliest explicit interpretation of the snake in the garden as Satan, we must look elsewhere.

James Kugel has collected several ancient interpretations of the snake. Some ancient interpreters (Josephus, Philo, Jubilees) represent the snake as merely a normal, talking snake.[10] For Philo, the snake is itself a symbol of pleasure.[11] Just as snakes lie on their stomach, eat dirt, and produce poison, so also the one who loves pleasure is so indulgent that he can hardly lift

---

[7] This interpretation is mentioned and rejected by Zurawski, "Separating the Devil from the Diabolos," 373–74. It is considered a possible interpretation by Stokes, *Satan*, 217 n. 63; Archie T. Wright, *Satan*, 32.

[8] For commentary on 1 Clement, see Lightfoot, *Apostolic Fathers*, pt. 1, vol. 2, 20–21. Lightfoot also points to the parallel in Theophilus, *To Autolycus* 2.29 (quoted in our previous chapter at note 70), which perhaps relies on both Wisd. of Sol. and 1 Clement.

[9] Zurawski, "Separating the Devil from the Diabolos," 398, suggests the translation: "But through an adversary's envy death enters the world, and those who belong to death's party put humanity to the test." See his article for a defense of this translation. Zurawski does not relate Wisdom 2:24 to any particular biblical story but to a general truth: that people motivated by evil (here: "envy") bring spiritual death upon themselves. For other suggestions on the identity of the *diabolos* in Wisdom 2:24, see Kelly, *Satan*, 70–79.

[10] Kugel, *Bible as It Was*, 73, who quotes Jubilees 3.28; Philo, *On the Creation* 156; Josephus, *Jewish Antiquities* 1.41.

[11] Philo says this several times: *On the Creation* 157; *Allegorical Interpretation* 2.74; *On Husbandry* 97. The following quote is from *On the Creation* 158.

his head; he feeds not on heavenly wisdom but food from the earth—wine and delicacies, so that he becomes a glutton, "making his aim not to reach satiety but to make sure that nothing of what has been laid out is left behind." So the temptation from the snake is really the temptation from pleasure—the basis of all temptation (§162). Not coincidentally, it was the woman that pleasure approached, not the man (§165).

Kugel also quotes several interpretations regarding the snake as Satan in disguise, but the only one of these passages that might be pre-Christian is in the Similitudes of Enoch (1 En. 69.6), where a rebel angel named Gadre'el, among many acts of wickedness, "led Eve astray."[12] The precise dating of the Similitudes is in dispute, though most scholars date it to around the time of Jesus,[13] so here we might have the earliest passage extant that (apparently) considers the snake in the garden not just a talking snake but the tool of an evil angel, in this case, Gadre'el. But "around the time of Jesus" allows for a pretty broad range of dates; it would be nice to be more precise. Richard Bauckham's recent argument—which he acknowledges as "not conclusive"—locates the composition of the Similitudes to the later end of the time period, perhaps as late as the early second century AD, mostly because of parallels he finds between the Similitudes and other literature of that time (Revelation, 4 Ezra, 2 Baruch).[14] Another relevant passage probably from the late first century AD is 4 Maccabees 18:7–8, where a character in the text maybe links "the deceitful serpent" to an evil

---

[12] For an interpretation of the passage, see Nickelsburg and VanderKam, *1 Enoch 2*, 301.

[13] For discussion, see Nickelsburg and VanderKam, *1 Enoch 2*, 58–63; Davila, *Provenance of the Pseudepigrapha*, 132–37: "I would not rule out the possibility that an Enochic work such as the Similitudes could have been written any time in the early centuries CE" (136–37). See also the discussion of Macaskill, *Entangled Enoch*, 90–113, who seeks to destabilize the discussion but does not essentially question the scholarly consensus dating the Similitudes to 50 BC–AD 100 (p. 112).

[14] Richard Bauckham, *"Son of Man,"* vol. 1, 112–18, 267–85. The "not conclusive" comment comes on p. 285.

spirit, but the matter is not clear.[15] It is clear, as we saw in Chapter Seven, that the Greek Life of Adam and Eve links the snake to Satan, but here again we face the problems of date. While some scholars would date the Greek form of this work to the first century BC, it could be from centuries later, and the trend attributes to it a date in the early centuries AD.

Another source that might link the snake to Satan and might date to the first century is the pseudepigraphic Assumption (or Ascension) of Moses or Testament of Moses. It was Origen who mentioned a work called the Assumption/Ascension of Moses and said that it represented the snake as inspired by Satan.

> First, a serpent is described in Genesis as having seduced Eve; regarding this serpent, in the *Ascension of Moses*—a little work which the Apostle Jude [verse 9] mentions in his Epistle—the archangel Michael, when disputing with the devil regarding the body of Moses, says that the serpent was inspired by the devil to become the cause of the transgression of Adam and Eve.[16]

What is this work that Origen mentions, this Ascension of Moses? Several early Christian writers mention something called the Ascension of Moses (Greek: Ἀνάληψις Μωσέως; Latin: *Ascensio Mosis*) and a few mention a work called the Testament of Moses (Διαθήκη Μωσέως;

---

[15]On this passage, see Cousland, "Adam and Evel," 141: "While Satan is not directly mentioned, the reference to the serpent as the 'destroyer' (λυμεών) might suggest that the devil and the serpent are implicitly identified." See also deSilva, *4 Maccabees*, 258. The other passages cited by Kugel, *Bible as It Was*, 73–74, were all written in the second century AD or later, though scholars have sometimes suggested (on rather weak evidence) dates as early as the first century. Most of these works are available in Charlesworth, *Old Testament Pseudepigrapha*, cited here as *OTP*: Apocalypse of Moses (= Greek Life of Adam and Eve) 16 (*OTP* 2:277), 17.4 (*OTP* 2:279); 2 (Slavonic) Enoch 31.4–6 (*OTP* 1:154); 3 Baruch 4.8 (Slavonic; *OTP* 1:666), 9.7 (Greek; *OTP* 1:673); Apocalypse of Sedrach 4.5 (*OTP* 1:610); Testimony of Truth 47.3–6. This last work, a Gnostic Christian text from Nag Hammadi, is available in English translation by Birger A. Pearson in Meyer, *Nag Hammadi Scriptures*, 613–28. Also relevant is the Apocalypse of Abraham 23 (*OTP* 1:700–1), late first century AD or so. See also the list of ancient sources at Papaioannou, "Sin of the Angels," 403 n. 41, who adds Apocalypse of Moses 18.1–6, 29.15–17; Apocalypse of Sedrach 5.1–7; Apocalypse of Abraham 23.11; 1 Enoch 64–69; John 8:44.

[16]Origen, *On First Principles* 3.2.1, trans. Behr, 192.

Testamentum Mosis).[17] In 1861, an untitled work about Moses was discovered in a sixth-century Latin palimpsest manuscript now in Milan. Scholars imagine that the Latin was translated from Greek, which was translated from an original text written in either Hebrew or Aramaic. It is probably this text that went under the title Ascension of Moses, and it may well have been written in the first century.[18] But, in any case, Origen probably got confused; while he may have been correct in identifying the source of Jude 9 with the Ascension of Moses, there is nothing in the extant Latin text of this latter work about the snake in the garden, and this detail of Origen's comment probably derives not from the Ascension of Moses but from the Life of Adam and Eve, a work that circulated in Greek under the title Apocalypse of Moses.[19] Despite Origen's comment, the evidence currently available does not indicate that the Ascension of Moses will help us determine the earliest explicit interpretation of the snake in the garden as Satan.

By the mid-second century AD, the identity of the snake as Satan was taken for granted. Justin Martyr several times in his *Dialogue with Trypho* mentions the serpent as an evil spirit, without always explicitly mentioning the story in Genesis 3 or the temptation of Eve (e.g., *Dialogue* 39, 45, 70, 91, 124, 125), but he also links the serpent language to the story in Genesis 3 several times (*Dialogue* 79, 88, 94, 100, 102, 103). A few decades later, Theophilus of Antioch says that "the maleficent demon, also called

---

[17] For discussion of these early Christian sources, see Tromp, *Assumption of Moses*, 87–89, 100. The two sources that mention a Testament of Moses are the *Synopsis* of Pseudo-Athanasius and the *Stichometry* of Nicephorus.

[18] For text, translation, and commentary, see Tromp, *Assumption of Moses*. On the title of the work, see 115–16. The evidence for the title is based on the ecclesiastical historian Gelasius (see Tromp, 88). Tromp presents arguments that it was the book of Jubilees that was sometimes labeled the Testament of Moses. Nevertheless, scholars often title the Latin text discovered in 1861 as the Testament of Moses, partly because the content fits so well the testamentary genre; see J. Priest, "Testament of Moses," *OTP* 1:919–34; Kenneth Atkinson, "Testament of Moses," in Feldman et al., *Outside the Bible*, 2:1856–68; Ronald Herms, "The Testament of Moses," in Embry et al., *Early Jewish Literature*, 2:639–51. See Bauckham, "Jude and the Testament of Moses," in *Jude and the Relatives*, 238–80. On the date of the work now preserved in the Latin manuscript (whatever its title), see Tromp, 116–17, who concludes: "The first quarter of the first century C.E. seems a reasonable date." See also Herms, 644, who argues that the bulk of the work was written even earlier.

[19] See Tromp, *Assumption of Moses*, 274–75.

Satan, . . . spoke to Eve through the serpent."[20] Theophilus's contemporary Irenaeus of Lyon (at the conclusion to a passage quoted in the previous chapter) said in reference to Genesis 3:15 that "God cursed the serpent, which bore the Devil—a curse which fell upon that animal itself and the angel hiding in it, that is, Satan."[21]

We have explicit and easily datable interpretations of the Genesis 3 snake as Satan in the mid-second century AD, after which the equation snake = Satan becomes axiomatic. Before Justin Martyr, we have ambiguous sources or sources that are difficult to date (and so perhaps they are not prior to Justin Martyr, after all). This equation may predate the second century AD, but it is hard to be confident.

Chart 8.1. Possibilities for the Earliest Reference to the Snake in the Garden as Satan

Work	Date	Identity of Snake
Wisdom of Solomon 2:24	first century BC	??? It is not certain that this verse is reflecting on Genesis 3.
Similitudes of Enoch (1 En. 69.6)	first century BC or later	Gadre'el
4 Maccabees 18.7–8	around AD 100	??? This passage is reflecting on Genesis 3 but perhaps not linking the snake to an evil spirit.
Greek Life of Adam and Eve	first century BC or later	Satan
Ascension of Moses	first century AD or later	??? The extant form of this work contains no reference to the snake in the garden.
New Testament	first century AD	See discussion below.
Justin Martyr	second century AD	Satan

New Testament

There are some New Testament passages that need to be mentioned, though we will see that they are also somewhat ambiguous. As I approach these

[20] Theophilus, *To Autolycus* 2.28, trans. Grant, 73.
[21] Irenaeus, *Demonstration of the Apostolic Preaching* 16, trans. Behr, 49–50.

New Testament passages, I will be asking about our interpretive options. Can these passages be understood as references to Genesis 3? Do they have to be understood as references to Genesis 3? Spoiler alert: My answer to these questions is going to be "yes" and "no," respectively.

There are three New Testament passages, two from the book of Revelation (which both basically say the same thing) and one from Paul's letter to the Romans.

> The God of peace will shortly crush Satan under your feet. (Rom. 16:20)

> The great dragon was thrown down, that ancient serpent, who is called the Devil and Satan, the deceiver of the whole world—he was thrown down to the earth, and his angels were thrown down with him. (Rev. 12:9)

> He seized the dragon, that ancient serpent, who is the Devil and Satan, and bound him for a thousand years. (Rev. 20:2)

Paul's comment at Romans 16:20 may allude to Genesis 3:15, the curse upon the snake, when God says that the seed of the woman will bruise the snake's head.[22] But Paul does not mention a snake, or a snake's head, or the woman's seed. He does mention feet, though the verse in Genesis does not. The actions—"crush" in Romans 16:20 and "strike" or "bruise" in Genesis 3:15—are different (though similar), for which the two verses use different words.[23] Perhaps Paul was thinking of Genesis 3:15, but the echo is not very strong.

The two verses in Revelation look much more promising. According to Ryan Stokes, "Scholars agree that Rev. 12:9 and 20:2 allude to the Gen. 3 story," but they disagree on whether Romans 16:20 does so.[24] Stokes himself

[22] Williams, *Spirit World*, 93–95, interprets Paul as having this view (snake = Satan), based on Rom. 16:20 (cf. Ps. 91:13) and especially 2 Cor. 11:3, 14. Perhaps already Jerome interpreted Paul in this way; *Hebrew Questions on Genesis* 3:15.

[23] It's even further apart when comparing the Septuagint of Gen. 3:15, which uses the word for "watch" (τηρέω, *tēréō*), "he will watch your head." See below for more on the translation of Gen. 3:15.

[24] Stokes, *Satan*, 216 n. 62. Aune, *Revelation*, 2:696: "Rev. 12:9 provides the only explicit biblical identification of Satan with the serpent who tempted Eve in Gen. 3:1–7."

agrees with this consensus—but he also notes that Revelation may allude to more than just Genesis 3.

> The serpent of Gen. 3 was one of several serpent traditions in the literature of early Judaism and was not the only serpent tradition with which NT authors connect the Satan. A number of texts in the Hebrew scriptures speak of mythological primordial serpents/dragons. These include Leviathan (e.g., Isa. 27:1; Job 3:8; Ps. 104:26) and Rahab (e.g., Job 26:12–13; Ps. 89:11 [Eng. 10]; Isa. 51:9). Revelation's portrayal of the Satan as the "dragon" and the "ancient serpent" reflects such primordial serpent/dragon traditions."[25]

In other words, while it may seem obvious to modern readers steeped in the mature Satan legend that Revelation 12:9 and 20:2 allude to Genesis 3, perhaps the apocalyptic seer had a more apocalyptic reference in mind, such as Isaiah 27.

> On that day YHWH with his cruel and great and strong sword will punish Leviathan the fleeing serpent, Leviathan the twisting serpent, and he will kill the dragon that is in the sea. (Isa. 27:1)[26]

Leviathan here is obviously an enemy of God, and the Greek translation of this verse labels the beast with the two animal terms that Revelation 12:9 applies to Satan: dragon and snake. When John called Satan "the ancient serpent," maybe he was thinking about Genesis 3, but maybe he was thinking instead about Isaiah 27, where we find not only the word "serpent" but also the word "dragon."[27] The reference to Isaiah 27—or a similar

[25]Stokes, *Satan*, 218. In note 66, Stokes says, "That Gen 3 also serves as a background to the depiction of the Satan in Rev. 12 is suggested by the enmity between the dragon and the woman's 'seed' in v. 17 (cf. Gen. 3:15) and perhaps also the dragon's role as deceiver (Rev. 12:9)." On the other hand, Archie T. Wright, *Satan*, 190, says only that Revelation 12:9 "hints at Genesis and the Garden."

[26]This verse describes YHWH's opponent in language reminiscent of the description of Lotan/Litan in the Baal Cycle from Ugarit (Tablet 5, column 1, line 1); see Coogan and Smith, *Stories from Ancient Canaan*, 139. For more on Leviathan, see Orlov, *Supernal Serpent*.

[27]This is the view of Dolansky, "How the Serpent," which you can find online at the website for the Biblical Archaeology Society.

Leviathan/Rahab tradition—and not to Genesis 3 seems the more plausible when we remember that we have failed to find a single interpretation of the Genesis 3 snake in terms of Satan that with any confidence can be dated before the book of Revelation.

In any case, Revelation does not offer an interpretation of either Old Testament passage, Genesis 3 or Isaiah 27, but rather it simply borrows the imagery to describe Satan. As John H. Walton and J. Harvey Walton have written, "the dragon character in Revelation (e.g., Rev. 12:3) can be understood as a reference to the Leviathan in Isaiah 27:1, but this allusion derives from a history of eschatological interpretation and apocalyptic imagery and is not intended to clarify the identity of the character in Isaiah."[28] Stokes makes the same point about the possible use of Genesis 3 in Romans and Revelation:

> Paul and John may have been among the Jewish interpreters of their era who believed that the Satan was involved in the rebellion of the first human couple, but they express no interest in explaining this story in light of their doctrine of the Satan. Instead, they evoke the Eden story allusively in order to communicate their doctrine of the Satan, vividly portraying his nefarious work and his eventual judgment.[29]

I fail to see any reason to say that a straightforward reading of the Christian Bible requires, or even indicates, a reading of Genesis 3 such that the snake is Satan. The Hebrew Bible does not make the identification. The New Testament might hint at it, or it might not. The relevant passages can be interpreted in multiple ways, but none of the relevant New Testament passages offer an interpretation of Genesis 3, even if they borrow imagery from Genesis 3 (which is not certain). The earliest reference to the Genesis 3 snake as Satan is perhaps one of the pseudepigrapha; the Similitudes of Enoch seems to be the best candidate, though the name of the evil spirit controlling the snake is Gadre'el and not Satan. The earliest clear and easily

[28] Walton and Walton, *Demons and Spirits*, 104.
[29] Stokes, *Satan*, 219–20.

datable interpretation of the Genesis 3 snake as Satan is that of Justin Martyr in the mid-second century AD.[30] We cannot assume that it was a common interpretation at the time of the New Testament.

We might think that even if the Bible nowhere comes out and says it, still the story of Genesis 3 is most straightforwardly interpreted as representing Satan with the snake. After all, here is a talking snake (!) that wants to trick Eve into disobeying God. Plus, there's the curse: The seed of the woman (!) will crush the head of the snake. Many readers would agree with D. A. Carson: "Some sort of prehistoric fall of the embodied serpent (Gen. 3) is doubtless presupposed by Genesis."[31] And doesn't the promise of Genesis 3:15, a messianic prophecy of Christ's victory over Satan, prove that the snake must be more than a snake?

In my view, this way of reading Genesis 3, such that the snake represents Satan, is one possibility among others. Let's take the last point (from the previous paragraph) first.

Genesis 3:15: Messianic Prophecy?

Is Genesis 3:15 obviously a messianic prophecy? The short answer is no. The verse reads perfectly sensibly in reference to human beings (the offspring of the woman) and snakes: Snakes strike people's heels, whereas people stomp on snakes' heads. In the context of the garden of Eden story, when there has been perfect harmony between people and animals, this verse (Gen. 3:15) explains why there is no longer such harmony. The present conflict between wild animals and humans becomes something of a theme in the Bible (e.g., Deut. 7:22; Ezek. 14:12–23, 34:25–29). Such enmity between humans and animals started in the garden with the snake, according to the Word of God in Genesis 3:15. In future, God will make a covenant of peace with the animals (Hos. 2:18; Isa. 11:6–9; cf. Mark 1:13).[32]

---

[30] See also Archie T. Wright, *Satan*, 226: "Justin makes what is likely the earliest connection between the satan and the serpent in the Garden." Stokes, *Satan*, 217, thinks that the identification of Satan with the Genesis 3 serpent happened "during or just prior to the first century CE." The earliest such text may be the New Testament (217 n. 63). Archie T. Wright, *Satan*, 31, regards 1 John 3:8 as also "likely an allusion to the serpent narrative in Genesis 3."

[31] Carson, "2 Peter," 1049.

[32] For a similar interpretation, see Theophilus, *To Autolycus* 2.17; Greek Life of Adam and Eve 11.1–2.

One problem with the interpretation of Genesis 3:15 is the meaning of the verb. What is it that the seed of the snake and the seed of the woman will do to each other? The KJV says "it shall bruise thy head, and thou shalt bruise his heel." The ESV also has bruise/bruise. The NRSV and NET Bible have strike/strike. As these translations reveal, the Hebrew word (שׁוּף, *shuph*) is the same both times, but it is a rare word, the meaning of which is contested. In the Bible, it appears only here and in Job 9:17 and Psalm 139:11. In the Dead Sea Scrolls, the word also appears once (CD 11.4), but that appearance doesn't really help define the word. One major dictionary of ancient Hebrew offers several suggestions: Maybe it means "crush; rub," or "conceal," or "sweep over," or "graze," or "spy."[33]

This last suggestion echoes the rendering in the Septuagint, which uses the verb *tēréō* (τηρέω), "watch": "he will watch your head and you will watch his heel" (NETS). What is this supposed to mean? Ancient Greek translators offered interpretations, which we will notice in a moment.

But some other ancient translators of the Hebrew Bible did not find "watch" to give an appropriate meaning, so they suggested alternatives: The second-century AD translator Aquila used the verb *prostríbō* (προστρίβω), "to inflict"; and the slightly later translator Symmachus used either *thlíbō* (θλίβω), "to rub, afflict," or *tríbō* (τρίβω), "to rub, wear away."[34] Jerome, in the Latin Vulgate, offered different Latin words for the two appearances of *shuph* in Genesis 3:15, first *contero* ("break, crush") and then *insidior* ("to lie in wait for"). Such a verb choice in the Latin translation coheres well with a messianic understanding of the verse—though Jerome himself interpreted the verse to mean that Satan would engage in constant warfare with humans (the descendants of the woman), who would finally gain victory over Satan, as Paul promised in Romans 16:20.[35] Jerome's translation of the Bible, the Latin Vulgate, actually does not say "he will crush" (*ispe conteret*) or "it will crush" (*ipsum conteret*) but rather "she will crush" (*ipsa*

[33] Clines, *Dictionary of Classical Hebrew*, 8:308.

[34] For the evidence for the translations by Aquila and Symmachus, see Wevers, *Genesis*, 93.

[35] See Jerome, *Hebrew Questions on Genesis* 3:15, in the translation of Hayward, *Saint Jerome's Hebrew Questions*, 33, with the corresponding note on 115–16.

conteret), so that medieval interpreters often applied the phrase to the Virgin Mary or the church.[36]

It was probably Irenaeus who provides our earliest datable interpretation of Genesis 3:15 in terms of a messianic prophecy. (Gen. 3:15 is never quoted in the New Testament, though perhaps alluded to at Rom. 16:20, as we have seen.) Near the end of the second century AD, Irenaeus wrote:

> He put enmity between the serpent and the woman with her offspring, who observed each other. On the one side there is the one whose sole was bitten but who has the power to tread on the head of his enemy; on the other side there is the one who bit and killed and hindered the steps of humanity until the offspring came who was Mary's child, who was destined beforehand to trample on his head.[37]

And in the next book, after quoting Genesis 3:15, Irenaeus offered this interpretation:

> This enmity the Lord recapitulated in himself by being made man from woman, and by *trampling on his* [*the Serpent's*] *head*, as we have shown in the preceding Book.[38]

The argument has been made that if we are looking for the earliest interpretation of Genesis 3:15 as a messianic prophecy, we find it not in Irenaeus but in the Septuagint. The Greek translation of Genesis was produced in the third century BC, long before Irenaeus. We have already noticed its translation of Genesis 3:15, but let's look at it again, now in more detail.

---

[36] For an example, see the interpretation of Remigius of Auxerre (ninth century) in Schroeder, *Book of Genesis*, 82. The reading *ipse* in the manuscripts of the Vulgate is attested, though very many manuscripts have *ipsa*, which is the reading chosen for the main text in the two standard editions of the Vulgate in the modern period (and every printed edition of the Vulgate): see *Biblia Sacra*, vol. 1: *Librum Genesis*, ed. A. Gasquet et al., 151; Weber and Gryson, *Biblia Sacra*, 7. This feminine reading in the Latin tradition is not considered significant enough to merit a mention in the apparatus of the recent critical edition of the Hebrew text of Genesis: Tal, *Genesis*, Biblia Hebraica Quinta, 9.

[37] Irenaeus, *Against the Heresies* 3.23.7, trans. Unger, 108.

[38] Irenaeus, *Against the Heresies* 4.40.3. trans. Unger, 121; italics in the original.

> καὶ ἔχθραν θήσω ἀνὰ μέσον σου καὶ ἀνὰ μέσον τῆς γυναικὸς καὶ ἀνὰ μέσον τοῦ σπέρματός σου καὶ ἀνὰ μέσον τοῦ σπέρματος αὐτῆς· αὐτός σου τηρήσει κεφαλήν, καὶ σὺ τηρήσεις αὐτοῦ πτέρναν.

> And I will put enmity between you and between the woman
> and between your offspring and between her offspring;
> he will watch your head,
> and you will watch his heel. (NETS)

Aside from the strange word *watch*, the other thing to note about this translation is "he will watch your head." The word "he" is specified in the Greek text, which is interesting. The antecedent of "he" is "seed" (σπέρμα, *sperma*), which in Greek is the neuter gender. Since "seed" is neuter, any pronoun referring to it should also be neuter ("it"), but the Greek text specifies that the one who will watch the snake's head is not "it" but "he" (αὐτός, *autos*). The argument has been put forward that this "he" must be the messiah, and the Septuagint provides the earliest messianic interpretation of Genesis 3:15.[39]

However, interpreting the Septuagint is no simple task. Ancient and modern readers of the Greek text have not always found the messiah in this verse. According to John William Wevers (the modern editor of the Septuagint Genesis), the Septuagint translator did not intend to point to the messiah; rather, the singular *autos*, "he," is merely collective for humanity, mankind. Mankind will watch the head of the snake.[40]

This collective interpretation is found in our earliest commentator on the Septuagint, the Alexandrian author Philo, roughly contemporary with Jesus.

> The sentence "he shall watch thy head, and thou shalt watch his heel" (Gen. 3:15) is a barbarism, but has a perfectly correct meaning. It is addressed to the serpent concerning the woman, but the woman is not "he" but "she." What is to be said then?

[39] Martin, "Earliest Messianic Interpretation," 425–27.

[40] Wevers, *Notes on the Greek Text of Genesis*, 44. Another example of this sort of interpretation of the Greek is Brayford, *Genesis*, 240.

> He has left off speaking about the woman and passed on to her seed and origin; but the mind is the origin of sense; and mind is masculine, in speaking of which we should use the pronouns "he" and "his" and so on. Rightly, then, is it said to Pleasure [i.e., the snake], "the Mind shall watch thy chief and principal doctrine, and thou shalt watch it, the Mind, as it acts and rests upon its accepted tenets." This basing of conduct and principle on tenets is naturally represented by the word "heels." The word "shall watch" has two meanings, one like "shall guard and preserve," the other equivalent to "shall watch for to destroy."[41]

Philo goes on to interpret *watch* as possibly meaning "watch in order to destroy." The good mind will keep an eye on its enemy, pleasure, "watching eagerly for the moment when it shall set upon it and achieve its utter destruction" (§189). No messianic interpretation here.[42]

A few centuries later, another Alexandrian author, this one a Christian named Didymus, also fails to see in Genesis 3:15 a promise of the messiah, though he does regard the snake as a cipher for Satan.

> And since reference is not being made to a material serpent, its *seed* is not to be taken as something material, either, but as people bearing its stamp, form, and genesis, or thoughts that are at variance with the truth, and teachings foreign to it. Likewise, the *seed* of the woman is to be taken as virtuous people issuing from her, as she is a type of the Church, or the tenets of divine teaching, against which the malice of the adversary directs his endeavors.[43]

---

[41] Philo, *Allegorical Interpretation* 3.188–89, trans. Colson and Whitaker, 1:429–31.

[42] The same can be said for the Targums, some of which (Neofiti and Ps-Jonathan, not Onkelos) do mention the messianic age as the time when the constant battle between people and snakes will come to an end. On Philo's (muted) messianism, see Termini, "Philo's Thought," 109–11; messianism does not arise as a topic of discussion in Niehoff, *Philo of Alexandria*.

[43] Didymus the Blind, *Commentary on Genesis*, trans. Hill, 97.

Didymus interprets the devil as "watching" the heel of people while people "watch" the head of the devil. Again, a collective interpretation, non-messianic. The same thing was found a century earlier in Origen.[44]

Now, messianic interpretations of Genesis 3:15 were also known in the ancient church, as we have seen with Irenaeus, who was himself interpreting the Septuagint. It is possible that the use of the masculine pronoun *autos*, "he," encouraged some Christians to interpret the verse messianically.[45] But according to John Skinner, while the interpretation of the snake in the garden as Satan has been very popular over the past two millennia, the messianic reading of Genesis 3:15 has been less popular.[46]

If Genesis 3:15 is not a messianic promise, then perhaps the snake in the garden is no more than a snake.

A Sneaky, Talking Snake

But surely the snake is more than a snake. I mean, it talks! And it wants to trick Eve! Why would it want to do that unless it's God's enemy?

Let's think about the story without Satan and see if we can make sense of it. One of the interesting features of the story, perhaps underappreciated, is that Eve engages in conversation with a snake. Most people would probably react differently if a snake began talking. Eve never asks the snake how he has the gift of speech. Is Eve not surprised to meet an articulate snake? Has she had conversations with snakes before? Was she accustomed to animals talking? So Josephus and others thought.[47] In the context of this story, I'm not sure that we're supposed to be surprised that a snake is talking. Eve is not.[48]

And as for the snake's motivation in tricking Eve, what does the text itself say? "Now the serpent was more crafty than any other wild animal

---

[44] Origen, *Homilies on Genesis* 15.5, trans. Heine, 211.

[45] As asserted by Wevers, *Notes on the Greek Text of Genesis*, 44.

[46] Skinner, *Critical and Exegetical Commentary*, 80–82.

[47] Josephus, *Jewish Antiquities* 1.40–44; Philo, *On the Confusion of Languages* 6; Jubilees 3.28. For a rabbinic passage suggesting that snakes alone among animals had the power of speech, see Deuteronomy Rabbah 5.10.

[48] There is another story in the Pentateuch about a talking animal: Balaam's talking donkey (Num. 22:28–30). Balaam does not react with surprise at his talking donkey, but the text does otherwise make it clear that donkeys—including this particular donkey—usually do not talk.

that YHWH God had made" (Gen. 3:1). The Bible says that the snake is sneaky, crafty. It doesn't say that this particular snake is sneaky, but that snakes in general are sneaky. That is the explanation for the trickery that then ensues. Many readers have been dissatisfied with this explanation for the snake's motivations, and so they have invented different motivations: jealousy or some such. But this is not a situation in which the Bible is silent on an issue, leaving us to take guesses. The Bible is not silent about the motivations of the snake; the Bible says he was motivated by craftiness. A lot of readers simply do not like the motivation mentioned by the Bible.

By the way, I find it interesting that Christian readers who think the snake was Satan disagree on whether Genesis 3:1 (snakes are crafty) applies to snakes in general or only to a snake inhabited by Satan. Augustine took the latter position: "Though this serpent could be called the wisest of all wild beasts not in its own non-rational soul, but with an alien spirit, the devil's, that is."[49] On the other hand, John Milton represented Satan as choosing the snake as his covering because the snake was already smart.[50] Martin Luther agreed with Milton.[51] For the sake of comparison, I note that in literature (especially children's literature) snakes are sometimes represented as wise or tricky, whether we're talking about Kaa in *The Jungle Book* or the Hamadryad in *Mary Poppins*, who is described by the Brown Bear as "the lord of our world—the wisest and most terrible of us all."[52]

If we take the story in Genesis 3 on its own terms, we have a talking snake that causes no obvious surprise to the woman, and we have a crafty snake that tricks the woman into eating the fruit. The trickery of the snake results in an ages-long conflict between the offspring of the snake and the offspring of the woman. Satan is never mentioned.

The story is open to multiple readings, an obvious point based on the history of interpretation. One might imagine an evil spirit disguising itself

[49] Augustine, *Literal Meaning of Genesis* 11.2.4, trans. Hill, 490.

[50] *Paradise Lost* 4.347–50.

[51] Luther, *Lectures on Genesis*, trans. Schick, 145.

[52] Travers, *Mary Poppins*, ch. 10. For *The Jungle Book*, I am relying on the Disney movie (1967), in which Kaa can hypnotize people with his eyes. The Hamadryad in *Mary Poppins* is also described as having eyes that can compel obedience. Another example is the Harry Potter series, in which the title character and his chief enemy—two of the best wizards on the planet—are both Parselmouths (people who can speak Parseltongue, the language of snakes).

as a snake or taking control of a snake. I do not want to argue against the comment of C. S. Lewis: "What Satan put into the heads of our remote ancestors was the idea that they could 'be like gods'—could set up on their own as if they had created themselves—be their own masters—invent some sort of happiness for themselves outside God, apart from God."[53] I also have no problem with preachers who say that Satan tempted David to sin in 2 Samuel 11. I would just like people to recognize that Satan is not mentioned in 2 Samuel 11, and that the only way to find him mentioned in Genesis 3 is through an interpretation that not everyone shares.

As it turns out, there are multiple profitable ways of reading Genesis 3. If I'm advocating anything, it is less confidence that any particular interpreter has the one right way of reading this wonderful, foundational story.[54] Many people have read this story without Satan's involvement—apparently nearly everyone did before Justin Martyr, who is the earliest datable author who clearly says that the snake was Satan. Many people have read this story as involving Satan, and that has proven profitable as well. Nevertheless, I doubt that the original author had Satan in mind (else, why not mention him?), or the earliest readers, and maybe not even the New Testament authors.

EZEKIEL 28

The book of Ezekiel contains a nine-verse section (28:11–19) that has often been interpreted as describing the origins of Satan. Ezekiel does not say that he is describing Satan at all; he says that he is talking about the king of Tyre (28:11). This is the final oracle against Tyre and its king in the book, concluding a series of oracles against Tyre that occupies three chapters of the prophetic collection (chs. 26–28).

It is not hard to understand why some people have thought Ezekiel is describing Satan even if he does not say so. He describes the king of Tyre as (using the ESV for a moment) "full of wisdom and perfect in beauty" (v. 12).

---

[53] Lewis, *Mere Christianity*, 39 (book 2, ch. 3).

[54] This point applies also to someone like Heiser, *Unseen Realm*, 73–75, who is very confident in the basic accuracy of the traditional Christian way of reading this story, though he dresses up his interpretation with some references to the ancient Near Eastern worldview.

And then he says something that, everyone agrees, could not possibly apply to the king of Tyre in any sort of literal way: "You were in Eden, the garden of God" (v. 13). And then there's this:

> You were an anointed guardian cherub.
> I placed you; you were on the holy mountain of God;
> in the midst of the stones of fire you walked. (Ezek. 28:14 ESV)

So, we have the king of Tyre being described as a very beautiful guardian cherub in the garden of Eden. Ezekiel continues by describing the fall of the king of Tyre: "You were blameless in your ways . . . until iniquity was found in you" (v. 15). This guardian cherub grew full of pride, so God expelled him from the garden (vv. 16–17).

Again, Ezekiel cannot be describing the king of Tyre in a literal way, and the passage sounds a lot like what we otherwise know about the fall of Satan. Many interpreters throughout history have promoted the idea that Ezekiel is comparing the king of Tyre to Satan. If we pursue this line of thought, we learn from Ezekiel that Satan began as a cherub appointed by God for the protection of Adam and Eve in the garden of Eden, and his pride and jealousy of the human couple led him to betray his charge and bring harm on his wards instead. Michael Heiser has explained: "Although Ezekiel 28 is about the prince of Tyre, in describing this prince's arrogance, downfall, and original state, the prophet utilizes an older tale of a downfall *in Eden*."[55]

This interpretation goes back all the way to the start of the third century AD, first attested in Tertullian. In his refutation of the doctrine of the early Christian heretic Marcion, Tertullian commented on Ezekiel 28.

> Also if you turn up Ezekiel's prophecy you will easily perceive that that angel was by creation good, and by his own act became corrupt. In the person of the prince of Tyre this pronouncement is made against the devil.

Here Tertullian quotes portions of Ezekiel 28:11–16, and then he says:

---

[55] Heiser, *Unseen Realm*, 77—emphasis in the original. For another modern example of the Satan interpretation, see Cooper, *Ezekiel*, 264–70.

> which [words] it is evident properly apply to the castigation not of that particular prince [of Tyre] but of an angel, because no one of mankind has ever been born in the paradise of God,[56] not even Adam himself, for he was translated thither [cf. Gen. 2:7–8]: nor has any man been set with the cherub in God's holy mountain, that is, in the height of heaven, from which our Lord testifies that Satan also fell [cf. Luke 10:18]: nor has any man dwelt amid the stones of fire, among the gleaming rays of the burning constellations, from whence also Satan like lightning was cast down. Rather was he, the author of sin, being stigmatized in the person of a sinful man: aforetime irreproachable since the day of his creation, created by God for goodness, as by a good Creator of creatures without reproach: adorned with all angelic glory: set in God's presence, as good in the presence of the good, yet afterwards by himself transposed into evil.[57]

Once Tertullian established the idea that Satan is described in Ezekiel 28, many other Christians have followed suit. A younger contemporary of Tertullian, Origen of Alexandria, in the early third century pointed out to his readers that the two prophecies against the prince of Tyre (28:1–10 and 28:11–19) cannot be understood about a human being, or at least the second one cannot, the one under discussion here. Rather, the passage must refer

[56] Why does Tertullian bring up this point about being "born" in the garden of Eden? Because the text of Ezek. 28:13 that he has quoted earlier mentions this fact about the person described, that he was born in the garden, whereas English translations say simply, "You were in Eden." The English translations correspond to the Hebrew text and also to its earliest translation, the Septuagint. These texts (Hebrew and Greek) say, "You were in Eden." But an alternative form of the Greek text, with only a slight change (the addition of a single letter), has the reading "were born" (ἐγεννήθης) instead of simply "were" (ἐγενήθης). Tertullian's alternative reading is not known in any extant Greek manuscript of Ezekiel, since it is unmentioned in the critical apparatus in Ziegler, *Ezechiel*, 223. But Tertullian is not the only early Christian to attest this alternative Greek text, as pointed out by Patmore, *Adam, Satan, and the King of Tyre*, 45, 53. It is this alternative reading in the Greek text that convinces Tertullian that Ezekiel could not be referring to Adam, in accordance with a prominent Jewish interpretation, as we will see.

[57] Tertullian, *Against Marcion* 2.10, trans. Evans, 1:115–19.

to "an adverse power" (*adversaria virtus*).[58] Origen's main goal (in his discussion in *On First Principles* 1.5.4)—as also for Tertullian in his arguments against Marcion—is to demonstrate that the evil angels were not created evil but were created good and became evil by their own choice. This is what Origen (and Tertullian) thinks Ezekiel 28 demonstrates. Origen even has an explanation for why the "adverse power" was called a "prince of Tyre" (28:2): because he was originally appointed as the angel in charge of the city of Tyre.[59] "We think, therefore, that these words were spoken of a certain angel who had been appointed to the office of governing the Tyrian people, and to whose care their souls also seem to have been entrusted."[60]

This Satan interpretation of Ezekiel 28 became the standard Christian reading of this passage for many centuries and is still prominent today, but not universal. Some conservative scholars continue to imagine that Ezekiel 28 might prove helpful in determining the origins of Satan.[61] Most scholars disagree.[62] The evangelical scholar Daniel Block gives the Satan interpretation of Ezekiel 28 only a brief glance before dismissing it.[63]

Those adhering to the Satan interpretation of this passage can argue that Ezekiel is clearly comparing the king of Tyre to some other individual that can be described as a cherub in the garden of Eden, who then fell because of pride, and that this description clearly refers to Satan. But I would argue that the only reason this passage sounds to us like it refers to Satan is because this passage has been interpreted as referring to Satan. It's circular reasoning. Earlier in this discussion I said that Ezekiel's description conforms to what we otherwise know about Satan—which is a bit

[58] Origen, *On First Principles* 1.5.4; see also Origen's *Homilies on Ezekiel* 13.1–2; *Against Celsus* 6.44.

[59] In the Greek text that Origen read, the king of Tyre is called in both verse 2 and verse 12 an *archōn* (ἄρχων), "ruler." As Origen knew, the Bible sometimes uses the word *archōn* to refer to spiritual beings, including evil ones (e.g., Eph. 2:2). See the discussion in Chapter Three.

[60] Origin, *On First Principles* 1.5.4, trans. Behr, 51.

[61] Hummel, *Ezekiel 21–48*, 860, is open to a version of the Satan interpretation. Earlier I also mentioned Heiser and Cooper as holding this interpretation.

[62] It has become increasingly difficult to find a commentary released by a major publisher that countenances the Satan interpretation. For examples of major scholars that fail to mention this interpretation at all, see Greenberg, *Ezekiel 21–37*, 579–93; Jensen, *Ezekiel*, 218–22.

[63] Block, *Book of Ezekiel*, 118–19.

of misdirection on my part. It is Ezekiel 28 itself that has contributed to the Satan legend that constitutes the "knowledge" we bring to Ezekiel 28. We don't "know" the origins of Satan from the Bible; the legend of Satan has been created based on this interpretation of Ezekiel 28, which never mentions Satan.

I admit, of course, that the description of the king of Tyre in Ezekiel 28:11–19 cannot apply literally to the king of Tyre or any other human being. The passage does not apply literally to the king of Tyre but rather metaphorically to him. It's figurative language. God is condemning the king for his arrogance, and he figuratively represents him as if he were a cherub in the garden of Eden—perhaps the loftiest status imaginable—who fell from his exalted position and is now condemned, cast down before kings and turned to ash, perhaps the lowest position imaginable.

Or maybe the king is not described as a cherub but as "with a cherub." Check out different translations of Ezekiel 28:14 and 16, and you will find some translations (KJV, ESV) that say "you were a cherub," whereas other translations (NRSV, NET) say "with a cherub." The manuscript evidence is not uniform. The medieval Hebrew text (Masoretic text) says "you were an anointed . . . cherub," but the original Hebrew text did not mark down the vowels, and the consonants could be read as "with a cherub." In fact, the Septuagint translates the passage in this way ("with a cherub").[64] There is debate about what the correct reading should be; scholars are not in agreement.[65] The early Christians whose views we examined above (e.g., Tertullian, Origen) read the Septuagint and assumed that Ezekiel did not equate Satan with a cherub but rather said that he was "with a cherub," and Ezekiel may have intended to say "with a cherub."

Another textual issue has to do with tenses of the verbs. The KJV and some other English translations have future tense verbs in certain parts of the oracle, for example in verses 16–18: "Therefore will I bring forth a fire from the midst of thee." Other translations (e.g., NRSV) put these same expressions in the past tense: "So I brought out fire from within you." Here the issues are also somewhat difficult; it seems to me that the Hebrew text

[64] See Patmore, *Adam, Satan, and the King of Tyre*, 189.

[65] Zimmerli, *Ezekiel 2*, 85; the traditional Hebrew text (the MT) is defended by Greenberg, *Ezekiel 21–37*, 583.

consistently reads as past tense, but the Septuagint sometimes has future tense verbs, and perhaps English translations have sometimes followed the verb tenses of the Septuagint. The verb tenses can make it easier to see a reference to Satan in the KJV than in the NRSV, under the assumption that the destruction of Satan is yet future. Readers should compare different translations to get a better understanding of what Ezekiel intended.

Earlier I said that Ezekiel's description of the king of Tyre could not literally apply to any human being. But if Ezekiel did not say "you were a cherub" but rather "with a cherub," maybe his description could apply to a human being—someone who was in Eden and fell through his own pride. The only biblical character that fits such a description is Adam. If Ezekiel is not just using figurative language to describe the king of Tyre but is comparing the king of Tyre to another biblical character, perhaps that biblical character is Adam, who fits the description fairly well. This interpretation, favored today by several scholars, is, in fact, the standard interpretation in ancient Judaism.[66] There are many examples of this interpretation in rabbinic literature; for instance, in the rabbinic commentary on Genesis (Genesis Rabbah), we read that a rabbi proposed that Eve "was adorned with twenty four kinds of finery, and then brought to him [Adam], as it says: 'In Eden, the garden of God you were, and all precious stones were your covering: the carnelian, the topaz . . .'" (Gen. Rab. 18.1, quoting Ezek. 28:13).[67]

It is not obvious that Ezekiel was talking about Satan in Ezekiel 28:11–19. This interpretation goes back to Tertullian in the early third century AD, but it goes back no further (that we know of). The traditional Jewish interpretation of the passage—again, going back to ancient times—does not see Satan in Ezekiel but rather Adam. Maybe Ezekiel did not intend to invoke either Satan or Adam in his description of the king of Tyre, but was simply using figurative language about the arrogant monarch.

---

[66] For modern scholars taking the Adam interpretation, see Blenkinsopp, *Ezekiel*, 123–25; Archie T. Wright, *Satan*, 41–48.

[67] I took the translation from the online version of Genesis Rabbah at sefaria.org. For many other examples of this interpretation in rabbinic literature, see Patmore, *Adam, Satan, and the King of Tyre*, 16–40.

ISAIAH 14

Isaiah 14 is another passage that does not mention the name Satan or the devil but has been instrumental in the development of the Satan legend. As in the case of Ezekiel 28, Isaiah 14 names the subject of the discourse as a pagan king, this time the king of Babylon (14:4). As in the case of Ezekiel 28, the main topic is both the arrogance of this pagan king and God's condemnation of him. The essential string of verses comes in the middle of the oracle.

> How you are fallen from heaven,
> O Day Star, son of Dawn!
> How you are cut down to the ground,
> you who laid the nations low!
> You said in your heart,
> "I will ascend to heaven,
> I will raise my throne
> above the stars of God;
> I will sit on the mount of assembly
> on the heights of Zaphon;
> I will ascend to the tops of the clouds,
> I will make myself like the Most High."
> But you are brought down to Sheol,
> to the depths of the Pit. (Isa. 14:12–15)

Does that sound like a passage that could be describing Satan? Yes, and especially so when we read the beginning of verse 12 in the KJV: "How art thou fallen from heaven, O Lucifer, son of the morning!" Instead of "Day Star," the KJV (and NKJV) gives us "Lucifer." Lucifer is a Latin word that means "light-bringer," and it is the word that appears in the Latin Vulgate in this passage. The Latin version of Isaiah 14:12 is the reason that people consider Lucifer to be one of the names of Satan. Of course, *lucifer*, being a Latin word, would not have been the name of an evil spirit in Hebrew or in Greek.

Isaiah 14 is not the only time that the term *lucifer* appears in the Latin Bible. It also shows up in Job 11:17 and 38:32, and 2 Peter 1:19. In those two passages in Job, *lucifer* clearly does not refer to Satan, but rather to a star.

This is the way the term *lucifer* was used in Latin literature outside the Bible, especially in reference to the morning star or the planet Venus.[68] The passage in 2 Peter is talking about Jesus: He is the light-bringer (or Day Star, *lucifer*) that arises in your hearts. Just because the term *lucifer* appears in the Latin Bible in Isaiah 14 does not mean that the passage refers to Satan or that *lucifer* is used as a name.

The idea that Isaiah is talking about Satan is perhaps not quite as popular as the idea that Ezekiel 28 refers to Satan. Nevertheless, this interpretation is almost as ancient as the corresponding interpretation of Ezekiel 28. It seems that Origen is the first writer to explicitly interpret Isaiah 14 in terms of an evil angel. After his statements on Satan in Ezekiel 28 (mentioned above), Origen continues: "Again, we are taught such things by the prophet Isaiah about another opposing power [*de alia virtute contraria*]." Origen quotes Isaiah 14:12–22 and comments, "Most clearly by these words is he, who formerly was the Day Star and used to arise in the morning, shown to have fallen from heaven."[69]

A couple of centuries later, Jerome's commentary on Isaiah is reluctant to claim that Isaiah 14 refers directly to Satan. Jerome first presents a historical interpretation of the passage (book 5 of his *Commentary on Isaiah*), where he interprets the oracle as concerning Nebuchadnezzar, king of Babylon, in conformity to the explicit wording of Isaiah. Then Jerome presents a spiritual interpretation of the passage (book 6 of the *Commentary*), in which he says that the text concerns "the true Nebuchadnezzar," that is, the devil.[70] Both Origen and Jerome seem to confirm the view of Everett Ferguson, who interpreted these early Christian uses of Isaiah 14 as meaning "that what is said about these kings is an even truer description of the devil"—in other words, the earliest Christians who proposed the Satan interpretation of Isaiah (and Ezekiel) recognized that the prophets were

---

[68] See Lewis and Short, *New Latin Dictionary*, 1080; Glare, *Oxford Latin Dictionary*, 1045.

[69] *On First Principles* 1.5.5, trans. Behr, 51–52. Origen wrote in Greek, but his *On First Principles* is not preserved in Greek but only in the Latin translation made at the beginning of the fifth century by Rufinus of Aquileia. The term "Day Star" in the English version quoted in the text translates Rufinus's word *lucifer*.

[70] See Jerome, *Commentary on Isaiah*, trans. Scheck. The phrase "true Nebuchadnezzar" appears at p. 307 (*Comm. Isa.* 6.23).

not really talking about the devil, but thought that their words were especially appropriate for the devil—"but this distinction was soon lost or at least not noted, and the passages were applied directly to the fall of Satan."[71] An example of the latter tendency is Augustine, who quotes Isaiah 14:12 and acknowledges that these words are spoken to someone "in the guise of the King of Babylon" before claiming that they "are certainly in the actual context understood of the devil."[72]

Despite the (surprisingly) muted popularity of the idea in the history of Christianity that Isaiah 14 refers to the devil, modern scholars are a little more ready in the case of Isaiah 14 than for Ezekiel 28 to interpret the passage in reference to an evil or wayward spiritual being. The Hebrew term translated in the KJV as "Lucifer, son of the morning" is *helel ben shaḥar* (הֵילֵל בֶּן־שָׁחַר). A prominent idea in the scholarship on Isaiah 14 is that *Helel ben Shaḥar* is the name of a deity associated with a particular story that would have been known to Isaiah and his audience, and that the king of Babylon is being compared to this presumptuous deity.[73] Was there such a deity? Well, the name Shaḥar (i.e., Helel's father) is very similar to a couple of names of deities in an Ugaritic text.[74] And since deities are often associated with light and with the stars, it's pretty easy to imagine that Helel ("Day Star") is the name of a deity, though this name appears only here in the Hebrew Bible and not often outside the Hebrew Bible—again, a couple of Ugaritic texts use the name, or something close to it, for a deity.[75]

That's not much evidence, is it? It's a lot of guesswork, but let's go with it for a moment. Let's assume that there was a pagan god named Helel ben

---

[71] Ferguson, *Demonology*, 108. On the history of interpretation of this passage, see Sawyer, *Isaiah through the Centuries*, 100–103, whose discussion also indicates that many interpreters have refused to see Satan described in Isaiah 14.

[72] Augustine, *On Christian Teaching* 3.37.55, trans. Green, 99. See also Heiser, *Unseen Realm*, 83–86.

[73] Kaiser, *Isaiah 13–39*, 38–40; Wildeberger, *Isaiah 13–27*, 62–68; Watson, "Helel," *DDD*, 392–94.

[74] *KTU* 1.23. *Die keilalphabetischen Texte aus Ugarit* (*KTU*) is the standard reference for the Ugaritic texts. For an English translation of *KTU* 1.23, see Wyatt, *Religious Texts*, 324–35, where the text is called "The Gracious Gods: A Sacred Marriage Liturgy," and the section with the name *Shaḥar* is at p. 332.

[75] *KTU* 1.23, 1.24, trans. Wyatt, *Religious Texts*, 336–41, where the text is called "The Wedding of Nikkal and Ib." For all the evidence for the relevant names, see Shipp, *Dead Kings and Dirges*, 67–79.

Shaḥar. What if there were also a story about this god trying to ascend to the highest place among the gods, and failing to do so? Then maybe that story would provide background for Isaiah's taunt song against Babylon's king. It would be like someone today alluding to a fictional story to make a point, perhaps: "That person lies so much he would make Pinocchio blush." (And, for our present purposes, it would show that Isaiah 14 is really about the fall of a supernatural being, in accordance with the interpretation that sees Satan as the subject of the oracle.)

So is there any evidence for a story about Helel ben Shaḥar trying to ascend to a high place only to be cast down? Well, there is Isaiah 14. And aside from that, um, no. But we can imagine such a story!—especially because we do have similar stories from the ancient world, not exactly like Isaiah 14, but sort of, though none of them uses the name Helel. For instance, the early Greek writer Hesiod mentions the children of Eos ("light," "morning"), among whom is "a splendid son [φαίδιμον υἱόν], powerful Phaethon, a man equal to the gods."[76] And we've got a myth about Phaethon (son of the dawn [= Eos]!), whose arrogance leads to his downfall, a myth told, for example, by the first-century Roman poet Ovid.[77] There's another myth told much earlier, in the Ugaritic tablets, about a god named Athtar who tried to sit on the throne of the high god, but he was too little for his feet to reach the footstool, so he was demoted.[78] Athtar was not referred to as "son of the dawn," but, still, maybe Isaiah had him in mind.

Does this all sound like complete silliness? It's hard not to agree with J. J. M. Roberts: "In the absence of any compelling textual evidence for such an explanatory narrative myth, it seems pointless to reconstruct it with the characters in this verse [Isa. 14:12], and then use the phantom reconstruction to interpret the text we actually have."[79]

---

[76] Hesiod, *Theogony* 984–91. English translation and Greek text taken from Hesiod, *Theogony*, trans. Most, 81–83.

[77] Ovid, *Metamorphosis* 1.747–2.400.

[78] This myth is told as part of the Baal Cycle, tablet 6, column 1; see the translation in Coogan and Smith, *Stories from Ancient Canaan*, 146.

[79] Roberts, *First Isaiah*, 210. See also Albani, "Downfall of Helel," who says of the Athtar myth that it "hardly offers an appropriate parallel" to the Isaiah passage (p. 63). Albani instead locates the background of this passage in the ancient Near Eastern royal ideology that kings would become gods (or stars) at death.

Though scholars (and various interpreters throughout history) have tried to find a spiritual being in Isaiah 14:12, whether Satan or one going under another name, readers who prefer evidence to fancy will apply the figurative language of the passage to the king of Babylon, in accordance with the explicit statement of the text.

CONCLUSION

If we insist on a plain-sense reading of Genesis 3, Ezekiel 28, and Isaiah 14, then we have no biblical testimony about the origins and nature of Satan and no explanation of his motivations for opposing God. We have, in fact, no information whatsoever about Satan in the Old Testament. He is entirely a New Testament concept.

Now, I recognize that we could say the same thing about Jesus—but there is a difference. The New Testament resolutely insists that the Son of God had been there all along, that he was in fact involved in creation (John 1:1–5), that he had been seen by Isaiah (John 12:41), that Moses had written about Jesus (John 5:46), that the prophets looked forward to his appearance (Matt. 1–2), that his death, burial, and resurrection were foretold (1 Cor. 15:3–4), and that he fulfilled all Scripture (Luke 24:44). But the New Testament is essentially silent regarding Satan's role in the Old Testament. Because Jesus taught his disciples to look for him in the Scriptures of Israel, a Christian reading of the Old Testament is justified in finding Jesus there. The New Testament does not similarly encourage readers to find Satan in the Old Testament.

Nevertheless, I think it makes sense to think of the appearance of Satan in the Old Testament along lines similar to how Christians often think of Jesus in the Old Testament. Let's consider the angel of YHWH. In the Hebrew Bible, a being called the angel of YHWH seems, on occasion, to have an identity that overlaps with God,[80] similar to the way the identity of Jesus is presented in the New Testament. It might make sense, then, to think about the angel of YHWH in the Old Testament as a preincarnate appearance of the Son of God—a traditional Christian view found already in Justin's writings.[81] However, we should also recognize that this interpre-

[80] Greenberg, *Understanding Exodus*, 58; Sommer, *Bodies of God*, 41–42.
[81] *Dialogue with Trypho* 58–60.

tation is not explicit in Scripture. The depiction of the angel of YHWH is very suggestive, but no more than suggestive. In my experience, Christian readers are happy to entertain the notion that the angel of YHWH may be connected to Jesus, but they are ready to admit that the connection is speculative. In fact, some conservative Christian readers I have encountered are so insistent on a literal reading of Scripture that they are quite dubious about a connection of the angel of YHWH with Jesus.

The same is not true with regard to Satan in the Old Testament, as far as I can tell. Christian readers devoted to a literal interpretation of Scripture are often quite insistent that Satan makes several appearances in the Old Testament, incognito, especially in Genesis 3 but also in Isaiah 14 and Ezekiel 28 and elsewhere. They often assert that the reading of these passages in terms of Satan is the obvious and straightforward reading, despite the absence of any mention of Satan or the devil in the text. Whereas they are doubtful of seeing Jesus in the Old Testament, despite Jesus's explicit and repeated declarations that he should be found there, these readers I am describing are without doubt that Satan appears in the Old Testament in several passages where he is unnamed. I would suggest that we see the two situations as at least a little more analogous. As it can be interesting and helpful to think about Jesus as the angel of YHWH while also recognizing that the text of Scripture does not make this connection explicit, so also we could read some Old Testament passages such as Genesis 3 or Ezekiel 28 in light of the New Testament character Satan—while also recognizing that the text of Scripture does not make this identification explicit, but rather makes other identifications explicit (a sneaky snake in Genesis 3; the king of Tyre in Ezekiel 28).

At any rate, a plain-sense reading of Scripture nowhere reveals the origins or nature of Satan. The Satan legend that is so familiar to Bible students is not found in the Bible but developed in the early Christian centuries with some influence from extrabiblical Jewish literature.

CHAPTER NINE

THE FALL OF ANGELS

The angels who did not keep their own position, but left their proper dwelling, he has kept in eternal chains in deepest darkness for the judgment of the great day.

—Jude 6

For if God did not spare the angels when they sinned, but cast them into Tartarus and committed them to chains of deepest darkness to be kept until the judgment.

—2 Pet. 2:4

Apparently angels can sin. Or, at least, there are some biblical verses that point in this direction. I'm not aware of any passage in the Hebrew Bible that outright says that angels have sinned, though one particular passage (Gen. 6:1–4) has long been interpreted in this way by some people. But the New Testament has several verses that say or imply that angels have sinned, and many ancient writings outside the Bible have stories about sinning angels. This chapter attempts to cover most of the material, starting with the New Testament.

EVIL ANGELS IN THE NEW TESTAMENT

The verses from Jude and 2 Peter quoted as epigraphs to this chapter are the premier examples in the New Testament about sinful angels, but some other New Testament passages should also be brought into the discussion.

> Then he will say to those at his left hand, "You that are accursed, depart from me into the eternal fire prepared for the devil and his angels." (Matt. 25:41)
>
> War broke out in heaven; Michael and his angels fought against the dragon. The dragon and his angels fought back. (Rev. 12:7)
>
> Therefore, to keep me from being too elated, a thorn was given me in the flesh, a messenger [Greek: *angelos*] of Satan to torment me, to keep me from being too elated. (2 Cor. 12:7)
>
> He went and made a proclamation to the spirits in prison, who in former times did not obey, when God waited patiently in the days of Noah, during the building of the ark, in which a few, that is, eight persons, were saved through water. (1 Pet. 3:19–20)[1]
>
> Do you not know that we are to judge angels? (1 Cor. 6:3)[2]
>
> It is clear that he did not come to help angels, but the descendants of Abraham. (Heb. 2:16)

---

[1] We will not deal further with this passage, but for a recent substantial discussion, see Travis B. Williams and Horrell, *1 Peter*, 2:185–294. As Williams and Horrell make clear in their excursus on the history of interpretation (215–21), there have been three major interpretations of this passage: (1) that Christ preached to deceased humans during the period between his death and resurrection; (2) that the spirit of Christ preached through Noah to the people alive during the construction of the ark; and (3) that Christ preached a message of victory to the fallen angels. This last view was proposed only in the modern period and is the most popular view now among scholars, but it is challenged by Williams and Horrell. In the Stone-Campbell Movement (which has influenced my own religious context), this passage from 1 Pet. became the focal point of a bitter dispute between Alexander Campbell and Jesse B. Ferguson; see Foster, *Life of Alexander Campbell*, 258–60; West, *Search for the Ancient Order*, 1:262–64.

[2] Apparently Paul had previously taught the Corinthians on this point. Williams, *Spirit World*, 117–18, does not think this verse concerns humans judging evil angels, but rather that humans become like angels.

> I am convinced that neither death, nor life, nor angels, nor rulers, nor things present, nor things to come, nor powers, nor height, nor depth, nor anything else in all creation, will be able to separate us from the love of God in Christ Jesus our Lord. (Rom. 8:38–39)

> For this reason a woman ought to have a symbol of authority on her head, because of the angels. (1 Cor. 11:10)[3]

None of these passages tell us how these angels became evil. Some of these passages (e.g., 1 Cor. 6:3, 11:10) may not be about evil angels at all. But it appears that the devil has his own band of angels (Matt. 25:41; Rev. 12:7; 2 Cor. 12:7), and Peter and Jude seem to know a story about sinful angels and expect their readers to be familiar with the story as well. Judging from the order of examples that Peter gives, we might guess that the story of sinning angels happened before the flood, since he seems to be going in chronological order: angels (2 Pet. 2:4), Noah (v. 5), Sodom and Gomorrah (v. 6), Lot (v. 7). (Not so Jude, who starts with the exodus [v. 5], then talks about sinning angels [v. 6], then Sodom and Gomorrah [v. 7].)[4]

There are two possibilities: Either Peter and Jude are referencing a story told in the Bible, or they are not. We might expect them to be referencing a story told in the Bible since their other examples come from well-known Bible stories. And there was a very prominent ancient Jewish interpretation of a strange and confusing biblical passage in terms of the sin of angels, specifically Genesis 6:1–4. We will look at this passage and its ancient interpretation in just a moment. In the context of Genesis, it appears immediately before the flood story, and maybe it serves as part of the reason for the divinely appointed deluge. But there are other stories told about angels who sinned much earlier than the flood, and we should think about the biblical roots of these stories first.

---

[3]Already Tertullian (*On the Veiling of Virgins* 7) connected this verse to the Watchers myth, but according to Doedens, *Sons of God*, 119, "the likelihood that Paul alludes to the angels-interpretation of Gen 6:1–4 is very minimal." For further discussion, see Stuckenbruck, "Why Should Women Cover?"; Wassen, "'Because of the Angels'"; Martin, *Corinthian Body*, 229–49.

[4]There is a slight parallel in the first-century work known as 3 Maccabees 2:4-5, which starts a list of evildoers with the antediluvian giants and then Sodom.

REBELLION IN HEAVEN?

Paradise Lost begins with Satan and his horde of rebel angels in agony in the flames of Hell, having lost their battle in heaven against the forces of good angels, led first by the archangel Michael and later by the Son of God himself. We saw in the previous chapter that there is nothing explicit in the Bible about such a primordial angelic rebellion.[5] Christians have often found this type of rebellion in Isaiah 14 or Ezekiel 28 or Luke 10:18 or Revelation 12.[6] The only one of these passages that overtly talks about an angelic battle in heaven is Revelation 12, but there it looks like the heavenly battle cannot have been the moment of the angelic rebellion because Satan is an active troublemaker before the battle takes place.

Were Peter and Jude talking about a rebellion of angels before creation, or before the snake tempted the human couple in Genesis 3? As we saw in the previous chapter, already around the time of the New Testament, or maybe just a little later, some interpreters saw in the snake of Genesis 3 a rebellious angel, one of a group of rebellious angels. So it's not impossible that Peter and Jude had this story in mind (though the story is not explicit in the Bible, but it was eventually discovered in Isaiah 14 and Ezekiel 28). And this is the interpretation of Peter and Jude that Augustine championed in the fourth century. He said that Peter "is speaking of those who rebelled against God in the beginning, and fell with the devil, their prince, who through envy dispossessed the first man by the deceit of the serpent."[7]

But this may not be the best candidate for what Peter and Jude were thinking about.

THE SONS OF GOD IN GENESIS 6

The story of the flood in Genesis is immediately preceded by a strange account about "the sons of God" and "the daughters of men," along with some beings called Nephilim (a Hebrew term difficult to translate), and a decree that humans are allotted 120 years (Gen. 6:1–4). I'm not sure what

[5]This fact is a major downfall (among others) of the argument in Kim Papaioannou, "Sin of the Angels."

[6]For a recent attempt, see the article by Papaioannou mentioned in the previous note.

[7]*City of God* 15.23, trans. Dyson, 681.

any of this means, and no one else is either. That does not make this passage of Scripture unique, by the way. The beginning of Genesis 6 contains several difficult elements.

Chart 9.1. The "sons of God" and "daughters of men" in Genesis 6:1–4

Verse	NRSV, adapted (Hebrew text)	NETS (Septuagint)
1	When people [*ha-adam*] began to multiply on the face of the ground, and daughters were born to them,	And it came about when humans [οἱ ἄνθρωποι] began to become numerous on the earth, that daughters also were born to them.
2	the sons of God [*benei-ha-elohim*] saw that they were fair; and they took wives for themselves of all that they chose.	Now when the sons of God [οἱ υἱοὶ τοῦ θεοῦ] saw the daughters of humans, that they were fair, they took wives for themselves of all that they chose.
3	Then YHWH said, "My spirit shall not abide[8] in mortals forever, for[9] they are flesh; their days shall be one hundred twenty years."	And the Lord God [κύριος ὁ θεός] said, "My spirit shall not abide [καταμείνῃ] in these humans forever, because they are flesh, but their days shall be one hundred twenty years."
4	The Nephilim were on the earth in those days—and also afterward—when the sons of God [*benei-ha-elohim*] went in to the daughters of humans, who bore children to them. These were the heroes [*ha-gibborim*] that were of old, warriors of renown.	Now the giants [οἱ γίγαντες] were on the earth in those days and afterward. When the sons of God [οἱ υἱοὶ τοῦ θεοῦ] used to go in to the daughters of humans, then they produced offspring for themselves. Those were the giants [οἱ γίγαντες] that were of old, the renowned humans.

According to these four verses, near the dawn of humanity, when people started to multiply, they had daughters (of course!). And some beings called "the sons of God" thought these women, or some of them, were very beautiful, and they married them. So far so good—a nice little romance. Verse 3 introduces a limitation on human life: 120 years; but to what does it refer? Is this a limitation on the individual life span, such that each individual will now live no longer than 120 years? But Genesis is filled with people who live much longer than that—like, basically,

[8] Day, "Sons of God," 437–40, discusses this difficult word (יָדוֹן, *yādōn*) and concludes that it probably has to do with strength.

[9] Day, "Sons of God," 440–41, discusses this word (בְּשַׁגַּם, apparently ב + ש + גם), saying that it means "in that also" or "since also." He proposes this translation: "My spirit shall not be strong in man for ever, since he is also flesh," i.e., in addition to spirit, just mentioned.

everybody—and, on the other hand, another verse of Scripture puts the human lifespan more reasonably at seventy to eighty years (Ps. 90:10). So is the 120-year limitation instead the timing of the flood? Maybe God is saying he will give people 120 years to repent before the flood comes.[10] Whatever the 120 years indicates, it is not explicitly related to the previous verses about the marriages, so we wonder whether the marriages somehow provoked God to limit human life, and if so, why? But the passage is not done. Verse 4 tells us that at the time of the marriages, there were some beings on earth called Nephilim. The verse also mentions the children produced by the marriages, and maybe it means that the Nephilim are those children, or maybe it just means that the children lived at the same time as the Nephilim. Finally, the end of the verse says that they were famous warriors—but is it the Nephilim who were the famous warriors, or the children from the marriages, or maybe they are all one and the same?

Furthermore, are readers supposed to imagine that Genesis 6:1–4 reports a sin? There is no explicit judgment on the various beings mentioned in this passage, but the very next verse declares that "YHWH saw that the wickedness of humankind was great in the earth" (Gen. 6:5), so maybe we should interpret the marriages as displeasing God for some reason. Are the Nephilim evil? Do they somehow cause the flood, which immediately follows? Scripture does not say.[11]

We can read what the text says, but what does it mean? I've already said that I do not know and no one else does either. "A reader who is confused by the paragraph [Gen. 6:1–4] may take comfort from the fact that the commentators are as well."[12] But I won't leave the matter there. Guesses have been made, some of which have been very influential, so we'll talk about the guesses.

---

[10] This is the interpretation of the first-century work called Book of Biblical Antiquities (3.2) by an unknown author whom scholars call Ps-Philo.

[11] On the view that the Nephilim, or the events of Gen. 6:1–4, do not necessarily have anything to do with the flood, or are not necessarily immoral, see Stokes, *Satan*, 60; Walton and Walton, *Demons and Spirits*, 179. In fact, Walton and Walton interpret the sons of God in Gen. 6 as divine beings (they don't like the term "angels" in this context) but still insist that what they did was not sinful, so they are not "fallen" divine beings (177–86).

[12] VanderKam, "Genesis 6:1–4," 1.

It seems pretty clear that the story in Genesis assumes some knowledge on the part of its readers. Probably the first people who read Genesis had heard about these marriages and the Nephilim, and so the Genesis text does not give more details because more details were not needed. In other words, there was once a larger story (I assume), and what we've got in Genesis 6:1–4 is just a summary of that larger story. Now, some people think that the larger story is preserved for us in 1 Enoch, or at least that 1 Enoch tells a story similar to the one Genesis 6 is summarizing. I consider that idea possible—that 1 Enoch provides the background to Genesis 6:1–4—but this way of looking at the matter is no more than a guess. Probably a better guess is that the author of 1 Enoch had no idea what Genesis 6:1–4 was about, but he decided to use the biblical text as the jumping-off point for a story that he wanted to tell. I agree with the scholar Philip S. Alexander, who many decades ago described 1 Enoch as "an elaborate midrash [interpretation] on Gen. 6:1–4."[13] In other words, I imagine that 1 Enoch is just a guess at what Genesis 6:1–4 means, but it also happens to be our earliest preserved guess.

The opening section of 1 Enoch is called the Book of the Watchers (chs. 1–36), and this section was probably written in the third century BC.[14] Fragmentary manuscripts of the Book of the Watchers were found among the Dead Sea Scrolls, and some of these manuscripts (particularly 4Q201 and 4Q202) were themselves produced in the second century BC. The text was written in Aramaic. The term *watchers* in the title is a designation for angels, just like in the book of Daniel (e.g., Dan. 4:13), apparently because angels are "those who sleep not," as the book of Enoch has it (e.g., 1 En. 39.12). The Book of the Watchers tells the story of these watchers (the sons of God in Gen. 6:1, according to this interpretation) sleeping with human women (the daughters of men) and producing a race of giants (the Nephilim; cf. especially 1 En. 6–7). The section describing this sin starts with this description:

[13] Alexander, "Targumim and Early Exegesis," 60.

[14] For an English translation, there are various options (e.g., *OTP* 1:5–89), but I will be using Nickelsburg and VanderKam, *1 Enoch*. *First Enoch* is a composite of several booklets, which were written at different times, sometimes centuries apart.

> When the sons of men had multiplied, in those days, beautiful and comely daughters were born to them. And the watchers, the sons of heaven, saw them and desired them. And they said to one another, "Come, let us choose for ourselves wives from the daughters of men, and let us beget children for ourselves." (1 En. 6.1–2)

Then two hundred of these angels mate with human women (1 En. 6.6), and the angels are punished by being locked in prison (1 En. 10; 21).

Some of this interpretation of Genesis 6 on the part of 1 Enoch makes sense (such as interpreting "sons of God" as angels, as we will see), but I want to stress again that the text of Genesis does not even say that the Nephilim were the offspring produced by the sons of God and daughters of men, so there is a lot of dot-connecting happening here.

The term "sons of God" often does refer to what we would call angels. That's the way it is in Job 1:6, 2:1, and 38:7; probably also in Psalm 29:1 and 89:7; and maybe in Daniel 3:25. As we have seen, in 1 Enoch, this idea that the sons of God were angels is the earliest interpretation we have for Genesis 6:1, and it is the only interpretation of which we have record until after the time of Jesus. It is presupposed by quite a bit of ancient Jewish literature.[15] In the second century BC, the book of Jubilees has this account: "And when the children of men began to multiply on the surface of the earth and daughters were born to them, the angels of the Lord saw in a certain year of that jubilee that they were good to look at. And they took wives for themselves from all of those whom they chose. And they bore children for them; and they were the giants" (Jub. 5.1; cf. 4.15). Josephus also passes on this interpretation, or something like it.

> For many angels of God, consorting with women, fathered children who were insolent and despisers of every good thing

[15] Aside from the sources mentioned above in the text, see the Genesis Apocryphon 2.1; the Damascus Document A 2.17–19; Testament of Reuben 5.6–7 (*OTP* 1:784); Testament of Naphtali 3.5 (*OTP* 1:812); 2 Baruch 56.10–14 (*OTP* 1:641); 2 Enoch 18 (*OTP* 1:130–32). Aside from the Book of the Watchers, other Enochic booklets now forming a part of 1 Enoch also mention (more briefly) the rebellious angels: the Similitudes (see 1 En. 39.1, 69.6); the Dream Visions (see 1 En. 86.3–6); the Epistle of Enoch (see 1 En. 106).

> because of the confidence that they had in their power. For, according to tradition, they are said to have committed outrages comparable to those said by the Greeks to have been done by giants.[16]

Josephus states that angels procreated with human women, but he seems not convinced that the children were giants but only like giants in their wickedness.

The original Septuagint offered a straightforward translation of the Hebrew, "sons of God."[17] The Greek translators did not offer a clear interpretation. But many later LXX manuscripts do make it clear by substituting "angels" for "sons," so that Genesis 6:2 talks about the "angels of God."[18] Apparently Philo in the first century AD had such a Greek text in front of him, for that is how he quoted the verse.[19]

If the "sons of God" were angels, so that it was angels who were marrying human women and having kids with them, then it would make sense (I suppose) for those kids to be giants—because they had angels for their fathers. Later in this chapter we will consider the Nephilim. The word *nephilim* does not necessarily mean "giants," but the Hebrew Bible does seem to indicate that the Nephilim were tall, and the LXX translates the word as "giants." If the Nephilim were the offspring of the marriages reported in Genesis 6:2, and if the sons of God were angels, and if the Nephilim were giants, then it would make some sense for angels to have very tall kids.

---

[16] Josephus, *Jewish Antiquities* 1.73.

[17] Wevers, *Genesis*, 108.

[18] This is the case for Codex Alexandrinus in the fifth century, though the reading "sons of God" was retained for Gen. 6:4. According to Alexander, "Targumim," 63, the reading "angels" in Codex Alexandrinus "has the reading over an erasure." A facsimile of the manuscript can be accessed at https://manuscripts.csntm.org/manuscript/View/GA_02, and the relevant page is labeled image 3b (bottom right of the image). There are also nine further Greek manuscripts with the reading "angels," as listed in the apparatus to Wevers's edition (previous note). In the early fifth century, Augustine seems to have had a text with a double rendering (or was he looking at two different copies of Genesis with different readings?): "in the same verse of Scripture where the sons of God are said to have loved the daughters of men, they are also called 'angels of God'" (*Civ.* 15.22, trans. Dyson, 680). According to Marguerite Harl (and contra the edition of Wevers), "angels" is the Old Greek reading; Harl, *La Genèse*, 125.

[19] See Philo, *On the Giants* 6–7; *Questions on Genesis* 1.92.

But can angels marry? Christians have often rejected the idea that the "sons of God" in Genesis 6:1–4 are angels because Jesus says that people in the resurrection "neither marry nor are given in marriage, but are like angels in heaven" (Matt. 22:30). John Chrysostom in the fourth century cited this passage against the angels interpretation.[20] But no one (as far as I know) believes or has ever believed that angels in heaven do marry, nor that Genesis 6:1–4 describes angels in heaven marrying. Even in the Book of the Watchers angels have no need of marrying and producing children because they are immortal (1 En. 15.7). Augustine—a champion of the non-angelic interpretation of Genesis 6 (we'll talk about his view later)—admitted that angels could take on physical bodies and therefore that it was possible for them to have sex, and that sometimes it still happened, but of course these would not be "God's holy angels."[21]

Outside the Bible, it was sometimes thought that angels had the proper physical features for reproduction. At any rate, Jubilees 15.25–27 says that angels are circumcised.[22] Also, remember that in the book of Tobit, the demon Asmodeus was in love with Sarah (Tob. 6:15).[23] And Paul's statement at 1 Corinthians 11:10 (quoted earlier) that women should wear a veil "because of the angels" was early on interpreted as a reference to the lustful angels associated with Genesis 6.[24] (Women need to wear a veil to cover their beauty so that the angels will be able to control themselves.) The Jewish work known as the Testament of Reuben (5.5–6) says that women should refrain from adorning their heads "for it was thus that they charmed the Watchers, who were before the flood." In ancient times it was commonly thought that angels, or spiritual beings, might have the means and the motives for procreating with human women.

The earliest Christian literature that reflects explicitly on Genesis 6:1–4 also interprets the "sons of God" as angels.[25] This includes Justin Martyr

[20] *Hom. Gen.* 22.7.

[21] *City of God* 15.23.

[22] Bernat, "Circumcision."

[23] See Fitzmyer, *Tobit*, 215, who discusses the textual evidence. 4Q196 does (apparently) preserve most of the Aramaic word for "love" here (רחם), for which see DJD 19:20.

[24] See, e.g., Tertullian, *On the Apparel of Women* 1.2; *On Virginity* 7; *On Prayer* 22.

[25] VanderKam, "1 Enoch, Enochic Motifs."

in the mid-second century, Irenaeus a little later, Clement of Alexandria and Tertullian near the turn of the third century, Commodian in the mid-third century, and Lactantius in the early fourth century.[26] The earliest Christian writer to propose a different (non-angelic) interpretation was Julius Africanus in the first half of the third century, whose view we will examine a little later.

By the time of Augustine in the early fifth century, the idea that Genesis 6 talked about angels had largely fallen out of favor both in Judaism and in Christianity.[27] In the late fourth century, Philaster of Brescia was willing to give the label "heresy" to the belief that angels had slept with human women.[28] Already in the second century AD, Jewish translators into Greek were guarding against this interpretation by rendering the crucial expression in Genesis 6:2 as either "sons of the gods" (Aquila; οἱ υἱοὶ τῶν θεῶν) or "sons of the mighty ones" (Symmachus; οἱ υἱοὶ τῶν δυναστευόντων).[29] The Aramaic translations of Genesis (the targumim) translate the disputed phrase in Genesis 6:2 similarly to Symmachus, showing that these translators did not think the sexual activity described in the verse involved

---

[26] Justin Martyr, *First Apology* 5.2; Irenaeus, *On the Apostolic Preaching* 18; Clement of Alexandria, *Paedagogus* 3.2; Clement of Alexandria, *Stromata* 5.1; Tertullian, *On the Apparel of Women* 1.2–3, 2.10; Tertullian, *Apology* 22; Tertullian, *On the Veiling of Virgins* 7; Tertullian, *On Idolatry* 9; Commodian, *Instructions* 3; Lactantius, *Divine Institutes* 2.15. In the third century, the Ps-Clementine *Homilies* 8.11–15 (*ANF* 8.272–73) promotes the angel-interpretation, whereas the Ps-Clementine *Recognitions* promotes a non-angelic interpretation; see VanderKam, "1 Enoch," 76–80. Also, the Cyprian in the mid-third century (*On the Dress of Virgins* 14) attributes the illicit transmission of knowledge of cosmetics to the sinful angels, obviously in reliance on the Book of the Watchers, but he does not say that angels had intercourse with women.

[27] Augustine's predecessor in the mid-fourth century, Hilary of Poitiers, regarded the idea that angels mated with human women to be absurd, but he mentioned this idea in relation to Ps. 133:3 and not in relation to Gen. 6; see his *Tractatus super Psalmos* on LXX Ps. 132, §6.

[28] Philaster, *Book of Diverse Heresies* 108.

[29] For these renderings, see the second apparatus in Wevers, *Genesis*, 108. Theodotion (probably around the turn of the era) is reported as retaining the LXX rendering οἱ υἱοὶ τοῦ θεοῦ. Since Aquila felt the need to revise the LXX to τῶν θεῶν, one might interpret the LXX (or, perhaps, Aquila did) as too close to the Watcher myth. According to Wevers, *Notes on the Greek Text of Genesis*, 76 n. 3, Aquila understood the term to refer to the pagan gods.

angels.[30] Rabbinic literature contains no references to angels mating with humans, but instead interprets the "sons of God" in Genesis as humans (as we will see below).[31]

The idea that Genesis 6:1–4 tells a story about angels who sinned is the earliest interpretation of the Genesis passage that we have, and it was a widespread interpretation at the time of the New Testament and before. But from the second century AD, other interpretations began to appeal to readers of Scripture. Let's examine those other proposals.

Human Interpretations of the Sons of God

Can the "sons of God" in Genesis 6:2 be humans? Sure they can. After all, the nation of Israel is identified as God's "firstborn son" (Exod. 4:22; cf. Hos. 11:1), and Israel is a human nation, not an angelic one. King David described his son Solomon as a son of God (1 Chron. 28:6). While the plural "sons of God," the few times it appears in the Old Testament, always seems to refer to supernatural beings, maybe Genesis 6 is the exception. The singular "son of God" can refer to humans after all.

Which humans? Who would be described as "sons of God" here? There are basically two lines of thought: Maybe these "sons of God" are especially righteous humans, or maybe they are especially exalted or powerful humans. If they are righteous people, then the usual idea is that they are the descendants of Seth, the third son of Adam and Eve (Gen. 4:25). The other idea, that they are exalted or powerful, identifies these "sons of God" with judges or rulers of some sort. A third idea was expressed by an early rabbi named Resh Lakish who suggested that these people were called "sons of God" "because they lived a long time without trouble or suffering"[32]

Jewish sources started to promote the human interpretation of Genesis 6:2 in the second century AD. Or, perhaps we should say in the first century AD. Philo of Alexandria, who wrote in Greek and read his Bible in

---

[30] On the targumim, see Alexander, "Targumim"; and see below.

[31] A couple pseudepigrapha are also relevant to the lack of popularity of the angels interpretation. Ps-Philo's Book of Biblical Antiquities (ch. 3; *OTP* 2:306) offers a straightforward translation of "sons of God" and spends little time on them, suggesting that they are not important (probably not angels, therefore). The Sibylline Oracles (uncertain date, perhaps second century AD) represents the Watchers as human beings (Sibylline Oracles 1.65–125; *OTP* 1:336–37).

[32] Genesis Rabbah 26.5, trans. H. Freedman, *Midrash Rabbah*, 1:213.

Greek, found in his Bible the word "angels" in Genesis 6:2 (in line with some later LXX manuscripts, as we've seen), but he interpreted these angels allegorically (as he routinely interpreted the Bible) so that the word "angels" symbolized people.[33] But in the allegory of Philo, there is no actual mating at all, because the "daughters of men" are allegories for the evil pleasures that seem beautiful to some men. So I'm not sure Philo should really count as the earliest interpreter to understand the "sons of God" in Genesis 6 as humans, since his interpretation is explicitly an attempt to read the text not according to the letter. So then, like I said, it was in the second century when the human interpretation began to surface in Judaism.

One rabbi who lived in the second century is attributed with the view that the "sons of God" were nobles and that it was improper for people to refer to them as "sons of God," probably because that phrase usually means "angels." The midrash called Genesis Rabbah contains this description of his view: "R. Simeon b. Yoḥai called them the sons of nobles [בני דיניא]; [furthermore], R. Simeon b. Yoḥai cursed all who called them the sons of God" (Genesis Rabbah 26.5). Another midrash, *Sifrei Numbers* 86, gives the same interpretation.[34] The (fictional?) Jew named Trypho who debates with the Christian philosopher Justin Martyr in the mid-second century also rejects the notion that angels rebelled against God.[35] This new Jewish view can also be seen in the translations produced in rabbinic circles, both Greek and Aramaic. We have already noticed above the second-century Greek translations of Aquila and Symmachus. The Aramaic Targums (of which there are three for the book of Genesis) also advance this new interpretation, while some of them also contain elements of the older angel interpretation in their translations of our passage.

---

[33] Philo has a treatise called *On the Giants*. He also addressed this text in his *Questions on Genesis* 1.92. Philo's interpretation is similar to that of Augustine (*City of God* 15.22). On Philo's interpretation, see Archie T. Wright, *Origin of Evil Spirits*, ch. 7.

[34] *Sifré to Numbers*, Neusner, 2:84. For another translation alongside the Hebrew text, see sefaria.org. Both translations render the term בני הדיינים as "sons of judges." Origen, *Against Celsus* 4.31, was aware that eminent judges were called "god," according to a Jewish tradition (though Origen did not mention this point in connection with Genesis 6).

[35] Justin, *Dialogue* 79.1.

Chart 9.2. Three translations of Genesis 6:1–4

Onqelo[36]	Pseudo-Jonathan[37]	Neofiti[38]
Now it happened when the sons of man started to multiply upon the face of the earth, and daughters were born to them, that the sons of the great ones [בני רברביא] saw how beautiful were the daughters of man; and they took for themselves as wives any they so chose.	When the children of men began to multiply on the face of the earth and beautiful daughters were born to them the sons of the great ones [בני רברביא] saw that the daughters of men were beautiful, that they painted their eyes and put on rouge, and walked about with naked flesh. They conceived lustful thoughts, and they took wives to themselves from among all who pleased them.	And it came to pass that the sons of man began to multiply on the face of the earth and female daughters were born to them. And the sons of the judges [בני דייניא] saw that the daughters of the sons of man were beautiful in appearance and they took wives for themselves from among whomseoever they chose.
Now the Lord said, "This wicked generation shall not endure before me forever, because they are flesh and their deeds are evil; let an extension be granted to them for 120 years (to see) if they will repent."	The Lord said in his Memra, "None of the evil generations that are to arise (in the future) will be judged according to the order of judgment applied to the generation of the Flood, (that is) to be destroyed and wiped out from the world. Did I not put my holy spirit in them that they might perform good deeds? But behold, their deeds are evil. Behold, I gave them an extension of a hundred and twenty years that they might repent, but they have not done so."	And the Lord said: "None of the generations yet to arise will be judged according to the order of the judgment of the generation of the flood. Behold, the order of the judgment of the generation of the flood has been sealed before him: to be destroyed and blotted out from the midst of the world. Behold, I have put my spirit in the sons of man because they are flesh and their deeds are evil. Behold I have given the span of one hundred and twenty years (in the hope that) perhaps they might do repentance, but they have not done so."

[36] *Targum Onqelos to Genesis*, trans. Grossfeld.
[37] *Targum Pseudo-Jonathan: Genesis*, trans. Maher.
[38] *Targum Neofiti 1: Genesis*, tran McNama.

Onqelos	Pseudo-Jonatha	Neofiti
The mighty ones [גיבריא] were on earth in those days, as well as later, when the sons of the great ones came unto the daughters of men who gave birth; they <in turn> were the mighty ones of old, men of renown.	Shamhazai and Azael fell from heaven and were on earth in those days, and also after the sons of the great ones had gone in to the daughters of men, who bore them children; these are called the heroes of old, the men of renown.	There were giants [גיברים] on the earth in those days and also later when the sons of the judges went in to the daughters of the sons of man and they bore children to them. These are the giants that (were there) from the beginning of the world, giants of distinguished names. Marginal reading: "There were warriors dwelling on the earth in those days, and also afterward, after the sons of the angels had joined (in wedlock with) the daughters of the sons (of man)."

Christian sources took the other approach, identifying the "sons of God" with the descendants of Seth.[39] As mentioned earlier, this view was first proposed by Julius Africanus in the third century.

> When humankind became numerous upon the earth, angels of heaven had intercourse with daughters of men. In some manuscripts, I found: "the sons of God." In my opinion, this is to be understood figuratively [μυθεύεται]: <the descendants> of Seth are called "the sons of God" by the Spirit, since the genealogies of the righteous and the patriarchs up until the Savior are traced from him. But the descendants of Cain it designates as human seed [ἀνθρώπων . . . σποράν], as having had nothing divine because of the wickedness of their line and the dissimilarity of their nature, so that when they were mingled together, God grew angry.
>
> But let us suppose they refer to "angels." Then it was they who transmitted knowledge about magic and sorcery, as well as the numbers of the motion of astronomical phenomena, to their

[39] Wickham, "Sons of God," 135–47. The fourth-century Ambrose (*Exp. Psalm 118* 4.8) interpreted the "angels of God" that he found in his Latin version of Gen. 6:2 as an allegorical reference to spiritual people, but he did not identify them with any particular group.

> wives, from whom they produced the giants as their children; and when depravity came into being because of them, God resolved to destroy every class of living things in a flood, after threatening that humankind would not live beyond 120 years.[40]

Later Christian authors appreciated Africanus's proposal that the "sons of God" in Genesis 6:2 were the descendants of Seth. This line of thought became the governing interpretation of Genesis 6:2. John Chrysostom in the late fourth century denied that angels were ever called in Scripture "sons of God," but only humans were.[41] In the early fifth century, Augustine, approaching the matter from a different direction, more correctly notes that "the Holy Scriptures attest in a great many places that men of God were often called 'angels,'" and he cites Mark 1:2 as well as the prophet Malachi, whose name means "my messenger" or "my angel." Both Chrysostom and Augustine interpreted the "sons of God" along the lines suggested by Africanus: They were sons of Seth.[42] Augustine mentioned the apocryphal writings attributed to Enoch and declared them untrustworthy, thus undermining the most influential representation of the angels interpretation. By the twelfth century, the descendants-of-Seth interpretation had become so well-accepted among Western Christians that it was recorded without discussion in the medieval study Bible called the *Glossa Ordinaria*.[43] The interpretation of the "sons of God" as descendants of Seth also found its way into Jewish sources, but only in the medieval period and probably in reliance on Christian interpretations.[44]

---

[40] This excerpt, translated by William Adler, is labeled F23 in Julius Africanus, *Chronographiae*, 48–51 (Greek and English on facing pages). The fragment is preserved by George Syncellus.

[41] *Hom. Gen.* 22.6. For a translation of Chrysostom's *Homilies on Genesis*, see John Chrysostom, *Homilies on Genesis 18–45*, trans. Hill, 72.

[42] Chrysostom, *Hom. Gen.* 22.8; Augustine, *City of God* 15.23.

[43] For a translation of the Genesis volume of the *Glossa Ordinaria*, see Klumpenhouwer, *Biblia cum Glossa Ordinaria*, 80.

[44] For the Jewish sources transmitting this interpretation, see Ginzberg, *Legends of the Jews*, 5:172 n. 14 (in the chapter on Noah in the section called "The Generation of the Deluge").

What about the Giants?

If the "sons of God" in Genesis 6:2 were just human beings and not angels, why would their offspring be gigantic? Or were the offspring indeed gigantic? Is that the right way to interpret the terminology in Genesis 6:4? And, for that matter, are the beings that are (possibly) described as giants in Genesis 6:4 the offspring of the unions mentioned two verses earlier? I already admitted at the beginning of this discussion of Genesis 6 that I do not know the answers to these questions, but it might be valuable to explore the possibilities, the evidence, and the proposed interpretations.

The word "giant" appears in some of the major English translations (e.g., KJV, NKJV, CSB). That interpretation goes back to the LXX, which has the Greek word "giants" (γίγαντες) twice in verse 4, where the KJV has the word "giants" the first time and "mighty men" the second.[45] For the LXX, the offspring of the sons of God and daughters of men were giants, but the Hebrew text reads differently. The NRSV represents the Hebrew well: "The Nephilim were on the earth in those days—and also afterward—when the sons of God went in to the daughters of humans, who bore children to them. These were the heroes that were of old, warriors of renown." No giants here, unless the Nephilim are giants. And to reiterate the other ambiguities of this verse in Hebrew: What is the relationship between the Nephilim and the "heroes"—the Hebrew term is *gibborim*—later in the verse, and are either of these the offspring of the sons of God?

The Hebrew allows for these possibilities:

- *nephilim* = *gibborim* = children of sons of God with daughters of men
- *nephilim* = *gibborim* ≠ children of sons of God with daughters of men[46]
- *nephilim* ≠ *gibborim* = children of sons of God with daughters of men

[45] According to the apparatus in Wevers, *Genesis*, there are no variants in the LXX manuscripts.

[46] This is the view taken (more or less) by John Day, "The Sons of God and the Daughters of Men and the Giants: Disputed Points in the Interpretation of Genesis 6:1–4," *Hebrew Bible and Ancient Israel* 1 (2012): 427–47, at 432–34.

The first option seems to be the interpretation of both the LXX and the targumim (quoted earlier). The LXX is often interpreted as indicating more clearly than the Hebrew that the offspring of the marriages are giants.[47] Certainly Philo, our earliest interpreter of the LXX version of this story, regarded the giants as offspring of the marriages, as did Josephus.[48]

What are *nephilim*, anyway? The Hebrew word seems to be related to the verb *naphal*, "to fall," and so perhaps the *nephilim* are "fallen ones." That is the interpretation of Aquila, the second-century Jewish Greek translator, who rendered the word as οἱ ἐπιπίπτοντες (*hoi epipiptontes*, "fallen/falling ones"). Aquila rendered *gibborim* as δυνατοί, "strong ones," or, according to a different report, δυσίατοι, "incurable ones." The slightly later translator, Symmachus, used the word οἱ βίαιοι, "violent ones," for both *nephilim* and *gibborim*.[49] Jerome's Latin Vulgate has "giants" (*gigantes*) for *nephilim* and "strong ones" (*potentes*) for *gibborim*. Despite his translation, Jerome understood that the Hebrew *nephilim* is more easily understood as "fallen ones," which, he pointed out, would work well as a description of the offspring of angels or righteous men who sinned.[50] In other words, for Jerome, the description of the offspring as "fallen ones" lends no support to the angel interpretation.

But even if the word *nephilim* doesn't mean "giants,"[51] it may be that the *nephilim* (whatever the word itself means) were, in fact, gigantic. At least, their incredible height is implied in the only other passage in the Bible that uses the term.[52] When the twelve spies returned to the camp after having scouted out the land of Canaan, they reported having encountered Nephilim.

---

[47] Harl, *Genèse*, 126; Wevers, *Notes on the Greek Text of Genesis*, 77–78; Brayford, *Genesis*, 261; Henze, *Mind the Gap*, 100–101.

[48] Philo, *Questions on Genesis* 1.92; Josephus, *Jewish Antiquities* 1.73.

[49] It seems that Theodotion kept the LXX renderings, γίγαντες, twice in verse 4. According to Wevers's apparatus, the word γίγαντες is attested for Theodotion for Gen. 6:2, but his reading for Gen. 6:4 is unattested, probably because it was the same.

[50] See Hayward, *Saint Jerome's Hebrew Questions*, 37.

[51] In fact, the *Dictionary of Classical Hebrew* does provide the gloss "giant" for the word.

[52] Other passages that use similar (but not identical) words include Ezek. 32:27, *nophlim*, "fallen ones" (same consonants, different vowels), connected in the verse to *gibborim*; and Job 3:16 and Ps. 58:8, both of which contain the word *nēphel*, "stillborn."

> There we saw the Nephilim (the Anakites come from the Nephilim); and to ourselves we seemed like grasshoppers, and so we seemed to them. (Num. 13:33)[53]

For this verse also, the LXX renders *nephilim* as "giants." Whatever the word means, it seems that the Nephilim in Canaan were really big people, and that the spies expected the other Israelites to be familiar with the group of people called Nephilim and to know that they were big people.

Numbers 13:33 connects the Nephilim also to another label, the Anakites, the descendants of Anak. Another reference to Anak appears in Deuteronomy, where Moses reminds the Israelites about the land of Moab.[54]

> The Emim—a large and numerous people, as tall as the Anakim—had formerly inhabited it. Like the Anakim, they are usually reckoned as Rephaim, though the Moabites call them Emim. (Deut. 2:10–11)

Again, the Anakim are tall, and other names associated with them are Emim (the Moabite name) and Rephaim. That last group comes up again later in the same chapter, again, in reference to Moab.

> It also is usually reckoned as a land of Rephaim. Rephaim formerly inhabited it, though the Ammonites call them Zamzummim, a strong and numerous people, as tall as the Anakim. (Deut. 2:20–21)

Moreover, there was a king named Og who was one of the Rephaim, in fact, their last surviving member (cf. Josh. 13:12). And Og was big—or, at least, he had a big bed, so big it became a tourist attraction.

> Now only King Og of Bashan was left of the remnant of the Rephaim. In fact his bed, an iron bed, can still be seen in Rabbah of the Ammonites. By the common cubit it is nine cubits long and four cubits wide. (Deut. 3:11)

---

[53] Robin Routledge argues that this report by the unfaithful spies was unreliable; Routledge, "The Nephilim," 27–28.

[54] For other biblical passages associating the Anakim with unusual height, see Deut. 1:28, 2:21, and 9:2.

There is also a valley called several times in Scripture "the valley of Rephaim," a term translated in the LXX as "valley of the Titans" (2 Sam. 5:18) or "valley of giants" (1 Chron. 11:15, 14:9). So, again, Rephaim had a reputation for being tall.[55]

If we put all these verses together, we can construct the following equivalencies:

Nephilim > Anakim = Rephaim = Emim (Moabite name) = Zamzummim (Ammonite name)

They are all very tall. It may be these tall people, and not all Amorites (= Canaanites; but see Gen. 14:5, 15:20), whom Amos had in mind when he described the Amorites as very tall.[56]

> Yet I destroyed the Amorite before them,
> whose height was like the height of cedars,
> and who was as strong as oaks;
> I destroyed his fruit above,
> and his roots beneath. (Amos 2:9)

What happened to the Nephilim (or the Anakim or Rephaim or whatever)? The Israelite conquest reduced their number (see Num. 13:22; Josh. 15:14; Judg. 1:10).[57] While Joshua made war on the Anakim (Josh. 11:21–23), he did not eliminate them completely; some remained in towns such as Gath (Josh. 11:22)—Goliath's hometown (1 Sam. 17:4). Gath was also the home of other warriors associated with a certain "Rapha" (the Hebrew word; cf. "Rephaim"), often translated "giant" (2 Sam. 21:16–22; 1 Chron. 20:4–8).[58]

---

[55] See Edelstein, "Rephaim, Valley of (Place)," *Anchor Bible Dictionary*, 5:676–77. The valley adjoins the valley of the sons of Hinnom (Josh. 15:8, 18:16). There is also another term, "Rephaim," which refers to the shades of people who inhabit the underworld (Job 26:5; Ps. 88:10; Prov. 2:18, 9:18, 21:16; Isa. 14:9, 26:14, 26:19); see Smith, "Rephaim," *Anchor Bible Dictionary*, 5:674–76. For a comprehensive examination of traditions about Rephaim from the Ancient Near East, see Yogev, *Rephaim*.

[56] If Amorites are tall, then Sihon (an Amorite king; Deut. 3:2) would have been tall, just like his comrade, Og, as we know—or strongly suspect—from his bed and his status as one of the Rephaim. (According to the Talmud, *Niddah* 61a §18, Sihon and Og were brothers.) Rabbinic tradition identifies Sihon as a giant; see Ginzberg, *Legends*, 3:339–42.

[57] Heiser, *Unseen Realm*, ch. 25, argues that the *ḥerem* (the "ban") of Joshua aimed to eradicate the giants; for the logic (such as it is) of the viewpoint, see 211 n. 13.

[58] On Rapha, see Becking, "Rapha," *DDD*, 687–88.

So, were the Nephilim giants? According to biblical scholar John Day, "It is clear that the Nephilim are to be understood as giants,"[59] an interpretation arising from the evidence we have just examined, particularly the appearance of the Nephilim in the promised land (Num. 13:33) and the association of the inhabitants of the promised land with great height (Amos 2:9), along with the association of the Nephilim with other tall people (Anakim, Rephaim, etc.; Deut 2:10, 20–21; 3:11). Of course, the problem with associating the Nephilim with the descendants of the sons of God in Genesis 6 is that there were still Nephilim in the land of Canaan in the time of the Israelite conquest. Why wouldn't they be destroyed by the flood? And, in fact, it may be that Genesis 6:4 means that the Nephilim were already on the earth, before the union between the sons of God and daughters of men, a point argued not only by Day in recent times but already by Augustine centuries ago.[60]

Various explanations have been proffered to explain how the Nephilim survived the flood. There is a rabbinic tradition that the giant Og (later king of Bashan; Num. 21:33) survived the flood by hitching a ride on board Noah's ark.[61] Michael Heiser, a modern scholar and proponent of the angel interpretation of Genesis 6:2, proposed either that Noah's flood was a local event (and so it did not kill all the Nephilim) or that after the flood more angels cohabitated with women and produced more giants.[62] Augustine's solution is that sometimes there are really tall people.[63] He acknowledges that some people think the sons of God must have been angels because the offspring were giants. But he counters that there are still sometimes really tall people in the world—he mentions an example of a really tall woman in Rome not long before Augustine's own day—and he points out that the

---

[59] Day, *From Creation to Babel*, 81.

[60] For Day's argument, see *From Creation to Babel*, 82; for Augustine's, see *City of God* 15.23.

[61] Talmud, *Zevaḥim* 113b §12. Other traditions about Og appear at Talmud, *Berakhot* 54b.

[62] Heiser, *Unseen Realm*, 189–91.

[63] Augustine, *City of God* 15.23. See also *City of God* 15.9, where he cites classical authors as demonstrating that people used to be taller than they were in Augustine's own day; see Vergil, *Aeneid* 12.899–900; *Georgics* 1.493ff.; Herodotus 1.68; Pliny the Elder, *Natural Histories* 7.16; Homer, *Iliad* 5.302ff, 12.378ff, 445ff. Augustine also reported that he himself had seen a very large tooth.

text of Genesis says that there were giants on the earth in those days and afterward, suggesting that the giants were not necessarily connected to this particular incident of sons of God mating with daughters of men. It seems that John Chrysostom also thought that the giants had nothing to do with the marriages of Genesis 6:2.[64]

Then again, giants may have survived the flood if the guy that built the ark was himself a giant. Some people in antiquity thought there may have been evidence for this view, that Noah was a giant, and they found it in Nimrod. In Genesis 10:8–12 there is a man named Nimrod, a "mighty hunter" or "mighty warrior." Here the term *gibbor* is used for Nimrod, which earlier had been used in connection with the Nephilim. Is the text telling us that Nimrod was a giant? Indeed, the LXX translates *gibbor* in this way (γίγας, Gen. 10:8–9).[65] But remember, Nimrod is the great-grandson of Noah. So if Nimrod is a giant, maybe it's in his genes? Some ancient Jewish sources speculated that Noah may have been (or may have been thought to be) the offspring of an angelic father and a human mother.[66] There has also been the belief that Abraham was connected to giants.[67]

Giants outside the Biblical Tradition

Ancient pagan myths included tales about giants or Titans. The Titans were the divine beings who preceded the Olympian gods more familiar to us, the latter including Zeus and Hera and others. According to this mythology, the father of Zeus and Hera (remember, they're siblings and they're married to one another) was a Titan named Cronus, whom Zeus defeated

---

[64] *Hom. Gen.* 22.12.

[65] On all things having to do with Nimrod, see van der Toorn and van der Horst, "Nimrod before and after the Bible." By the way, the popularization of the term "nimrod" in English in reference to a dolt may be connected to Elmer Fudd; see Wikipedia, "Nimrod," last modified March 10, 2025, https://en.wikipedia.org/wiki/Nimrod, under the section, "Idiom."

[66] The possibility is broached and rejected in 1 Enoch 106; Genesis Apocryphon col. ii. See the discussion in Glaser, "Demigods and the Birth of Noah."

[67] This view is recorded by the Christian historian Eusebius, *Preparation for the Gospel* 9.18.2, who attributed the view to an anonymous source sometimes labeled today Pseudo-Eupolemus, a source perhaps originating in the second century BC; for text, translation, and notes, see Holladay, *Fragments*, vol. 1: *Historians*, 176–77 (fragment 2). See also the comments on this extract in van der Toorn and van der Horst, "Nimrod before and after the Bible," 16–17; Stuckenbruck, *Myth of Rebellious Angels*, 7–12.

and imprisoned in a place called Tartarus. In the seventh century BC, the Greek poet Hesiod described the battle of the Olympian gods against the Titans.[68] The Olympian gods won.

> They sent them down under the broad-pathed earth and bound them in distressful bonds after they had gained victory over them with their hands, high-spirited though they were, as far down beneath the earth as the sky is above the earth.
>
> For it is just as far from the earth to murky Tartarus: for a bronze anvil, falling down from the sky for nine nights and days, on the tenth day would arrive at the earth; [and in turn it is the same distance from the earth to murky Tartarus;] and again, a bronze anvil, falling down from the earth for nine nights and days, on the tenth would arrive at Tartarus. Around this a bronze barricade is extended, and on both sides of it night is poured out threefold around its neck; and above it grow the roots of the earth and of the barren sea.
>
> That is where the Titan gods are hidden under murky gloom by the plans of the cloud-gatherer Zeus, in a dank place, at the farthest part of huge earth. They cannot get out, for Poseidon has set bronze gates upon it, and a wall is extended on both sides.[69]

Some Christians saw a connection between the giants descended from angels in Jewish tradition and the giants in pagan Greek tradition. For example, in the late second century, Athenagoras explained that the offspring of the angels and humans were the giants, written about even by Greek poets.[70] No doubt Athenagoras found compelling the stories about giants not only because of the testimony of the Enochic writings and other Jewish and Christian traditions, but also because they find a close parallel in classical Greek accounts.[71]

---

[68] Hesiod, *Theogony* 617–720.

[69] Hesiod, *Theogony* 717–33, trans. Most, 61–63.

[70] Athenagoras, *Plea* 24.6.

[71] See Stuckenbruck, *Myth of Rebellious Angels*, 36–57. For another example of a Christian connecting the Enochic giants and pagan giants, see the fragment labeled F24 in Julius Africanus, *Chronographiae*, 52–57.

So Were They Angels?

I repeat: I do not know what Genesis 6:1–4 means. I'm not going to offer an interpretation. As far as I can see, there are only possibilities and questions, few definite details. But one of those definite details is that many people throughout history regarded the sons of God in Genesis 6 as angels—and those people include our earliest Jewish and Christian interpreters of the passage and modern scholars. John Day is willing to say that there is widespread agreement among modern scholars that the sons of God are divine beings, basing this view on the use of the term "sons of God" elsewhere in the Hebrew Bible, the possibility that their offspring were giants, and that it was the earliest interpretation.[72]

BACK TO PETER AND JUDE

Peter and Jude mentioned some angels that had sinned and are being held in chains (in Tartarus, according to Peter) until the day of judgment. Who are these angels?

It seems obvious to me that the angels must be the ones we have been talking about, the ones that were thought to be the sons of God in Genesis 6, the ones described by 1 Enoch as being kept in chains. Part of the reason I think this interpretation is obvious is because Jude 14–15 quotes 1 Enoch. In fact, it quotes the Book of the Watchers, the very section of 1 Enoch that deals so extensively with those sinning angels based on Genesis 6.[73] So Jude obviously knew about that interpretation of Genesis 6. Also, given the popularity in ancient Judaism of the angel interpretation of Genesis 6, I think Jude and Peter—if they weren't referencing the angel interpretation of Genesis 6—would have had to specify that they meant some other group of sinful angels, not the group everyone knows about, the group that married the human women.

I am not alone in this view that Jude and Peter were referring to the angel interpretation of Genesis 6. Most modern scholars would say so,

[72] Day, *From Creation to Babel*, 77. The evangelical scholars Walton and Walton agree that the "sons of God" are divine beings (*Demons and Spirits*, 177–86).

[73] On Jude's quotation of 1 Enoch, see Gallagher, *Apocrypha through History*, 77–82.

including conservative Christian scholars.[74] For example, D. A. Carson agrees that Jude and Peter had Genesis 6 in mind when they talked about sinful angels, and that the Book of the Watchers helps us understand the story that the early Christians apparently presupposed: "Both Jude and 2 Peter apparently pick up on at least some of these themes. Yet what is picked up is not the entire 'package' taught by *1 Enoch* but rather only that these 'angels' (*angeloi*) are kept in darkness, bound in eternal chains awaiting the day of judgment."[75] Carson stresses (and Augustine long before him; *City of God* 15.23) that the reference to sinful angels in 2 Peter and Jude is not sufficient reason to accept all of 1 Enoch—or, even, all of the Book of the Watchers—seriously as an account of these angels. The fact is that Genesis 6 is the only biblical account of the fall of angels—if it is that.[76]

Some Christians have taken it further; they have thought that Jude's use of 1 Enoch (both his quotation of 1 En. and his reference to the sinful angels) entails the acceptance of 1 Enoch as Scripture. This is the position of the Ethiopian church, which includes 1 Enoch in its Bible.[77] The early Christian author Tertullian, near the turn of the third century, also thought that Jude confirmed the inspiration of the books associated with Enoch. But, again, I think Augustine has the better argument, that just because Jude might find some value in the Book of the Watchers does not mean he thinks the whole thing is the Word of God.[78] After all, Paul quoted pagan poets (e.g., Titus 1:12).

In fact, I'm not even sure to what extent Peter and Jude expect readers to affirm the angel interpretation of Genesis 6. Do they mean for their readers to agree that the "sons of God" in Genesis 6 were, indeed, angels, and that they begot giants? Or are they referring to this common belief just to provide an example? Might it be similar to a modern preacher taking Christian moral lessons from Star Wars or Batman? "Just as the young Luke Skywalker felt the urge to give in to his hate but ultimately resisted,

[74] For an attempt to overturn this near consensus, see Papaioannou, "Sin of the Angels." But his argument is deeply flawed, based on assumptions and inaccurate accounts of the ancient data.

[75] Carson, "2 Peter," 1048.

[76] Heiser, *Unseen Realm*, 324 n. 3.

[77] For a recent argument along these lines, see Bruk, *1 Enoch as Christian Scripture*.

[78] Tertullian, *On the Apparel of Women* 1.3; Augustine, *City of God* 15.23.

so also you must resist the desires of your flesh." You don't have to tell people that you don't really believe that Luke Skywalker was a real person. It doesn't matter for the point you're trying to make. Or what about someone about whom there might be some doubt, like King Arthur—some people think he's fake, and some think he's real, but a Christian preacher could still cite him as an example without taking a position on the historicity. "Just as King Arthur dedicated himself to finding the holy grail, in the face of opposition from a killer rabbit and the terrifying Knights Who Say Ni, so also you must dedicate yourself to the things of God." Let the reader understand.

The point I'm trying to make is that Peter and Jude could be referring to a popular idea without affirming the truthfulness of that popular idea, because the truthfulness of the idea was beside the point. The point was: "Don't be wicked like those angels we've all heard about." If Peter and Jude are not intending to affirm the validity of the angel interpretation of Genesis 6, but only to reference that interpretation for their own moral exhortation, then this use of the angel interpretation would be an example of what Christian theologians call "accommodation" in Scripture, when the writers of Scripture accommodate their language to the popular views simply for the purposes of communication. Like when Mark 1:32 mentions the setting sun—Mark is not intending to affirm the idea that the sun truly sets, that the earth is stationary and the sun revolves around the earth. That's not the point of his language.[79] Maybe the exhortation based on the common idea about angels is the same type of thing.[80] Note that whether Peter and Jude believed the story in the Book of the Watchers is irrelevant. I'm not talking about what was going on inside their heads; I'm talking about what they wrote and why they wrote it.

I probably wouldn't make this suggestion about accommodation if Jude and Peter made a bigger deal about the angel interpretation, if it were a bigger part of their argument. But it's not; it's just one of a series of examples about how to behave. Peter and Jude weren't writing a treatise on angels.

---

[79] For a helpful discussion, see Provan, *Reformation*, chs. 13–14.

[80] I'm not the only one who has thought this; see Walton and Walton, *Demons and Spirits*, 226–27.

All that to say that I still don't know what Genesis 6:1–4 is about, even though I do believe that Peter and Jude were referring to the interpretation most popular in their day. And since I'm not convinced that Genesis 6 mentions an angelic rebellion, I do not find anywhere in Scripture a description of the fall of angels. The New Testament mentions some evil angels, but it does not say how they became evil.

CHAPTER TEN

DEMONS

Beelzebub has a devil put aside for me.

—Queen, "Bohemian Rhapsody"

What does the word "demon" bring to mind? Gargoyles? Pea soup? Screwtape? I hope you think of Screwtape.

What is a demon? What does a demon do? These questions are not easily answered, but for different reasons. The substance and origin of demons are not things the Bible is interested in discussing, but other people have proffered thoughts. As for the activity of demons, we gain a pretty clear picture in the Gospels, but Christians have disagreed on whether demons continued in the same activities after the time of the apostles. I myself have never encountered anyone that seemed to be possessed by a demon, but I have talked to people (both in my home country and elsewhere) who think they've encountered demons, or people possessed by demons. As interesting as reports of demonic activity in the modern world are, the ancient period provides so much to consider that it demands our full attention in this chapter.

Once again, I do not have answers to our questions about demons, and the Bible does not supply the answers. Where do demons come from? The Bible does not say. But there have been various guesses about the origins of demons, and we'll talk about those guesses—how popular the guesses are and how old. I don't know if any of the guesses are right. For the most part, the same goes for just about everything I discuss in this chapter. Nevertheless, the Bible does say some things about demons, and we'll notice those things as well.

TERMINOLOGY

The terminology of demons can get complicated.[1] The English word "demon," to my mind, always designates a wicked spirit, harmful to humans and hostile toward God. The English word "demon" derives from the Greek *daimōn* (δαίμων), which does not always mean that. In fact, there are two closely related Greek words to consider: *daimōn* and *daimonion* (δαιμόνιον). It is the latter, *daimonion*, that appears almost exclusively in the New Testament and is routinely translated "demon," though scholars are beginning to wonder whether *daimonion*, even in the New Testament, always means what we mean by "demon."[2] One thing that is clear is that in classical Greek, a *daimōn* could be a beneficent spirit. Then we come to another complication: Outside of Greek (and even in Greek, as we have just seen), there is no standard word for harmful spirits, so we can't rely on terminology but have to identify demons by their activities. But—and here's a further complication—the activities of demons do not necessarily entail opposition to God. In fact, we have seen in previous chapters (especially Chapter Four) that sometimes the Old Testament represents harmful spirits as working for God rather than against him. Should we call these harmful spirits "demons"?

So, the complications again: I think of a "demon" as a harmful spirit opposed to God—but (1) the Greek word *daimōn* does not always mean a harmful spirit; (2) the Bible shows that sometimes harmful spirits work for God; and (3) there is no standard word for harmful spirits, whether in Greek or Hebrew or other languages.

As I mentioned, the Greek word *daimōn* can refer to a good spirit or a bad spirit, especially in classical Greek. On the other hand, in Christian usage, evident usually in the New Testament and certainly thereafter, a

---

[1] For a helpful brief study, see Martin, "When Did Angels Become Demons?"

[2] See Frankfurter, "Master-Demons"; Bazzana, *Having the Spirit of Christ*; Reed, "When Did *Daimones* Become Demons?"

daimōn/daimonion is almost always wicked.[3] In classical Greek, a *daimōn* was something like what Christians think of as angels: minor deities.[4] That is precisely what Philo says when talking about angels in the Pentateuch: "The beings that other philosophers refer to as *daimones* are customarily given the name 'messengers' (*angeloi*) by Moses—which are souls flying in the air."[5] As Philo says, pagan Greek literature does have a name for powerful supernatural beings that are inferior to God or the gods; that label is not "angels" but "demons" (*daimones*). Earlier (Chapter One), we explored the meanings of the Hebrew word *elohim* and found that it could refer to a variety of supernatural beings. It turns out that the Greek word *daimōn* is similarly elastic. For example, Plato described Eros as neither god nor mortal but *daimōn*, that is, a minor deity.[6] This same sense is found in Acts 17:18, when some philosophers in Athens asserted that Paul was proclaiming foreign *daimonia*. According to Plutarch, it was the philosopher Xenocrates in the fourth century BC who described the *daimones* as having "human emotions and godlike power" (πάθος θνητοῦ καὶ θεοῦ δύναμιν).[7]

This positive angle on *daimōn* as referring to a minor deity is illustrated by Socrates at the turn of the fourth century BC, when he was defending himself from the charge of denying the existence of the gods. Socrates famously believed that a minor deity, a *daimōn*, guided him.[8] In fact, Socrates represented himself as merely doing the bidding of his personal *daimōn*. If Socrates believed in *daimōnes*, minor deities, could

---

[3] For a brief account of how the word *daimōn* went from neutral to negative, see Koskenniemi, "Miracles of the Devil," 84–87; but also Reed, "When Did *Daimones* Become Demons?"

[4] Thus, it is curious that the LXX translators never rendered Hebrew *malak* ("angel") by Greek *daimōn*; for a consideration of this point, see Martin, "When Did Angels Become Demons?," 664–66. In later Christian tradition, as we will see, the demons are identified with the fallen angels, as Martin's article also demonstrates.

[5] *On the Giants* 6. For a different translation see Philo, trans. Colson and Whitaker, 2:449.

[6] Plato, *Symposium* 202e.

[7] Plutarch, *On the Obsolescence of Oracles* §13 (416d); trans. Frank Cole Babbitt in Plutarch, *Moralia*, 5:387. The opinion of Xenocrates is referenced in Plutarch's work by the character Cleombrotus. See the entire speech by Cleombrotus, §§10–15.

[8] See Plato, *Apology* 31d. This claim from Socrates became a topic of discussion in antiquity. See, e.g., Plutarch, *On the Daimonion of Socrates*; Apuleius, *On the God of Socrates*.

he have been an atheist? The charge against Socrates had been brought by a certain Meletus, to whom Socrates addressed himself in his defense speech, called the *Apology*.

> But if I believe in *daimonia*, it is quite inevitable that I believe also in *daimones*; is it not so?

Let me pause here to point out something about Socrates's terminology. It seems that Socrates is distinguishing a *daimonion* from a *daimōn*. The Loeb translation, which I am following but slightly adapting, translates *daimonion* here as "spiritual being" and *daimōn* as "spirit." "If I believe in spiritual beings, it is quite inevitable that I believe also in spirits." *Daimonion* is an adjective (used nominally here), "spiritual (thing)," while *daimōn* is the noun, "spirit." They both refer to minor deities or demigods. The word *theos*, normally translated as "god" or "God," refers to a "full-fledged deity." As Socrates says, belief in *daimonia* implies belief in *daimones*. Now back to the speech of Socrates, right after he asked, "Is it not so?" He answers his partially rhetorical question in the affirmative.

> It is; for I assume that you agree, since you do not answer. But do we not think that *daimones* are gods [θεούς] or children of gods [θεῶν παῖδας]? Yes, or no? "Certainly" [answers Meletus]. Then if I believe in *daimones*, as you say, if *daimones* are a kind of gods [θεοί τινές], that would be the puzzle and joke which I say you are uttering in saying that I, while I do not believe in gods [θεοὺς], do believe in gods [θεοὺς] again, since I believe in *daimones*; but if, on the other hand, *daimones* are a kind of bastard children of gods [θεῶν παῖδές εἰσιν νόθοι τινές], by nymphs or by any others, whoever their mothers are said to be, what man would believe that there are children of gods [θεῶν παῖδας], but no gods [θεούς]?[9]

Socrates is relying on a very close connection between the word *daimōn* and the word *theos* ("god"). Just about the earliest Greek literature we have,

[9] Plato, *Apology* 27c–d, trans. Fowler, 1:101–3.

the *Iliad* of Homer, uses *daimōn* as basically an equivalent of *theos*.[10] Such a neutral or positive meaning of *daimōn* continued in later Greek as well. In a speech before the Roman senate in 27 BC, the emperor Caesar Augustus declared himself more like a *daimōn* than anyone else.[11] But by the fifth century AD, Augustine reported that the special negative meaning of "demon" among Christians had become prevalent even among pagans.[12]

Once we leave the safe confines of the Greek language, terminology gets hairier. What's the Hebrew word for demon? Is there one? What about the Egyptian word, or the Akkadian word? Other cultures often had a variety of spiritual beings in their religious conceptions, but they did not always, of course, use the Greek term *daimōn* for any of these beings, so it can be difficult to know whether it is proper to label any of their supernatural beings as "demons." For example, Egyptologists have often described some of the minor deities in the Egyptian religion as "demons," but according to a recent assessment, "There was not a clear class of demons in the Egyptian divine hierarchy."[13] The same issue complicates the search for demons in the Hebrew Bible and the examination of the terminology for demons there. Since even the Greek *daimōn* does not always refer to a "demon" as we usually think of such a being (a wicked and harmful spirit), it is not surprising that other languages also lack specific terminology for such beings.

Old Testament

Demons in the Bible are especially characteristic of the New Testament, where they appear frequently, particularly in the Synoptic Gospels and Acts. In the Old Testament, the word "demon" probably appears very rarely in your Bible, or maybe not at all. The ESV uses the word "demons" three times in the Old Testament: Leviticus 17:7, Deuteronomy 32:17, and

---

[10] See *Iliad* 1.222, 5.438–41, 3.420. This equation of *theos* with *daimōn* in Homer was pointed out by Cleombrotus in Plutarch's *On the Obsolescence of Oracles* 10. Cleombrotus immediately notes that for Hesiod, *daimones* were lower than *theoi* but above the class of heroes and the class of humans.

[11] The speech is recorded by the third-century AD historian Dio Cassius, *Roman History* 53.8.1.

[12] Augustine, *City of God* 9.19.

[13] Quack, "Demons, Demonology," *EBR*, 6:532.

Psalm 106:37.[14] The paucity of appearances of the word demonstrates that demons do not play a very prominent role in the Old Testament. (However, possibly some demonic beings are never labeled "demons"; at the end of this chapter, we will consider whether Azazel and Lilith are demons.)

We should probably pause at this point and reflect on this scarcity of demons in the Old Testament. It is something of which to take note, in light of the prominence of demons in the ancient Near East, the prominence of demons in ancient Jewish literature, and the prominence of demons in the Synoptic Gospels. The Hebrew Bible is distinctive in its minimizing of demonic activity. I have no point to make beyond simply noting this fact, which I think is interesting in itself.

As we examine the Hebrew terminology for demons, we will use the Septuagint (LXX) as a guide.[15] In the LXX, the word *daimōn* never appears, but *daimonion* appears eight times in the Greek translation of the Hebrew Bible (and another ten times in the Greek versions of the deuterocanonical books).[16]

Deuteronomy 32:17. The Hebrew text is translated in the NRSV in this way:

> They sacrificed to demons, not God,
> to deities [*elohim*] they had never known,
> to new ones recently arrived,
> whom your ancestors had not feared.

This translation of the Hebrew text is very similar to the Greek text, which uses in the first line the word *daimonia*, possibly "minor deities" (like in the case of Socrates). The relevant Hebrew word is *shēd* (שֵׁד, or actually, the

---

[14] The KJV uses the word "devils" in all these cases, just as it does in the New Testament where most other English versions have "demons." The KJV also has "devils" at 2 Chron. 11:15 (Heb. *seirim*; ESV: goat idols).

[15] For a study of the LXX's uses of the terminology for demons, see Reed, "When Did *Daimones* Become Deomons?" who shows that the word *daimonion* does not seem to mean "wicked spirit" in the LXX.

[16] Martin, "When Did Angels Become Demons?," 658 n. 4, asks why the LXX translators preferred *daimonion* to *daimōn*. One suggestion is because the longer form could be interpreted as a diminutive and thereby may have reduced the significance of these beings.

plural, שֵׁדִים, *shēdim*), a word that appears only twice in the Hebrew Bible, here and in Psalm 106:37 (see below).

Psalm 91:6. The Hebrew text is translated in the NRSV in this way:

> or the pestilence that stalks in darkness,
> or the destruction that wastes at noonday.

It's the word "wastes" that corresponds to what the LXX has as *daimonion*. The Hebrew term is a verb, *yashud*, that probably reminded the Greek translators of the noun *shēd* (see on Deut. 32:17 above), so that they translated with *daimonion*. Instead of "that wastes at noonday," the LXX mentions a "noonday demon" (NETS) or, maybe, "noonday demigod."

Psalm 96:5. The Hebrew text is translated in the NRSV in this way (slightly adapted):

> For all the gods [*elohim*] of the peoples are idols,
> but YHWH made the heavens.

The LXX renders that first line as "all the gods [*theoi*] of the nations are *daimonia*." It is interesting to imagine what Socrates would have made of this claim. Since he thought of *daimonia* as minor deities, distinct from a *theos*, which was a full-fledged deity, I suppose he might have thought that the psalmist was insulting the foreign deities not by equating them with evil spirits but by reducing their status to that of merely minor deities in a spiritual hierarchy ruled by YHWH, the God of Israel. That, indeed, may have been what the Greek translator of Psalms intended.[17]

The Hebrew word rendered by the NRSV as "idols" and by the LXX as *daimonia* is *elil* (אֱלִיל), which appears twenty-one times in the Hebrew Bible. The Hebrew word basically means "worthless," and it is translated this way once in the LXX (μάταιος; Zech. 11:17). The word is often translated "idol" (εἴδωλον; Lev. 19:4; Hab. 2:18; Ps. 97:7; 1 Chron. 16:26) or "made by hand" (χειροποίητος; Lev. 26:1; Isa. 2:18, 10:11, 19:1, 31:7) or "abomination" (βδέλυγμα; Isa 2:8, 20), but it is translated *daimonion* only once, at

[17] See the discussion of Angelini, *L'imaginaire du démoniaque*, 216–19.

Psalm 96:5.[18] Even at the parallel passage in 1 Chronicles 16:26, the Greek translator offers a different word, "idol" (εἴδωλον). Probably the writer of the Hebrew Psalm 96 was not thinking about demons (harmful spirits). The LXX use of the word *daimonia* for the gods of the pagan nations ties into—and contributes toward—a growing perception that the pagan gods are demons, a concept we explored in Chapter Three.

Psalm 106:37. The Hebrew text is translated in the NRSV in this way:

> They sacrificed their sons
> and their daughters to the demons.

The Hebrew term translated "demons" is *shēd*, the same term we encountered earlier at Deuteronomy 32:17, its only other appearance in the Bible. Both times it is translated by the LXX as *daimonion*.

Isaiah 13:21. The Hebrew text is translated in the NRSV in this way:

> But wild animals will lie down there,
> and its houses will be full of howling creatures;
> there ostriches will live,
> and there goat-demons will dance.

The NRSV gives the rendering "goat-demon" for the Hebrew term *sair* (שָׂעִיר).[19] The NRSV translates this word as "goat-demon" also at Leviticus 17:7 (the LXX has μάταιος, "worthless"), Isaiah 34:14 (see below), and 2 Chronicles 11:15 (LXX: μάταιος, "worthless"). The same word, *sair*—or, maybe a homonym—appears fifty-two times in the Hebrew Bible and just means "goat." The ESV translates the word as just "goat" at Isaiah 13:21 and 34:14, though it does have "goat demon" at Leviticus 17:7 and "goat idols" at 2 Chronicles 11:15. For the two Isaiah passages, the KJV uses "satyr" (and "devils" for Lev. 17:7; 2 Chron. 11:15). So there seems to be some agreement among English versions that the Hebrew word for "goat" can sometimes

[18] The Hebrew word *elil* is also translated as θεός at Isa. 19:3; μεγιστάν at Ezek. 30:13; κακός at Job 13:4; and is left untranslated in the LXX at Isa. 10:10 and Jer. 14:14.

[19] See Stokes, *Satan*, 145, who points out that Pseudo-Ezekiel in the Dead Sea Scrolls (4Q386 1 iii 4) relies on this verse but reads *shēdim* (שֵׁדִים) rather than *seirim* (שְׂעִירִים).

be used for a supernatural being or an object of worship ("goat demon" or "goat idol" or "satyr"), even if there is disagreement on whether that is what it means in Isaiah 13:21 ("goat" or "goat demon"?). The LXX for this verse has nothing about goats at all, but translates the word as *daimonion*.

Isaiah 34:14. The Hebrew text is translated in the NRSV in this way:

> Wildcats shall meet with hyenas,
> goat-demons shall call to each other;
> there too Lilith shall repose,
> and find a place to rest.

Here we find our term "goat-demons" again, representing the Hebrew *sair*, but this time the LXX has rendered the term ὀνοκένταυρος (*onokentauros*), "donkey-centaur." For the Hebrew term *lilith*, which we will discuss later, the LXX has also given "donkey-centaur," so that in the LXX "donkey-centaur" appears twice in the verse. The LXX has the word *daimonion* in the place where the NRSV has "wildcats." The Hebrew word is *tsi* (צִי), or in the plural, *tsiyim*; it appears six times in the Bible and apparently means "inhabitant of the desert."[20] At Isaiah 34:14, the LXX has at the beginning, "*Daimonia* shall meet with donkey-centaurs."

Isaiah 65:3. The Hebrew text is translated in the NRSV in this way:

> a people who provoke me
> to my face continually,
> sacrificing in gardens
> and offering incense on bricks.

The LXX has a little bit extra at the end of the verse: "offering incense on bricks to the *daimonia*, which are not."[21] The Hebrew text has nothing corresponding to this line, so this verse does not help us track down the Hebrew term translated as *daimonion* in the LXX.

---

[20] See Clines, *Dictionary of Classical Hebrew*, 7:113. The six appearances of *tsi* in the Bible include (in addition to Isa. 34:14) Isa. 13:21 (LXX: wild animal), 23:13 (LXX omits); Jer. 50:39 (LXX: ἴνδαλμα, *indalma*, "phantom"); Ps. 72:9 and 74:14 (for both psalms, LXX: Ethiopians).

[21] On this LXX plus, see Angelini, *L'imaginaire du démoniaque*, 82.

Isaiah 65:11. The Hebrew text is translated in the NRSV in this way (slightly adapted):

> But you who forsake YHWH,
> who forget my holy mountain,
> who set a table for Fortune [גַּד, *gad*]
> and fill cups of mixed wine for Destiny [מְנִי, *meni*].

The Hebrew word *gad* appears in the Bible only here and in Genesis 30:11,[22] where it provides the explanation for why the matriarch Leah named one of her sons Gad (because he represented good fortune). In that verse in Genesis, *gad* is translated into Greek as τύχη (*tuchē*), "fortune." Maybe in Isaiah 65:11, "Fortune" is thought of as a deity. At any rate, the LXX gives the translation *daimonion.*[23]

The other Hebrew word I've indicated in this verse, *meni*, "Destiny," appears only once in the Bible and is translated in the LXX here as τύχη. Maybe it is also supposed to be the name of a deity.[24]

Those are all the passages in which the Greek term *daimonion* appears in the LXX (excluding the deuterocanonical books).[25] English versions of the Bible translated from the Hebrew text often use the term "demon" in one other passage, which has already been mentioned: Leviticus 17:7 (goat-demon or some such). Aside from the beings mentioned in these passages, other beings that we might want to consider include the evil spirit that came on King Saul in 1 Samuel 16:14. After all, in the New Testament,

[22] See also Josh. 11:17, 12:7, 13:5, where it appears as part of a place-name, Baal-gad.

[23] The reading varies in the Greek manuscripts between *daimōn* (several manuscripts, including Codex Sinaiticus) and *daimonion* (Codex Vaticanus and Codex Alexandrinus). The text of the critical edition of the LXX prints *daimonion*; Ziegler, *Isaias*, 361. Anna Angelini makes an argument for the originality of *daimōn*; "Δαίμονες and Demons," 57–58.

[24] There is a textual variant in the Greek manuscripts such that the Greek terms are reversed; see Angelini, *L'imaginaire du démoniaque*, 82–83. On the LXX, see also Reed, "When Did *Daimones* Become Demons?"

[25] As for the deuterocanonical books, the term *daimonion* appears especially in Tobit (3:8, 17; 6:8, 15–17; 8:3), in which a harmful spirit plays an important role in the plot. See also Baruch 4:7, 35.

as we will see, "evil spirit" can be equivalent to "demon" (cf. Luke 8:2; more often "unclean spirit"). But in 1 Samuel 16, the evil spirit is controlled by YHWH (see Chapter Four), so I guess it is not the same kind of thing we read about in the New Testament, and it would be inappropriate to think about this spirit afflicting Saul as a demon, since we usually think about demons as opposed to God. So we can concentrate on the eight passages mentioned above.

Our Hebrew words in play are the following, all translated in the LXX as *daimonion*, at least one time.[26]

- *shēd*, appearing twice (Deut. 32:17; Ps. 106:37), translated *daimonion* both times. Also, at Psalm 91:6, the Greek translator probably was thinking of *shēd* (ושד rather than MT's ישוד, *yashud*) when he used the term *daimonion*. The term *shēd* appears fourteen times among the Dead Sea Scrolls (six times in Hebrew and eight times in Aramaic).[27]
- *gad*, appearing twice (Gen. 30:11; Isa. 65:11), but only once translated *daimonion* (Isa 65:11)
- *elil*, appearing twenty-one times, but only once translated *daimonion* (Ps. 96:5)
- *sair*, appearing four times, only once translated as *daimonion* (Isa. 13:21)
- *tsi*, appearing six times, only once translated *daimonion* (Isa. 34:14)

It is *shēd* that is most strongly associated with *daimonion*. Though in its two appearances in the Hebrew Bible (Deut. 32:17; Ps. 106:37), it is difficult to tell whether the term means "wicked spirit" or perhaps "divine being that is not YHWH," it would come to mean "wicked spirit" (i.e., what we mean by "demon") in later Hebrew and Aramaic (Qumran, targumim, modern Hebrew).[28] Most scholars also identify the *sair* as a demon or supernatural

[26] Martin, "When Did Angels Become Demons?," 658–66.

[27] See Stuckenbruck, "Demonic World," 56–57; Stokes, *Satan* 144–45. Out of the eight appearances of *shēd* in the Aramaic scrolls, five of them are from Tobit 6.

[28] Angelini, *L'imaginaire du démoniaque*, 81. For biblical Hebrew and Qumran Hebrew, see Clines, *Dictionary of Classical Hebrew*, 8:266. For Qumran Aramaic, see Cook, *Dictionary of Qumran Aramaic*, 230. For Rabbinic Hebrew and Aramaic, see Jastrow, *Dictionary of the Targumim*, 1523.

being, at least in some contexts. There are some other possible demons, such as Lilith (Isa. 34:14) and Azazel (Lev. 16). About other possible demons (pestilence? destruction?) there is more debate and very little evidence.[29]

New Testament

The New Testament uses the term *daimōn* once (Matt. 8:31) and *daimonion* sixty-three times. Matthew's *daimōn* in 8:31 is paralleled by Luke 8:27 with *daimonion*. There is also the related verb *daimonizomai*, "to be possessed by a demon," which appears thirteen times in the New Testament (all in the Gospels), and the adjective *daimoniōdēs*, "demonic," which appears once (James 3:15). Every appearance of *daimonion* in the New Testament could refer to a wicked spiritual being except one, Acts 17:18 (a passage we looked at earlier), where the term is neutral. That one use of the term in a definitely neutral way is also the only time that *daimonion* appears in Acts. Wicked spirits appear in Acts, but they are not called *daimonia* but rather "evil spirits" (Acts 19:12–16) or the like. Aside from the Gospels (and the single time in Acts), the term *daimonion* appears in the New Testament only a handful of times: four times in 1 Corinthians (all in 1 Cor. 10:20–21), once in 1 Timothy (4:1), once in James (2:19), and three times in Revelation (9:20, 16:14, 18:2). The Gospel of John contains no stories about demons, only a few accusations that Jesus has a *demon* (like Socrates? cf. 7:20; 8:48–49, 52; 10:20–21). The vast majority of appearances of the word *daimonion* in the New Testament are in the Synoptic Gospels (47x).

As we saw with the Old Testament, hunting for demons and hunting for the word *daimonion* are not necessarily the same thing. The word *daimonion* can mean "minor deity," even in the New Testament (Acts 17:18; perhaps elsewhere, e.g., 1 Cor. 10:20–21), but whatever the word connotes for the New Testament authors, the Gospel writers use it to designate wicked or harmful spirits. But they do not rely on solely on the term *daimonion*. Sometimes demons are called spirits, with various adjectives attached. For instance, in Luke 4:31–37, Jesus expels a demon from a man in a synagogue. Luke first calls the evil being a "spirit of an unclean demon"

[29] See the brief discussion of proposed demons in the Hebrew Bible in Kuemmerlin-McLean, "Demons," 2:138–40; Blair, *De-Demonising the Old Testament*; Walton, "Demons in Mesopotamia and Israel," 229–46.

(4:33), and then a "demon" (v. 35), and then an "unclean spirit" (v. 36).[30] Mark tells the same story in terms of an unclean spirit (1:21–28). As biblical scholar Dale Martin says, "All three Synoptic Gospels clearly identify demons with unclean or evil spirits."[31] But they all three had their own preferences: Matthew uses the term "unclean spirits" more than "demons," whereas Mark and Luke do the reverse.

This terminology might bring to mind again the evil spirit that afflicted King Saul, which was not a demon (or so I have usually thought), because it was sent by God. But in the New Testament, every being called an evil spirit or an unclean spirit seems to be in rebellion against God. The equation of evil spirits with demons had already been made in the Jewish literature before the New Testament.[32]

ORIGIN OF DEMONS

What is a demon?[33] There were different answers to this question in antiquity, and the Bible has no interest in deciding which answer is correct.[34] We can examine the suggestions.

---

[30] On the impurity of these spirits, see Thiessen, *Jesus and the Forces of Death*, 123–48.

[31] Martin, "When Did Angels Become Demons?," 673. Compare Mark 3:22 with verse 30; or, on the one hand, 5:2, 8, 13, and on the other hand, 5:15, 16, 18; or 6:7 and 6:13; or 7:25 and 7:26, 29. For a slight qualification of this statement, see Glover, "Mark's Demonic Christology," 47 n. 3.

[32] My evidence for this statement is Tobit 6:8 (attested at Qumran: 4Q197 4 i 13; DJD 19:44–47). In 1 Enoch 19.1–2, demons are distinct from evil spirits, though they are both wicked. (On 1 En. and Jub., see Martin, "When Did Angels Become Demons?," 667–69.) In this passage, the evil spirits encourage people to worship demons. On the other hand, in 1 Enoch 99.7–9, both demons and evil spirits receive worship.

[33] As for "what" a demon is—what it is made out of—there was some discussion on this question in antiquity—quite a bit of discussion. Just to cite one prominent theologian, Origen said that the body of a demon "is naturally fine and thin like air, and because of this is considered or called 'bodiless' by many" (*On First Principles*, preface §8), though a demon is not bodiless, strictly speaking (Origen thought). Origen insisted that only God is bodiless (*On First Principles* 1.6.4, 2.2.2, 4.3.15). We will not pursue this topic further, but a good place to start is Smith, "How Thin Is a Demon?"

[34] See Barth, *Church Dogmatics*, vol. 3, pt. 3, 522–23, who insists "The only possible answer is that their origins and nature lie in nothingness," but then Barth explains that demons "are null and void, but they are not nothing." For ancient suggestions on the origin of demons, see Ferguson, *Demonology*, ch. 2.

We have noted that the words *daimōn* and *daimonion* can be used in reference to spiritual beings who are not necessarily wicked. The term can be a synonym for "god," *theos*, or it can refer to a minor deity, a demigod, or it can refer to a personal guardian spirit (think Socrates).[35] But the dominant view of *daimonia* in Christianity is that they are negative beings, wicked, harmful, opposed to God and his people, and this view is closely associated with the New Testament depiction of the unclean spirits/demons.[36] Where is the origin of the wicked demons?

Again, this is a question that the Bible displays little interest in addressing. As for the Old Testament, Anna Angelini identifies three streams in which the LXX uses the term *daimonion*: (1) *daimonia* are pagan gods; (2) they live in the desert; and (3) they harass humans.[37] There is nothing about origins or nature, just characteristics.

Before pursuing further the origins of demons, let me just dwell a bit on the second characteristic mentioned by Angelini. Demons, at least sometimes, live in the desert. We have seen that idea already in our discussion of Isaiah 34:14. We will see it again when we talk about Azazel and Lilith at the end of this chapter. We see some hints toward this idea in the Gospels. The man with the legion was driven by the demons into deserted places (Luke 8:29). In the parable of Jesus regarding the demon that brings seven more demons into the person who had been cleansed, the demon initially wandered "through waterless places" (Luke 11:24–26). As Everett Ferguson points out, such avoidance of water by this demon is reminiscent of *The Legend of Sleepy Hollow*.[38] Ferguson even connects this idea to Christian baptism: "This belief about ghosts not crossing water may have something to do with the early church's doctrine about baptism freeing

[35] For *theos*, cf. Plato, *Apology* 24b–c and Acts 17:18; for *demigod*, see again Plato, *Symposium* 202e–203a (on Eros); Plutarch, *The Obsolescence of Oracles* 10–15 (*Moralia* 415a–418d [LCL 5:380–396]).

[36] In pagan literature after the classical Greek period, there was a trend toward viewing demons more negatively. See Ferguson, *Demonology*, 49–51; Angelini, "Δαίμονες and Demons," 60–61. Earlier (note 12), I noted Augustine's comment to this effect.

[37] Angelini, "Δαίμονες and Demons," 56–62.

[38] Ferguson, *Demonology*, 23–24.

one from the power of demons."[39] In a comment on Azazel in Leviticus 16, scholar Jacob Milgrom says, "In the Mesopotamian world, the wilderness (*ṣēru*) is one of the symbolic designations of the netherworld."[40]

Now, back to demonic origins. Perhaps the biblical authors assumed the ideas about the origins of demons that were current in the ancient world—but there were different ancient accounts of demonic origins. Here we will look at the major contenders.

Created as Demons

There is a view expressed in the Mishnah such that demons were created at the very end of creation week, as the Sabbath was beginning (m. Avot 5:6). Rabbi Judah the Prince explained that God created the souls of the demons but did not have time to create their bodies before the Sabbath started, with the result that demons are bodiless souls (Genesis Rabbah 7.5). Obviously, Rabbi Judah is just having a little fun here, but the point for us is that apparently some people thought that the demons were not byproducts of something else (corrupted creatures of some sort) but they had been created directly by God. In a first-century work called the Book of Biblical Antiquities, we read about how David described the evil spirit that afflicted Saul as being "created from an echo in the abyss" (§60).[41]

As the last mentioned example shows, this view coheres well with the depiction of the evil spirits in the Hebrew Bible, such as the evil spirit sent by YHWH to afflict King Saul (1 Sam. 16:14). Those spirits, which are servants of God, were presumably created directly by God and are not fallen or corrupted beings. But, again, this evil spirit sent from YHWH is not "demonic" in the sense that it is not opposed to God.

Most Christians throughout history have not been willing to accept the notion that God created demons as wicked beings, because, according to the Genesis account of creation, everything God created was "very good" (Gen. 1:31). For that reason, most people have thought that demons must have been created good and turned wicked somehow. As Origen said in the third century: "They are not God's creation in so far as they are daemons,

[39] Ferguson, *Demonology*, 25. See also pp. 126–27, with a citation of Cyprian, *Epistle* 71.15.

[40] Milgrom, *Leviticus*, 1:1072.

[41] The translation is from Howard Jacobson in Feldman et al., *Outside the Bible*, 1:602.

but only in so far as they are rational beings of some sort."[42] In other words, God did not create them as *demons* (wicked spirits); they became demons through their own choice. This kind of objection would probably not apply to those harmful spirits that we see God employing in the Hebrew Bible (e.g., the spirit that afflicted Saul). But, again, those harmful spirits are apparently not demons.[43]

Souls of Dead People, i.e., Ghosts

The archaic Greek poet Hesiod described the first race of humans, a golden race, who were generous and wise, who succumbed to peaceful deaths. "But since the earth covered up this race, by the plans of great Zeus they are fine spirits [δαίμονες . . . ἐσθλοί] upon the earth, guardians [φύλακες] of mortal human beings: they watch over judgments and cruel deeds, clad in invisibility, walking everywhere upon the earth, givers of wealth; and this kingly honor they received."[44] The terminology is going to get tricky here. Hesiod says that he's describing *daimones*, but he is not describing wicked spirits (our "demons"), or even necessarily harmful spirits; he's describing demigods, as we've discussed earlier. But it is the same term in Greek.

A few centuries later, Socrates quoted this very passage from Hesiod and commented:

> This, then, I think, is what he certainly means to say of the *daimones*: because they were wise and knowing [δαήμονες, *daēmones*] he called them *daimones*; and in the old form of our language the two words are the same. Now he and all the other poets are right, who say that when a good man dies he has a great portion and honour among the dead, and becomes a *daimōn*, a name which is in accordance with the other name of wisdom. And so I

[42] Origen, *Contra Celsum* 4.65, trans. Chadwick, 237. See the similar thoughts of Irenaeus at *Against the Heresies* 4.41.1–2.

[43] Barth, *Church Dogmatics*, vol. 3, pt. 3, 519–31, argues that the basic feature of a "demon" is its opposition to God and not its harmfulness.

[44] Hesoid, *Works and Days* 121–26. The Greek text with facing English translation is in Hesiod, *Theogony*, trans. Most, 97. The same view can be found in Campbell, "Demonology."

assert that every good man, whether living or dead, is *daimonic*, and is rightly called a *daimōn*.[45]

In the second century AD, the Greek writer Pausanias described an event in the days of Odysseus: A rapist was punished by stoning, but then his "ghost" (*daimōn*) tormented people in a certain city, Temesa, until he was placated by being offered a maiden. Then a certain Euthymus wanted to marry the maiden, so he fought the ghost. Pausanias does not tell us how they fought, but he says that Euthymus won, so that the *daimōn* "was driven out of the land and disappeared, sinking into the depth of the sea."[46]

We see, then, that a common pagan view was that the *daimones* were the ghosts of dead people, and sometimes specifically evil dead people.[47] Some Jewish writers took the same position. Josephus defined *daimonia* in this way: "the spirits [*pneumata*] of wicked men which enter the living and kill them unless aid is forthcoming."[48]

Souls of the Giants

Athenagoras, a second-century Christian author, advocates this view straightforwardly: "The souls of the giants [αἱ τῶν γιγάντων ψυχαί] are the demons [δαίμονες] who wander about the world."[49] Remember from our previous chapter that the giants are often considered to be the offspring of the union between angels and human women, an interpretation of Genesis 6:1–4. When the flood came and killed the giants, the bodies of the giants died but their spirits lived on as demons. In some tellings, the demons and the evil spirits are two separate classes of beings, whereas in

---

[45] The speech of Socrates is contained in Plato's *Cratylus* 398b; translation in Plato, *Cratylus; Parmenides; Greater Hippias; Lesser Hippias*, trans. H. N. Fowler, 55. This passage from Plato is later cited by Augustine, *City of God* 9.20. Socrates quoted the same passage of Hesiod at *Republic* 5.469a.

[46] Pausanias, *Description of Greece* 6.6.10, trans. Jones, 3:41.

[47] See Ferguson, *Demonology*, 41–42.

[48] Josephus, *Jewish War* 7.185. Earlier in the same work, Josephus quoted the Roman general (and later emperor) Titus who admonished his troops in their assault on Jerusalem with the idea that even if they died in battle they would have the hope of coming back as *daimones* and meeting their living family members (*Jewish War* 6.47). On demons in Josephus, see Martin, "When Did Angels Become Demons?," 672. For a Christian writer discussing this view, see Tertullian, *On the Soul* 57.

[49] Athenagoras, *Plea on Behalf of the Christians* 25, in *Legatio and De Resurrectione*, trans. Schoedel, 60–61.

other accounts they are equated. The idea that the demons are related to the giants from Genesis 6:4 was popular in second-century Christian texts. Another example is Justin Martyr: At creation, God "appointed His angels, whom He placed over mankind, to look after men and all things under heaven. But the angels violated their charge, fell into sin with women and begot children who are called demons."[50] Justin says that the demons are the offspring of the angels, but he probably means that the demons are the spirits of the offspring, the giants.

This same idea is found in some Jewish texts of the Second Temple period.[51] In the Book of the Watchers (1 En. 1–36), God explained the following to Enoch:

> And now the giants, the ones born from the spirits and flesh, they will be called evil spirits on the earth and their dwelling place will be on the earth. Evil spirits came out from their bodies [the giants], because from humans they came into existence, the beginning of their creation and origin is from the Holy Watchers; they will be evil spirits on the earth and they will be called evil spirits. The spirits of the giants commit injustice, consume, attack, wrestle, and hurl to the ground, cause sorrow, and they eat and drink nothing, but abstain from food and they thirst, and they are offensive. And these spirits will rise up against humanity and the women because they came out of them. (1 En. 15.8–10).[52]

Even if these evil spirits are (in the thought world of the Book of the Watchers) not exactly the same as demons (see 1 En. 19, where the spirits sacrifice to demons), they are closely related, and they are equated in other literature.

---

[50] Justin Martyr, *Second Apology* 5, trans. Falls, 124. But Justin seems to equate demons with the spirits of dead people at *First Apology* 18 in a passage quoted by Campbell, "Demonology," 386.

[51] See the fragmentary *Book of Giants*, as translated, e.g., by Archie T. Wright in Embry et al., *Early Jewish Literature*, 2:211–26.

[52] Trans. Archie T. Wright in *Early Jewish Literature*, 2:204–5.

For example, this long passage from Jubilees first mentions demons and then talks about evil spirits:[53]

> In the third week of that jubilee the polluted demons began to lead astray the children of Noah's sons and to lead them to folly and to destroy them. And the sons of Noah came to Noah, their father, and they told him about the demons who were leading astray and blinding and killing his grandchildren. And he prayed before the Lord his God and he said, "God of the spirits which are in all flesh, who has acted mercifully with me and saved me and my sons from the water of the Flood and did not let me perish as You did the children of perdition, because
>
> Great was your grace upon me,
> and great was your mercy upon my soul.
> Let your grace be lifted upon my sons,
> and do not let evil spirits rule over them,
> lest they destroy them from the earth.
>
> But bless me and my sons. And let us grow and increase and fill the earth. And you know that which your Watchers, the fathers of these spirits, did in my days and also these spirits who are alive. Shut them up and take them to the place of judgment. And do not let them cause corruption among the sons of your servant, O my God, because they are cruel and were created to destroy. And let them not rule over the spirits of the living because you alone know their judgment, and do not let them have power over the children of the righteous henceforth and forever."
>
> And the Lord our God spoke to us so that we might bind all of them. And the chief of the spirits, Mastema, came and he said, "O Lord, Creator, leave some of them before me, and let them obey my voice. And let them do everything which I tell them, because if some of them are not left for me, I will not be able to exercise the authority of my will among the children of men

[53] Unfortunately, we do not have this passage preserved in Hebrew but only Ethiopic, so we do not know what the original said. Possibly the Hebrew did not equate demons with the evil spirits, as suggested by Martin, "When Did Angels Become Demons?," 668.

> because they are (intended) to corrupt and lead astray before my judgment because the evil of the sons of men is great." And he said, "Let a tenth of them remain before him, but let nine parts go down into the place of judgment."
>
> And he told one of us to teach Noah all of their healing because he knew that they would not walk uprightly and would not strive righteously. And we acted in accord with all of his words. All of the evil ones, who were cruel, we bound in the place of judgment, but a tenth of them we let remain so that they might be subject to Satan upon the earth. (Jub. 10.1–12; *OTP* 2:75–76)

The chief evil spirit, whom Jubilees names Mastema, asked for permission from God to keep some of these evil spirits (demons) out of confinement so that he could use them to accomplish his mischief on the earth, and God permitted 10 percent of spirits to remain under the charge of Mastema. It has been argued that some concepts related to demons as displayed in this ancient Jewish literature find echo in passages in the New Testament.[54]

Fallen Angels[55]

The *Catechism of the Catholic Church* says it this way: "Satan or the devil and the other demons are fallen angels who have freely refused to serve God and his plan. Their choice against God is definitive. They try to associate man in their revolt against God" (§1.2.1.7.2.414). An early proponent of this view was Tatian in the second century AD, who wrote that the devil and the other angels who sinned with him all became demons.[56] But apparently the equation of demons with evil angels goes back no further than Tatian. The scholar Dale Martin says that idea "was an invention of late ancient Christian writings."[57] One might cite on behalf of this idea some passages in the New Testament, which attribute to the devil control of angels (Matt. 25:41; cf. Rev. 12:7) as well as demons (Mark 3:22–27); it is

---

[54] See, e.g., Elder, "Porcine and Polluted Spirits."

[55] It is the burden of Martin's article ("When Did Angels Become Demons?") to track down the early history of this idea, which he traces to Tatian in the second century AD.

[56] Tatian, *Oration* 7.

[57] Martin, "When Did Angels Become Demons?," 657.

a simple matter to equate Satan's angels with his demons.[58] Moreover, this view has connections with the Old Testament passages relating the pagan gods to demons, as we will see (and just as early Christian authors said, such as Commodian and Athenagoras).

So what are demons, or where do they come from? Ancient authors did not enjoy consensus on these questions, and Christian Scripture does not care even to broach them. Indeed, our term "demon" might encompass multiple types of spiritual beings. Further, the beings we think of as demons are not always given that label in ancient literature. It may be that when the writers of the New Testament (especially the Gospels and Acts) described demons or evil spirits, they did not have any particular nature or origin in mind for these spirits, other than wickedness and harmfulness and opposition to God.

ACTIVITIES OF DEMONS

In the Synoptic Gospels—remember: demons never appear in the Fourth Gospel—demons distress people in various ways. Most concerningly, they enter into the bodies of people. Exorcism was a well-developed skill in the ancient world,[59] but Jesus performed exorcisms with such uncomplicated force—no spells or potions—that people accused him of being in league with Beelzebul (Mark 3:22–30). In fact, the name of Jesus proved so powerful that others could invoke it over demons (Mark 9:38). Indeed, the man named Legion attempted to overpower Jesus by naming him and adjuring him, but to no avail (Mark 5:7). What demons don't do in the Gospels is tempt people to sin, or deceive them. Satan, known as the ruler of the demons, performs these activities (temptation and deception), but the demons themselves do not. "The main activity of demons in the New Testament ministry of Jesus is not to tempt to sin but to cause disability,

[58] But Karl Barth is very much opposed to this idea for theological reasons; see his *Church Dogmatics*, vol. 3, pt. 3, 531.

[59] For one recent discussion of exorcism outside the New Testament, see Ronis, *Demons in the Details*, 195–222.

disease and insanity: even though they are clearly associated with the activity of the Devil."[60]

Outside the New Testament, we read about demons doing similar things. Once again I will remind you that in the Old Testament there are "evil spirits" under God's control who do things harmful to humans.[61] And again I am assuming that we should not think of these evil spirits as demons. At any rate, in later Jewish literature, such as the Book of the Watchers and Jubilees and Tobit, demons afflict humans. In the book of Tobit, a demon named Asmodeus is in love with a woman named Sarah (Tob. 6:15), so he causes her problems each time she marries. "Sarah had been given in marriage to seven husbands, and the wicked demon Asmodeus [Ασμοδαυς τὸ πονηρὸν δαιμόνιον] had killed each of them before they had been with her as is customary for wives" (Tob. 3:8 NRSVCE).[62] In the Book of the Watchers and in Jubilees, demons cause all kinds of trouble, including deception.[63] As Matthew Thiessen shows in his summary of Jewish demonology of the Second Temple period, Jews at the time of Jesus almost always regarded demons as evil beings with the goal of harming or deceiving humans.[64]

People long after the time of the New Testament continued to experience trouble that they interpreted as demonic. Medieval rabbinic literature has a great deal to say about demons.[65] A modern biography of the early fifth-century Latin writer Augustine summarizes his thoughts on demons: "Their powers of influence were enormous: they could so interfere with the physical basis of the mind as to produce illusions [*Epistle* 9.3; *City of God* 18.18.12–22]. Thrust into the turbulence of the lower air, below the moon, these condemned prisoners, awaiting sentence in the Last Judgement [*Epistle* 102.3.20; *City of God* 11.33.1–2], were always ready to swoop, like

---

[60] Riley, "Demon," *DDD*, 237–38.

[61] According to Josephus, *Jewish Antiquities* 6.166, the evil spirit of 1 Sam 16:14 caused Saul "suffocations and strangulations." For other examples, see Judges 9:23; 1 Kings 22:19–23. Note that the spirit from God in 1 Kings 22, as described (imagined?) by Micaiah, is a deceiving spirit. For further discussion of these types of spirits, see Chapter Four.

[62] Asmodeus is identified as a giant in Testament of Solomon 5.1–11, especially verse 3.

[63] Stokes, *Satan*, 88–89. As Stokes points out, the deception of humans is not as prominent in the Book of the Watchers (only in 1 En. 19) as in Jubilees.

[64] Thiessen, *Jesus and the Forces of Death*, 132–38.

[65] Ronis, *Demons in the Details*.

birds, upon the broken fragments of a frail and dissident humanity [*City of God* 16.24.60]."[66]

Of course, many people (Christian and other) believe in the influence of demons today.[67] The *New York Times* columnist Ross Douthat, a conservative Catholic, recently published a book for a secular audience in which he argues for belief in the supernatural, including continuing demonic activity.[68] The best-selling spiritual author John Mark Comer affirms that spiritual growth includes deliverance from demonic activity.[69] And there are today Roman Catholic exorcists that are hard at work in all parts of the world, including my home country. While I haven't experienced anything myself that I would attribute to demons, I know enough not to make confident statements in this arena. Let's get back to the ancient sources.

The following section will concentrate on the ideas about demonic activity found in the New Testament, particularly the Synoptic Gospels, and even so we will be selective, concentrating on four aspects of demonic behavior: their testimony to Christ, their possession of human bodies, their connection to disease, and their connection to pagan gods.

Demons and Christology

The letter of James says that "even the demons believe" (James 2:19), and we see illustration of this idea in the stories of their encounters with Jesus. While most people in the Gospels struggle to understand the identity of Jesus or his significance, the demons that meet Jesus exhibit no such

---

[66] Brown, *Augustine of Hippo*, 311. For much more, see Wiebe, *Fallen Angels*.

[67] Keener, *Miracles*, 2:788–856, an appendix titled "Spirit Possession and Exorcism in Societies Today." Two other examples that I find interesting: James VI of Scotland—who later became James I of England and gave his name to the KJV—wrote a book on *Daemonologie* (1597), arguing for the continuing activity of demons in the world. And the mid-nineteenth-century religious reformer Alexander Campbell, a fierce advocate of rationality in religion, considered it possible that demons do still influence people in lands where Christianity is not strong; Campbell, "Demonology," 398. On Campbell's "logical, rational hermeneutic," see Boring, *Disciples and the Bible*, 101–5; Hughes and Gorman, *Reviving the Ancient Faith*, 27–28.

[68] Douthat, *Believe*.

[69] Comer, *Practicing the Way*, 145–46.

trouble.[70] For instance, when Jesus visited the synagogue in Capernaum, a demon-possessed man knew Jesus's name and labeled him "the Holy One of God" (Mark 1:24). Later, Jesus "cast out many demons; and he would not permit the demons to speak, because they knew him" (Mark 1:34; cf. Mark 3:11–12). Most famously, the man with the legion of demons recognized Jesus as "Son of the Most High God" (Mark 5:7).

The demons seem to have insight into the identity of Jesus not shared by the human characters in the story. Possibly this theme is related to stories of divine possession in Greek or Roman pagan contexts, in which a person possessed with a spirit has special insight and can sometimes predict the future (as we will see in just a moment). There is also at least one other story, outside the Gospels, in which a possessed person seems to have special insight—the demon-possessed girl in Acts 16 (though the term *daimonion* does not appear) who follows Paul and Silas, declaring "These men are slaves of the Most High God, who proclaim to you a way of salvation" (Acts 16:17). Luke tells us that this girl had "a python spirit" (or "spirit of divination," v. 16), a term related to the Greek pagan oracles at sites such as Delphi. The idea that these people embodied by spirits would have special insight would not have been surprising in the ancient world.

Demon Possession

Ancient people often believed that spirits sometimes entered people, or "possessed" them, and the experience was usually not pleasant.[71] In the *Aeneid*, when Aeneas finally arrived in Italy, he visited the cave of the Cumaean Sibyl, a prophetess of Apollo (a.k.a., Phoebus). As Vergil put it (in the recent translation by Sarah Ruden), "The priestess ran amok, resisting Phoebus and trying hard to shake the great god out of her soul," though she was unable to do so, and Apollo tamed her.[72] While the Cumaean

[70] On this aspect of demons, see Henze, *Mind the Gap*, 93–94. For an argument that these demons display a faulty christology, see Glover, "Mark's Demonic Christology," who argues that the titles used by the demons in reference to Jesus should be (or could be, by Mark's readers) associated with a militant messianism that the Gospel demonstrates is inaccurate. Still, even if the demons have an inaccurate perception of the messiah, they still seem to exhibit greater awareness of Jesus's identity than other characters in the Gospels.

[71] On the phenomenon in antiquity, see Bazzana, *Having the Spirit of Christ*.

[72] Vergil, *Aeneid* 6.77–80, trans. Ruden, 142.

Sibyl was most famous to the Romans, probably more famous to modern readers will be the Oracle at Delphi, Apollo's priestess named Pythia, who also uttered prophecies while possessed by the god.[73] She too, according to ancient report, disliked the sensation of inspiration. The first-century Latin writer Lucan stated that "the priestesses of Delphi feel no grief that utterance is denied them: nay, they rejoice in the cessation of the oracle."[74]

Spirit-possession is not fun. We get the same impression from the Gospels. Mark includes four main stories that focus on demon possession: the man in the Capernaum synagogue (1:23–27); Legion (5:1–20); the daughter of the Syrophoenician woman (7:24–30); and the young boy whose father begged to be aided in his unbelief (9:17–29). As we have seen, there are also other references to the exorcism ministry of Jesus and his disciples (Mark 1:32–34, 39; 3:11–12, 14–15; 6:7, 13). While the demons might be nervous about their encounter with Jesus, the people affected all seem grateful after the exorcism.

What does demon possession do to a person? What are the symptoms? As we noticed already, sometimes a demon grants special insight. In the story of the legion, the man has superhuman strength (5:4). But he also hurts himself (5:5). (Is the demon hurting the man, or is the man hurting himself to try to get rid of the demon?) The demon-possessed man in the synagogue is convulsed by the demon (1:26), similar to the demon-possessed boy (9:18, 20). This boy is also made mute by the demon (9:17). Legion did not live with people but among the tombs, whereas the other demon-possessed people in Mark all seem to be living with their parents (the Syrophoenician woman's daughter or the other boy in Mark 9) or at least living around people (the man in the Capernaum synagogue). The boy seems to have had his demon for some time (years? See 9:21).

It does not seem that demons afflicted only sinners, or only people who opened themselves up to the influence of demons. That is my impression because of the Gospel stories of the young girl (θυγάτριον; Mark 7:25) and

---

[73] See the discussion in Keener, *Miracles*, 2:776–79. For possession by a god or demon in classical Greek, see Martin, "When Did Angels Become Demons?," 663, who cites Sophocles, *Oedipus Tyrannus* 1300–1306; Aeschylus, *Persians* 725, 739–53; Euripides, *Hippolytus* 141–50.

[74] Lucan, *Civil War* 5.114–16, trans. Duff, 247.

young boy (Mark 9:21) possessed by demons. After the time of the New Testament, at least some Christians thought that demons could not possess the righteous. Origen tried to make the case that demons influence people only after the people have started down the sinful road.[75] In a later work, Origen said: "We do not deny that there are many demons on the earth, but we say that they exercise power among the wicked because of their own evil, but they have no power over those clothed with the whole armor of God."[76] Even before the New Testament, in Jubilees 10, for instance, it seems that demons have no power over the righteous (Jub. 10.6, 13).[77] But in Tobit, as we have seen, the demon Asmodeus afflicts—but does not possess—the righteous Sarah.

Jesus was not the only exorcist around; we observe that fact even in the New Testament (Mark 9:38; Acts 19:13–16).[78] According to a prominent ancient tradition, attested already in Josephus, King Solomon was a mighty exorcist.[79] The book of Tobit describes a recipe for expelling a demon (Asmodeus): the angel Raphael tells Tobias, "As for the fish's heart and liver, you must burn them to make smoke in the presence of a man or woman afflicted by a demon or evil spirit, and every affliction will flee away and never remain with that person any longer" (Tob. 6:8 NRSVCE). A brief and fragmentary text from Qumran contains instructions for exorcising various types of demons (4Q560).

> I adjure you, all who enter into the body: the male Wasting-demon and the female Wasting-demon . . . I adjure you by the name of the Lord, "He Who removes iniquity and transgression" (Exod. 34:7), O Fever-demon and Chills-demon and Chest Pain–demon . . . You are forbidden to disturb by night

---

[75] *On First Principles* 3.2.2–3.

[76] *Against Celsus* 8.34.

[77] See the commentary of VanderKam, *Jubilees*, 1:408–9.

[78] Keener, *Miracles*, 2:781–87. For exorcism in rabbinic literature, aside from Ronis, see Ferguson, *Demonology*, 86–95. See the exorcism story narrated by Josephus, *Jewish Antiquities* 8.46–49.

[79] Josephus, *Jewish Antiquities* 8.45; see especially the Testament of Solomon (*OTP* 1:935–87).

> using dreams or by day during sleep, O male Shrine-spirit and female Shrine-spirit, O you demons who breach walls.[80]

Another Dead Sea Scroll (11Q11) contains "Songs to Disperse Demons," as the scroll is named in one of its editions.[81]

When these formulas for expelling demons, and other stories of exorcism, are compared with the Gospels, the differences are stark. Jesus needs no formulas, no incantations, no burning of fish guts. It's nothing like *The Exorcist.* Jesus gives commands, and the demon obeys. It doesn't take much time. Luke tells a story about some Jewish exorcists (Acts 19:11–16) who have to say a magic formula, starting with "I adjure you" and followed by the invocation of some powerful name. These Jewish exorcists tried to invoke the name of Jesus over the demons they encountered, a strategy which in itself might have been successful (Luke 9:49–50; Acts 16:18; Luke 10:17), but it did not work well for everyone. (Of course, not everyone who casts out demons in Jesus's name is known to Jesus; Matt. 7:21–23.) But when Jesus himself wanted to expel a demon from someone, he had no need to "adjure" the demon. We have noticed that a demon once tried to "adjure" Jesus (Mark 5:7).

It was the obvious power that Jesus had over the demons that led some of his contemporaries to suspect that it was all a ruse, that Jesus was in cahoots with the demons, because no one could be that powerful. As Jesus stresses at Mark 3:22–30, the correct way to interpret the exorcisms that Jesus performs is victory over Satan, as the strong man being bound by one stronger. According to Everett Ferguson, "An important factor in the Christian success in the Roman world was the promise which it made of deliverance from demons."[82]

Why do demons enter people's bodies? Loren Stuckenbruck thinks the demons are supposed to be the souls of the giants, a view connected to Genesis 6:1–4, and he offers this explanation: "Being jealous of humanity who have survived the cataclysm [i.e., the flood] with their bodies

---

[80] Translation from Wise et al., *Dead Sea Scrolls*, 566–67. I have omitted all the brackets showing which parts of this translation are reconstruction.

[81] Wise et al., *Dead Sea Scrolls*, 588–90. This scroll is called "11Qapocryphal psalms" in DJD 23.

[82] Ferguson, *Demonology*, 129.

intact, these spirits instinctively attempt to rejoin themselves to a corporeal existence that they once had and so are especially inclined to afflict by attacking or entering the bodies of humans."[83]

Christians in the second century continued to believe that demons possessing people could be expelled through the power of Jesus.[84] Justin Martyr asserted, "Even to this day they are overcome by us when we exorcize them in the name of Jesus Christ."[85] A few decades later, Irenaeus claimed that Christians were able to perform various wonders, among which was exorcism: "There are some who certainly and really drive out demons, so that very often those who were cleansed of the most wicked spirits become believers and are in the church."[86] Irenaeus's contemporary Theophilus of Antioch also claimed, "Up to the present day those who are possessed by demons are sometimes exorcized in the name of the real God, and the deceiving spirits themselves confess that they are the demons who were also at work at that time in the poets [Homer and the like]."[87]

Demons and Disease

The Gospels represent demonic influence to be the cause of some bodily ailments and diseases. The demon-possessed boy in Mark 9 was mute (v. 17), suffered convulsions, foamed at the mouth (v. 18), and could not hear (v. 25). Matthew describes demons that caused muteness (9:32–33), blindness (12:22–23), and epilepsy (17:15). Luke describes a woman who was bent over because of a spirit (13:11). Not every physical malady is attributed to demons; the lady with the hemorrhage, for instance, was not associated with demons (Mark 5:25–34), nor was blind Bartimaeus (10:46–52). The summary of Jesus's healing ministry at Mark 1:32–34 seems to distinguish those whose illness derived from demons from those sick from other causes. Though many people have thought that the attribution

[83] Stuckenbruck, "Demonic World," 54. The passage he cites in support (1 En. 15.12) does not explicitly promote this view.

[84] Ferguson, *Demonology*, 129–33; Ferguson, *Early Christians Speak*, 2:135–57, who quotes and discusses several passages from Justin, Athenagoras, Irenaeus, Clement of Alexandria, Tertullian, Minucius Felix, Origen, and Ps-Clement.

[85] *Dialogue with Trypho* 30.

[86] Irenaeus, *Against the Heresies* 2.32.4, trans. Unger, 105. This passage from Irenaeus is quoted by Eusebius, *Church History* 5.7.3–5.

[87] Theophilus, *To Autolycus* 2.8, trans. Grant, 39.

of disease to demons reflects primitive notions before the development of modern medicine, the New Testament recognizes that not all diseases derive from demons.[88]

Demons and Pagan Gods

The apostle Paul asserted in 1 Corinthians 10:20 that meat sacrificed to idols was actually sacrificed to demons (see also Rev. 9:20). Only in this passage and at 1 Timothy 4:1 does the term *daimonion* appear in the canonical Pauline letters, though the apostle does elsewhere (apparently) refer to evil angels (1 Cor. 6:3; 2 Cor. 12:7; 1 Cor. 11:10?; 1 Cor. 2:6–8, "rulers"; cf. Rom. 8:38; Eph. 6:12). According to Ferguson, Paul's statement at 1 Corinthians 10:20 would have found ready acceptance among the pagan worshipers themselves, who thought that their cultic practices applied to demigods (*daimones*) rather than gods (*theoi*).[89] And, as Guy Williams summarizes the apostle's thought, "Idols may be nothing [1 Cor. 8:4], but that does not demand that the same is true of the demons which lurk behind them [1 Cor. 10:20–22]."[90] But is Paul really saying that the "god," the divine being, represented by the idol is a demon? What does Paul mean by "demon"—a wicked and harmful spirit (à la the Gospels)? Or a demigod? Or is it all one and the same for the apostle? And does he mean that the pagan gods—Zeus and Aphrodite and Artemas and Apollo—are real, true spiritual beings, though not worthy of the name "gods" but rather some lesser title, "demons"? And if this is what the apostle means, where would he have gotten such notions?

From his Bible.[91] Earlier in this chapter, we looked at Psalm 96:5 in the Hebrew that says "all the gods of the nations are *elilim*." That last word is usually translated "idols," but it also means "nothing." But the ancient

---

[88] The nineteenth-century preacher and educator Alexander Campbell, "Demonology," 389–91, explored and rejected the charge that demon-possession was a mere metaphor for disease.

[89] Ferguson, *Demonology*, ch. 2, with the sources cited at 138 n. 37. Ferguson also shows that "Paul follows the usual Jewish interpretation that idols are nothing, but that the pagan gods are actually demons" (144); on the Jewish view, see also Williams, *Spirit World*, 143–45. For pagan Greek writers (especially Plutarch and Porphyry) associating *daimones* with pagan gods, see Eusebius, *Demonstration of the Gospel*, book 5.

[90] Williams, *Spirit World*, 147.

[91] See Christopher Wright, *Mission of God*, 144–47.

Greek translation of this verse says that all the gods of the nations are *daimonia*. Similarly, Deuteronomy 32:17 says that the pagan nations offered sacrifice not to the one true God but to lesser divine beings (*daimonia*).

Does that mean that there is a real power to the pagan gods? The Bible does not provide a straightforward answer to that question. Sometimes it seems that the pagan gods are presented as figments of the imaginations of the worshipers. This is the impression some readers get from the narrative of Elijah's contest with the prophets of Baal on Mt. Carmel (1 Kings 18). On the other hand, perhaps an ancient Israelite would have understood the story to mean that Baal's power was real but no match for YHWH, who disallowed Baal to display any wonders for his worshipers. There are, in fact, some Old Testament passages that seem to presuppose some power possessed by pagan deities. How else to explain the prophet in Deuteronomy 13:1–5 who is able to perform signs but counsels the amazed crowds to worship foreign gods? Maybe that is part of the reason that witchcraft was forbidden in Israel (Lev. 19:26; Deut. 18:10–15). Did the magicians in Egypt, the opponents of Moses, truly have some power (Exod. 7:11, 22; 8:7, 18–19)? Justin Martyr, for one, believed that the devil supplied power to these magicians.[92] Did the Witch of Endor have any power (1 Sam. 28)? According to the Book of the Watchers, it was the wicked angels who taught magic practices to people (1 En. 7–8).

There are different ways of interpreting these biblical passages, and most Christians I know would probably gravitate toward explanations that do not involve any actual power possessed by these pagan gods. But some Christian readers throughout the ages have thought differently. Commodian, in the third century, considered demons to be the spirits of the giants: "and to them, when they died, men erected images. . . . Wandering they now subvert many bodies, and it is such as these especially that ye this day worship and pray to as gods."[93] A little bit earlier, Athenagoras and Theophilus had also associated the idols with demons.

[92] *Dialogue with Trypho* 69. These Egyptian magicians were named Jannes and Jambres (etc.) in Jewish and Christian tradition (cf. 2 Tim. 3:8), and these traditions usually assumed that the pair was able to practice dark magic. On the traditions associated with these magicians and the pseudepigraphic text eventually written about them, see *OTP* 2:427–42.

[93] Commodian, *Instructions* 3 (*ANF* 4:203).

Similar statements can be found in the writings of Justin, Clement of Alexandria, and Origen.[94] As we saw in Chapter Three, Milton made use of this tradition in book 1 of *Paradise Lost* by representing the pagan gods as the angels who rebelled with Satan before creation (1.364–521), naming Moloch (line 392), Chemos (406), Baalim and Ashtaroth (422), Astoreth (438), Thammuz (446), Dagon (462), Rimmon (467), Osiris, Isis, Orus (478), Belial (490), and the Greek gods (508–21).

To explore one viewpoint a little further, Athenagoras goes to great lengths to show that the pagan gods do not exist (*Plea* 18–22), though he then admits that there is a power behind the idols: "Not even we deny that in some places, cities, and nations certain things are brought about in the name of images."[95] He argues that it is demons who empower the idols—for which argument he cites Greek pagan philosophers who distinguished demons from gods, starting with Thales of Miletus in the sixth century BC.[96] He also approvingly quotes Plato in this regard.[97] Later Athenagoras clarifies the relationship between demons and idols: "The demons associated with matter, because they are greedy for the savour of fat and the blood of the sacrifices, and because their business is to delude men, take hold of these deceitful movements in the soul of the many, and by invading their thoughts flood them with illusory images which seem to come from the idols and statues."

NAMED DEMONS?

Before we conclude this chapter, we will investigate two beings named in the Hebrew Bible that have been associated with demons: Azazel and Lilith.

Azazel

The name Azazel (עֲזָאזֵל) appears four times in Leviticus 16 (v. 8, twice in v. 10, and in v. 26) and nowhere else in the Bible. Traditionally in English

---

[94] Athenagoras, *Plea to the Christians* 25–26; Theophilus, *To Autolycus* 1.10; Justin, *First Apology* 5; *Dialogue* 73.2; Clement of Alexandria, *Exhortation to the Greeks* 4; Origin, *Against Celsus* 7.69. See Ferguson, *Early Christians Speak*, 2:149–50; Ferguson, *Demonology*, 137 ns. 27–30.

[95] *Plea* 23.2, trans. Schoedel, 55.

[96] *Plea* 23.4.

[97] Athenagoras, *Plea* 23.5–10, quotes Plato, *Timaeus* 40d–e. The following quote is from Athenagoras, *Plea* 27.2.

(since William Tyndale) it has been translated as "scapegoat." Leviticus 16 describes the Day of Atonement ritual, which involves a couple of goats.

> Aaron shall cast lots upon the two goats; one lot for YHWH, and the other lot for the scapegoat. (Lev. 16:8 KJV)

The remainder of the passage shows that the goat for the Lord ends up getting sacrificed and his blood sprinkled on various objects around the tabernacle. The scapegoat carries the sins of Israel into the wilderness. But is "scapegoat" the right translation? Apparently Tyndale related the term *azazel* to two different Hebrew words: *az* (or ēz, עֵז), "goat," and *azel* (or *azal*, אזל), "to go away," thus "the goat that went away." This traditional interpretation of Azazel goes back to the LXX, which renders the word as ἀποπομπαῖος (*apopompaios*), "the one to be sent off" (Lev. 16:8; cf. 16:26, εἰς ἄφεσιν, "for release").[98] Jerome's Latin Vulgate gives *emissarius*, which Wycliffe rendered as "the goot that schal be sent out." More recent translations often do not translate the term at all.

> Aaron shall cast lots over the two goats, one lot for YHWH and the other lot for Azazel. (Lev 16:8 ESV)

In fact, we do know that Azazel is used as the name of a demon in some later literature. In the Ethiopic text of the book of Enoch, Azazel (rather than the Aramaic "Asael") is the name of one of the leaders of sinful angels.[99] In the Apocalypse of Abraham, a late first-century AD work preserved in Slavonic (*OTP* 1:681–705), Azazel is the name of an unclean bird

[98] See Wevers, *Notes on the Greek Text of Leviticus*, 244: "The translator in my opinion did not know what [the Hebrew word] meant, but from the ritual it was clear that this kid was sent away into the desert." For Philo's interpretation of the LXX here, see *Who Is the Heir of Divine Things?*, 179, where Philo says that "the one to be sent off" is the name of this goat "because creation is a homeless wanderer, banished far away from wisdom" (trans. Colson and Whitaker, 4:373). According to the second apparatus in Wevers, *Leviticus*, 186, among the later Jewish translators, Symmachus offered a rendering similar to the LXX (ἀπερχόμενον, "gone away") whereas Aquila provided a different rendering (κεκραταιωμένον, "fortified") that parallels a rabbinic suggestion at b. Yoma 67b §6. For more on the history of interpretation, see Angelini, "Is Azazel a Goat?"

[99] See 1 Enoch 8.1, 9.6, 10.4–8, 13.1, 54.5–6, 69.2. The name Azazel interchanges with other forms of the name (e.g., Asael) in the various languages in which the book of Enoch is preserved; see Nickelsburg and VanderKam, *1 Enoch 2*, 202. On Azazel, see Janowski, "Azazel," *DDD*, 128–31; Milgrom, *Leviticus*, 1:1020–21.

who apparently is a fallen angel (chs. 13–14). In *Paradise Lost*, Azazel is one of Satan's angels, described as "a cherub tall" (1.534).

Is it possible that Azazel is the name of a demon? We've seen that demons are associated with the desert. Maybe ancient Israelites thought that a demon named Azazel lived in the wilderness, and on Yom Kippur the second goat, the one carrying the sins of Israel, went away to the wilderness to the demon Azazel.[100] While not every ancient interpretation supported this line of thinking (e.g., the LXX), a strong ancient tradition associated Azazel with demonic activity. Even Judit Blair, generally dubious of demons in the Old Testament, acknowledges that the little information we have about Azazel suggests "a supernatural being whose place is in the desert," though she also prefers to understand Azazel as "a personification of the forces of chaos that threaten the order of creation."[101]

Lilith

In *The Lion, the Witch and the Wardrobe*, Mr. Beaver explains to the four Pevensie children that their enemy, the White Witch, has a father who is a giant and a mother named Lilith, who is Adam's first wife.[102] What is Mr. Beaver thinking here? A close reading of the opening chapters of Genesis yields no information at all about a person named Lilith, or about Adam's having a wife before Eve. Indeed, just the opposite: It is clear from Genesis 2 that Adam had no suitable companion until the creation of Eve, so there was no possibility of a previous wife—unless the first wife was not a suitable companion. In fact, Lilith was not suitable, or so the story goes. This first wife, Lilith, refused to be in subjection to Adam, and so she left the garden. She is now a demon that murders children in the night and whose beauty seduces men to their own destruction.

---

[100] For other possibilities on the original meaning of Azazel, see Angelini, "Is Azazel a Goat?" She points out that some manuscripts of the Samaritan Pentateuch, as well as the Temple Scroll (11QT 26.13), spell the name as עזזאל (*Azaz'el*, connected to *el*, "god") rather than עזאזל (*Aza'zel*).

[101] Blair, *De-Demonising the Old Testament*, 62.

[102] Lewis, *Lion, the Witch and the Wardrobe*, 87–88, in ch. 8, "What Happened after Dinner." Of course, Mr. Beaver was explaining this to only three children, though he didn't realize it at the time.

Lilith has been a popular character for centuries. She continues to make appearances in various media (books, movies, television series, etc.).[103] One well-known depiction of Lilith is the painting *Lady Lilith* (1873) by Dante Gabriel Rossetti, who also wrote a poem ("Body's Beauty," originally titled "Lilith") to accompany the painting. The poem's first stanza follows.

Of Adam's first wife, Lilith, it is told
(The witch he loved before the gift of Eve,)
That, ere the snake's, her sweet tongue could deceive,
And her enchanted hair was the first gold.
And still she sits, young while the earth is old,
And, subtly of herself contemplative,
Draws men to watch the bright web she can weave,
Till heart and body and life are in its hold.

Since the Bible says nothing about Lilith, Adam's first wife, where did this idea come from?[104] The story about Lilith as Adam's first wife is first told in a writing called the *Alphabet of Ben Sira*, a work of absurdity written possibly as early as the eighth century AD.[105] In earlier Jewish literature (earlier than the *Alphabet of Ben Sira*), Lilith is mentioned sometimes, but only as a demon, not as Adam's wife. The Talmud mentions Lilith a few times and gives very few details about her, but she does have long hair (b. Eruvin 100b §26) and wings (b. Niddah 24b §10).[106] She is mentioned in a couple of Dead Sea Scrolls, again, only as a demon.[107] And she is mentioned once in the Bible, neither as Adam's wife nor, perhaps, as a demon. Isaiah 34:14 contains the Hebrew word *lilith* alongside terms for some desert-dwelling creatures. What is *lilith* here? The LXX gives the rendering "donkey-centaur" (ὀνοκένταυρος). English translations vary in how they treat the term *lilith*: "screech owl" (KJV), "Lilith" (JPS 2023, NRSV), "night-monster" (JPS 1917, NASB 1995), "night hag" (RSV), "night

---

[103] For a guide to some of the appearances of Lilith in pop culture, see the Wikipedia entry on "Lilith," https://en.wikipedia.org/wiki/Lilith.

[104] See Waldman, "Lilith: Judaism," *EBR*, 16:663–65.

[105] There is a translation in Stern and Mirsky, "Alphabet of Ben Sira," 183–84.

[106] See also b. Shabbat 151b §10; Bava Batra 73a §11.

[107] *Song for a Sage* (4Q510–511) in DJD 7. See Henze, *Mind the Gap*, 110–13.

bird" (ESV, NASB 2020). Very possibly *lilith* is not a demon here but some more mundane desert-dwelling creature.

Lilith (Akkadian *Lilītu*) is the name of a demon in the ancient Near East.[108] The earliest mention of the demon Lilith is in a Sumerian text called *Gilgamesh and the Huluppu-Tree*, written around 2000 BC. In this text, Lilith "escapes to the desert places," the same location Lilith inhabits in Isaiah 34:14.[109]

In Isaiah, is Lilith a demon? Most scholars think so, based on the ancient Near Eastern background and the reception of Lilith in Judaism, in which she clearly is a demon.[110] But some scholars think Lilith in Isaiah may be a bird or some other non-demon entity, such that the biblical mention of Lilith should be read in contrast to the ancient Near Eastern depiction and not in harmony.[111]

CONCLUSION

So, what shall we say about demons? Despite their prominence in the Synoptic Gospels, we don't really know what they are or where they came from, though there are only a limited number of good guesses. I myself have never encountered a demon (that I know of), though I know people who think they have. Christians (and Jews and others) have frequently interpreted their troubles in terms of demonic attack. One vivid and influential example is the *Life of St. Anthony*, written by Athanasius in the fourth century. As told by Athanasius, the monk Anthony frequently battled demons, and these battles became a frequent subject of paintings.[112] It is the subject of the earliest known painting (*The Torment of Saint Anthony*) by Michelangelo, which he produced at age twelve or thirteen. Anthony's experiences as depicted in literature and art may caution us against the

---

[108] See Hutter, "Lilith," *DDD*, 520–21; Ben-Amos, "From Eden to Ednah"; Gaines, "Lilith."

[109] For text and translation, see Kramer, *Gilgamesh and the Huluppu-Tree*. The quotation is from line 97. See also line 42.

[110] See, e.g., Römer, "Lilith," *EBR*, 16:661–63.

[111] See Blair, *De-demonising*, 63–94; Walton, "Demons in Mesopotamia and Israel," 237–43.

[112] Wikipedia, "Temptation of Saint Anthony in Visual Arts," last modified September 29, 2024, https://en.wikipedia.org/wiki/Temptation_of_Saint_Anthony_in_visual_arts.

attacks of demons. On the other hand, Anthony also assures us that demons are powerless in comparison with Jesus.

The Bible encourages us not to worry about demons but to trust in Jesus. While many people have looked for the best concoction or incantation to drive away demons, Jesus himself talked about a particularly difficult demon by saying, "this kind can come out only by prayer" (Mark 9:29)—he never said that a particular demon could be driven away only by burning fish guts or pronouncing a correct spell. According to the New Testament, the chief of the demons is Satan or Beelzebul (Mark 3:22–27), whom people should not fear but rather resist, and they can expect that such resistance will cause Satan to flee (1 Pet. 5:8–9; James 4:7–8). Again, the New Testament tells us that evil spiritual forces might be able to bring suffering on people, but nothing—"neither death, nor life, nor angels, nor rulers, nor things present, nor things to come, nor powers, nor height, nor depth, nor anything else in all creation, will be able to separate us from the love of God in Christ Jesus our Lord" (Rom. 8:38–39).

CHAPTER ELEVEN

THE VICTORY OF CHRIST

How remarkable it is that in what Scripture says and does not say about the demonic sphere it could be overlooked that the fear of God and fear of the devil do not belong together but are mutually exclusive, the sole task of theology in this matter being to show and say that it is the fear of God which overcomes and excludes the fear of the devil!

—Karl Barth[1]

One of the results of this study about which I feel pretty confident is that we know a lot less about the subject of this book than we often seem to think. Or, let me put it this way: Scripture does not contain most of the elements about spiritual forces—especially the dark spiritual forces—that have become so prominent in the past couple millennia. I have argued that the Old Testament has nothing to say about a chief agent of evil who is leading other spirits in a war against God; indeed, the Old Testament has almost no interest in any supernatural opponents of God. The New Testament—especially the Synoptic Gospels—depicts wicked spirits harming people and attempting to mislead them, though one of the major themes of the New Testament is the powerlessness of these spirits

[1] Barth, *Church Dogmatics*, vol. 3, pt. 3, 522.

in their encounters with Jesus. This brief final chapter explores the New Testament portrayal of Christ's victory over the evil powers.

Let me say this again: The Christian Bible is not interested in narrating a major conflict between the forces of good and the forces of evil. That's not what the Bible is about. Now, you cannot summarize the major elements of the Bible or the Christian story without mentioning sin, but you can do so without mentioning Satan. For a demonstration of this assertion, return to Chapter Six of this book and see how little a chief agent of evil appears in Paul's letters. Christian Scripture would have us believe that there is no big spiritual conflict—except within our own hearts. Will we submit to Jesus as Lord, or not?

Paul does, of course, talk about spiritual warfare, and he tells us that the Christian battle is not against human beings (flesh and blood) but against "the rulers, against the authorities, against the cosmic powers of this present darkness, against the spiritual forces of evil in the heavenly places" (Eph. 6:12). Paul does accept the reality (so it seems to me) of wicked spirits afflicting people (2 Cor. 12:7) and attempting to mislead them. The protection from demons recommended by the apostle is simply good Christian behavior: filling your mind with Scripture, praying, and behaving faithfully in conformity to the gospel. Such commitments constitute the armor of God (Eph. 6:13–20). Indeed, the shield of faith is able to extinguish "all the flaming arrows of the evil one" (6:16). In other words, act like a Christian, and you need fear no evil beings. Jesus gives the same advice (Matt. 10:28).

Christianity is not, in this manner, like *The Lord of the Rings*. It's not like there's some amazingly powerful evil force to which all of our attention should be directed. We're in a world much more like Narnia, especially the Narnia after the crucial event at the Stone Table (of course), as narrated in *The Lion, the Witch and the Wardrobe*. Sure, in *Prince Caspian* and *The Voyage of the Dawn Treader* and all the way to *The Last Battle*, there is evil in the world, but it's nothing like Sauron.[2] So also in our world, the peril facing us has much more to do with whether we will choose to be noble

[2]On the relationship between Sauron and Satan, see Freeman, *Tolkien Dogmatics*, 213–24. I recognize that Freeman and (to some extent, perhaps) Tolkien disagree with my assessment.

or not, to be brave or cowardly, to do what we know is right or to shrink from the challenging aspects of our faith. Yes, we could talk about the devil afflicting us or tempting us, because such affliction or temptation is a constant of the human condition. But what is much more important is the choice that we make: Will we succumb to the temptation?[3]

And if we do succumb, it does no good claiming "the devil made me do it." The devil is a defeated enemy, or, as Everett Ferguson puts it, "Satan is a lame-duck ruler."[4] To the extent that the New Testament presents some sort of war between God and Satan, it is clear that the war is basically over, the decisive blow having been delivered long ago by Jesus. In the days after the crucial events narrated in the Gospels, we are involved in the mopping-up operation. Consider the term "disarmed" (KJV: "spoiled"; ἀπεκδύομαι, *apekduomai*) in Colossians 2:15.

CHRISTUS VICTOR

The Latin phrase *Christus Victor* ("Christ is victor/conqueror") is often used today to describe an idea prominent in the New Testament that among the things accomplished by the crucifixion of Jesus, perhaps the most important was conquest.[5] In fact, the victory of Christ is not tied merely to the death of Jesus but to his whole life and to his resurrection and his current reign as messianic king. The entire idea of a "messiah" is bound up with the notion of victory. Remember that the messiah is the "son of David" (see, e.g., Matt. 1:1, 22:42), with the expectation that just as David was a successful warrior (1 Sam. 18:7), so also would be the son of David, the messiah. This is the hope expressed in Psalm 2 and so many other passages in which the Old Testament anticipates the coming of an ideal king. The depiction in Daniel 2 of the coming kingdom of God involves the complete annihilation of the kingdoms of the world. When ancient Jews looked forward to the coming of the messiah, they looked forward to the victory of God over his enemies.

---

[3] If you want help thinking about the temptation and spiritual warfare, let me recommend to you Lewis, *Screwtape Letters*.

[4] Ferguson, *Demonology*, 162. Ferguson thinks demons are still at work today, but their power has been limited since the victory of Christ (pp. 170–72).

[5] The classic study of this view of atonement theology is Aulén, *Christus Victor*.

These ideas explain a great deal both about what Jesus was up to and why his contemporaries—even his own disciples—routinely misinterpreted his intentions. The basic disconnect between Jesus and the people of his day is that they had their minds focused on the things of humans rather than the things of God (Matt. 16:23). When they heard Jesus announcing the coming of God's kingdom (Mark 1:15), they thought of Daniel 2 and Psalm 2 and the destruction of the nations of the world—and they assumed that Jesus must be raising an army against Rome. First-century Jews knew that the messiah was the one who was supposed to bring victory to God's people (à la David), but they misunderstood what that victory would entail. Peter and the rest of the apostles were ready to die alongside Jesus in a battle against Rome (Mark 14:31), but they were thinking too small. Rome was small potatoes. Rome was not the enemy that Jesus had come to defeat. The messiah had come to defeat the cosmic enemies of God: Satan, sin, death.

Jesus entered into battle against the wicked spiritual forces as soon as his ministry began. Immediately after his baptism, the Spirit drove Jesus into the wilderness to face the tempter, and Jesus overcame (Mark 1:12–13). We saw in the previous chapter that Jesus regularly met people who were possessed by evil spirits, and Jesus always overcame. He was able to give his disciples the same authority over these spirits (Mark 6:7). His healing of people's physical maladies represented, at least sometimes, victory over Satan (Luke 13:16; Acts 10:38). Jesus explained the ease with which he expelled evil spirits from people as resulting from his having first "bound the strong man," the ruler of those spirits (Matt. 12:29; Luke 11:21–22). Second-century Christians recognized the significance of Jesus's description. Irenaeus repeatedly refers to Satan as the strong man whom Christ has bound.[6] Melito of Sardis puts this speech into the mouth of Jesus: "I am the one that destroyed death and triumphed over the enemy and trod down Hades and bound the strong one and carried off man to the heights of heaven."[7]

The Old Testament verse that is quoted in the New Testament more than any other biblical passage is Psalm 110:1, "YHWH says to my lord, 'Sit

---

[6] A few examples: Irenaeus, *Against the Heresies* 3.8.2, 3.18.6, 3.23.1, 5.21.3; cf. 3.23.7.
[7] Melito, *On Pascha and Fragments*, 102.

at my right hand until I make your enemies your footstool.'" You recall, of course, that Jesus asked about the best interpretation of this verse, querying how the messiah could be considered David's son if David here calls the messiah "my lord" (Mark 12:35–37). Jesus assumes that David is the speaker of this psalm—in accordance with the psalm's superscription—and that David is talking about someone that he himself calls "my lord." In fact, Jesus said that this "lord" mentioned by David was the messiah, and apparently Jesus's conversation partners agreed that the messiah is the subject of the psalm. (See the parallel accounts of this statement from Jesus at Matt. 22:41–46; Luke 20:41–44). We readers of this statement should recognize that the messiah is depicted in a warfare context; the messiah has enemies, and they will become his footstool. This verse represents succinctly the complete victory of the messiah over his enemies. No wonder it's so popular in the New Testament.[8]

Other verses similarly depict the victory of Christ over the dark forces.

> The Son of God was revealed for this purpose, to destroy the works of the devil. (1 John 3:8)

> Our Savior Jesus Christ, who abolished death and brought life and immortality to light through the gospel. (2 Tim. 1:10)

> For he must reign until he has put all enemies under his feet. The last enemy to be destroyed is death. (1 Cor. 15:25–26)

> Baptism which this prefigured, now saves you—not as a removal of dirt from the body, but as an appeal to God for a good conscience, through the resurrection of Jesus Christ, who has gone into heaven and is at the right hand of God, with angels, authorities, and powers made subject to him. (1 Pet. 3:21–22)

---

[8]In addition to the New Testament passages already mentioned, Psalm 110:1 is directly quoted at Acts 2:34; Hebrews 1:13. This psalm also provided the background for the numerous New Testament references to Jesus sitting at God's right hand: Matt. 26:64 // Mark 14:62 // Luke 22:69; Acts 2:33–34; Rom. 8:34; Eph. 1:20; Col. 3:1; Heb. 1:3, 8:1, 10:12, 12:2; 1 Pet. 3:22. There is another such reference in the long ending of Mark (16:19). Stephen saw Jesus "standing at the right hand of God" (Acts 7:55–56).

This victory over Satan and his angels derives some of its significance from the biblical depiction of Satan as ruler of the nations, a theme we have observed in previous chapters. Satan is the "ruler of the power of the air" (Eph. 2:2), the "god of this world who has blinded the minds of the unbelievers" (2 Cor. 4:4).[9] He is "the ruler of this world" who, according to Jesus, was about to be cast out (John 12:31; see also 14:30, 16:11). This authority has resulted in people being in "the snare of the devil, . . . held captive by him to do his will" (2 Tim. 2:26). In the wilderness, Satan offered this rule to Jesus (Luke 4:5–8), an offer that Jesus refused. Instead, Jesus bound the strong man and took the power for himself. "All authority in heaven and on earth has been given to me" (Matt. 28:18).

As the context of this last-quoted verse indicates, Jesus's greatest victory over evil forces came in his death and resurrection. The writer of Hebrews says that (at least part of) the reason for the incarnation was so that "through death he might destroy the one who has the power of death, that is, the devil, and free those who all their lives were held in slavery by the fear of death" (Heb. 2:14–15). It may at first seem strange that one should gain victory through dying, but parallels are not wanting, those in fiction being especially familiar. "If you strike me down, I shall become more powerful than you can possibly imagine." Many readers will remember how evil was defeated at the Cracks of Doom by the death of a wretched creature, and I have already referenced the deeper magic that led to the cracking of the Stone Table. The parallels with Obi-Wan, Gollum, and Aslan are not exact but potentially helpful. In the New Testament we witness the death of the one appointed both Lord and messiah (Acts 2:36), but then "God raised him up, having freed him from death, because it was impossible for him to be held in its power" (Acts 2:24).

VICTORY THROUGH DEATH

Though the victory of Christ over the evil forces involved more than his death, it was his crucifixion that was the least expected part of that victory, and certainly the most difficult part for Jesus himself to accomplish. I do not mean to discount the difficulty of the incarnation, which, as Paul

---

[9] It is possible that 2 Cor. 4:4 does not refer to Satan; see Chapter Six, note 20.

mentioned, involved Christ emptying himself (Phil. 2:7), but we do know that the human Jesus prayed that, in reference to his impending death, "this cup" would pass from him (Mark 14:36). And clearly few anticipated the death of the messiah, certainly not Jesus's own disciples, though he explicitly and repeatedly told them to expect it (Mark 8:31–38, 9:30–32, 10:32–34). After the resurrection, when the disciples had heard the report of the empty tomb, they were still uncertain how the death of the messiah fit into God's plans (Luke 24:21).

One way the New Testament depicts the significance of Jesus's death is in terms of conquest. We have seen that Hebrews 2:14–15 makes this viewpoint explicit. Another relevant passage is Colossians 2:14–15, which mentions "the handwriting of ordinances" and that Christ nailed this to the cross: "having spoiled principalities and powers, he made a show of them openly, triumphing over them in it" (KJV). The translation difficulties of this verse do not render Paul's thought incomprehensible, as Ferguson shows.

> Colossians 2:15 has its difficulties in translation and interpretation. Although I am not particularly happy with the RSV rendering, I shall stay with it since I am not satisfied how to take the verse: "He disarmed the principalities and powers and made a public example of them, triumphing over them in him." Whether the subject is God or Christ, whether we say "disarming" or "stripping off," whether the triumph was "in Christ" or "in the cross," the various ways the verse may be translated does not affect the point of utmost importance, which we want to make here. The principalities and powers have been defeated by Christ. This defeat was connected with the canceling of the debt of sin at the cross (vs. 14). The power of the world rulers over mankind is the result of human sin. When our trespasses are forgiven, the world rulers no longer have a claim on human life. Christ's victory thus was secured on the cross.[10]

[10] Ferguson, *Demonology*, 157.

Just as the messiah's crucifixion was unanticipated by Jesus's followers and opponents, so also the spiritual forces failed to foresee it. Paul seems to make this point in a passage in 1 Corinthians.

> Yet among the mature we do speak wisdom, though it is not a wisdom of this age or of the rulers of this age, who are doomed to perish. But we speak God's wisdom, secret and hidden, which God decreed before the ages for our glory. None of the rulers of this age understood this; for if they had, they would not have crucified the Lord of glory. (1 Cor. 2:6–8)

The "rulers of this age" mentioned twice in this passage could possibly be human rulers (Pontius Pilate, Caiaphas, etc.) but more probably are spiritual powers. Daniel 10 refers to angels as "princes," and the Greek word used in the LXX there is the same as the Greek word used by Paul here (*archōn*).[11] Probably Paul has in mind "hostile angelic beings defeated by the cross," as argued by Guy Williams.[12] This interpretation of the passage appears very early in the second century; moreover, the language of "this age" suggests that the rulers are cosmic powers, not human.[13] If that is the correct interpretation, Paul makes the point that God's supernatural enemies brought about the death of Jesus in part because they failed to recognize that they were playing into God's plans for the redemption of humanity and their own defeat.

The victory that Jesus achieved through his sacrificial death—a victory promised to all who imitate him (e.g., Rev. 2:10)—forms the background for the painting called *Calvary* by Josse Lieferinxe at the turn of the sixteenth century. While Jesus hangs on a cross, the spiritual war between angels and demons rages behind him. The sign above Christ's head, INRI,

---

[11]The Greek word *archōn* appears in the more popular Greek version of Daniel, known as the Theodotion text, several times in Dan. 10:13, 20–21. In the version labeled by modern scholars as the Old Greek, the same Greek word appears once in Dan. 10:13.

[12]Williams, *Spirit World*, 232–39; the quotation is from p. 232.

[13]Both of these arguments are from Williams, *Spirit World*, 236–37. The early interpretations taking the "rulers of this age" as angelic powers include Ignatius, *Epistle to the Ephesians* 19; Marcion (in Tertullian, *Against Marcion* 5.6.5).

stands for the Latin phrase, *Iesus Nazaraenus Rex Iudaeorum* (cf. John 19:19), proclaiming him king at the moment of his death.

Calvary, by Josse Lieferinxe, ca. 1500, Wikimedia Commons

CONCLUSION

Throughout this book we have used Milton's *Paradise Lost* as one of our guides into the tradition concerning Satan and his friends. I have frequently argued that the view enshrined in Milton's classic is not the only possible view that can be derived from Scripture. But when it comes to Christ's conflict with the evil spiritual forces, or at least one aspect of that conflict, Milton's depiction agrees completely with Scripture. I mentioned in the introduction that during the primordial battle between Satan's army and heaven's army led by Michael (this is all extraneous to Scripture)—as narrated by Raphael to Adam in book 6 of *Paradise Lost*—the two armies are evenly matched, until the Son of God becomes involved. At that point, the forces of evil stand no chance and are quickly expelled from heaven.

The battle between God and Satan as presented in Christian Scripture is not much of a battle. It's certainly not the kind of battle that causes any tension or anxiety on God's part. Satan is merely one of God's creatures, and anytime the Lord wishes, he may extinguish the life of any creature, including that of Satan and his host. Though the New Testament Satan is an enemy of God destined for punishment, we must imagine that his continued existence is owing only to his serving (unwillingly) God's purposes for the testing and refinement of people. Satan's power—like our own—is utterly contingent, a gift from his creator that can be withdrawn at any moment.

Once again, Luther had the right idea.

Did we in our own strength confide,
Our striving would be losing;
Were not the right Man on our side,
The Man of God's own choosing.
Dost ask who that may be?
Christ Jesus, it is he;
Lord Sabaoth is his name,
From age to age the same,
And He must win the battle.

And though this world, with devils filled,
Should threaten to undo us,

We will not fear, for God hath willed
His truth to triumph through us.
The Prince of Darkness grim,—
We tremble not for him;
His rage we can endure,
For lo! His doom is sure,—
One little word shall fell him.[14]

[14]Luther clarified that the powerful "little word" is *liar*; see *Against Hanswurst* (1541), trans. Gritsch, 185–86. The hymn appears under the title "Our God He Is a Castle Strong," in *Liturgy and Hymns*, ed. Leupold, 283–85. The original German of the hymn is found in *D. Martin Luthers Werke* (Weimarer Ausgabe), 35:455–57. The line in question runs "Ein wörtlein kan ihn fellen."

BIBLIOGRAPHY

BIBLE VERSIONS AND EDITIONS

Aly, Zaki, and Ludwig Koenen, eds. *Three Rolls of the Early Septuagint: Genesis and Deuteronomy*. Rudolf Habelt Verlag, 1980.

Biblia Sacra iuxta latinam vulgatam versionem. 18 vols. Polyglottis Vaticanis, 1926–1995.

Harl, Marguerite, trans. *La Genèse*. La Bible d'Alexandrie. Cerf, 1986.

McCarthy, Carmel, ed. *Deuteronomy*. Biblia Hebraica Quinta. Deutsche Bibelgesellschaft, 2007.

Tal, Abraham, ed. *Genesis*. Biblia Hebraica Quinta. Deutsche Bibelgesellschaft, 2015.

Targum Neofiti 1: Genesis. Translated by Martin McNamara. The Aramaic Bible 1A. Liturgical Press, 1992.

The Targum Onqelos to Genesis. Translated by Bernard Grossfeld. The Aramaic Bible 6. Michael Glazier, 1988.

Targum Pseudo-Jonathan: Genesis. Translated by Michael Maher. The Aramaic Bible 1B. Liturgical Press, 1992.

Weber, Robert, and Roger Gryson, eds. *Biblia Sacra iuxta vulgatam versionem*. 5th ed. Deutsche Bibelgesellschaft, 2007.

Wevers, John William, ed. *Deuteronomium*. Septuaginta 3.2. Vandenhoeck & Ruprecht, 1977.

———, ed. *Genesis*. Septuaginta 1. Vandenhoeck & Ruprecht, 1974.

———, ed. *Leviticus*. Septuaginta 2.2. Vandenhoeck & Ruprecht, 1986.

Ziegler, Joseph, ed. *Ezechiel*. 3rd ed. Septuaginta 16.1. Vandenhoeck & Ruprecht, 2006.

———, ed. *Isaias*. Septuaginta 14. Vandenhoeck & Ruprecht, 1983.

ANCIENT AND MEDIEVAL WORKS

Anderson, Gary A. "Life of Adam and Eve." In volume 2 of *Outside the Bible*, edited by Louis H. Feldman, James L. Kugel, and Lawrence H. Schiffman, 1331–58. 3 vols. Jewish Publication Society, 2013.

Anderson, Gary A., and Michael E. Stone, eds. *A Synopsis of the Books of Adam and Eve*. Scholars Press, 1994.

Anselm of Canterbury. *The Major Works*. Edited by Brian Davies and G. R. Evans. Oxford World's Classics. Oxford University Press, 1998.

The Ante-Nicene *Fathers*. Edited by Alexander Roberts and James Donaldson. 10 vols. 1885–1887.

Apuleius. *Apologia; Florida; De Deo Socratis*. Edited and translated by Christopher P. Jones. Loeb Classical Library. Harvard University Press, 2017.

Athenagoras. *Legatio and De Resurrectione*. Edited and translated by William R. Schoedel. Clarendon, 1972.

Augustine. *On Christian Teaching*. Translated by R. P. H. Green. Oxford University Press, 1997.

———. *On Genesis*. Translated by Edmund Hill. The Works of Saint Augustine. New City Press, 1999.

Charlesworth, James H., ed. *The Old Testament Pseudepigrapha*. 2 vols. Doubleday, 1983–1985.

Coogan, Michael D., and Mark S. Smith, eds. and trans. *Stories from Ancient Canaan*. 2nd ed. Westminster John Knox, 2012.

Dalley, Stephanie, trans. *Myths from Mesopotamia: Creation, the Flood, Gilgamesh, and Others*. 2nd ed. Oxford University Press, 2000.

Didymus the Blind. *Commentary on Genesis*. Translated by Robert C. Hill. Fathers of the Church. Catholic University of America Press, 2016.

Die keilalphabetischen Texte aus Ugarit. Edited by M. Dietrich, O. Loretz, and J. Sanmartín. Neukirchener Verlag, 1976.

Discoveries in the Judaean Desert. 40 vols. Oxford University Press, 1955–2010.

Enchiridion Symbolorum: A Compendium of Creeds, Definitions, and Declarations of the Catholic Church. Edited by Heinrich Denzinger and Peter Huenermann. Ignatius, 2012.

Eusebius. *Preparation for the Gospel*. Translated by Edwin Hamilton Gifford. 2 vols. Clarendon, 1903. Reprint, Baker, 1981.

———. *The Proof of the Gospel*. 2 vols. Translated by W. J. Ferrar. Macmillan, 1920.

Frey, Albert, J.-P. Pettorelli, J.-D. Kaestli, and B. Outtier, eds. *Synopsis Vitae Adae et Evae: Latine, Graece, Armeniace et Iberice*. 2 vols. Corpus Christianorum Seris Apocryphorum 18–19. Brepols, 2012.

Gathercole, Simon, trans. *The Apocryphal Gospels*. Penguin, 2021.

George, Andrew, trans. *The Epic of Gilgamesh*. 2nd ed. Penguin, 2020.

Hesiod. *Theogony; Works and Days; Testimonia*. Edited and translated by Glenn W. Most. Loeb Classical Library. Harvard University Press, 2006.

Holladay, Carl R. *Fragments from Hellenistic Jewish Authors*. 4 vols. Scholars Press, 1983–1996.

Irenaeus of Lyons. *Against the Heresies: Book 2*. Translated by Dominic J. Unger. Ancient Christian Writers 65. Newman, 2012.

———. *Against the Heresies: Book 3*. Translated by Dominic J. Unger. Revised by Irenaeus M. C. Steenberg. Ancient Christian Writers 64. Newman, 2012.

———. *Against the Heresies: Books 4 and 5*. Translated by Dominic J. Unger. Edited by Scott D. Moringiello. Ancient Christian Writers 72. Newman, 2024.

———. *On the Apostolic Preaching*. Translated by John Behr. Popular Patristics 17. St. Vladimir's Seminary Press, 1997.

Jerome. *Commentary on Daniel*. Translated by Gleason L. Archer Jr. Baker, 1958.

———. *Commentary on Isaiah*. Translated by Thomas P. Scheck. Ancient Christian Writers 68. Newman, 2015.

John Chrysostom. *Homilies on Genesis 18–45*. Translated by Robert C. Hill. Fathers of the Church. Catholic University of America Press, 1990.

John of Damascus. *On the Orthodox Faith*. Translated by Norman Russell. Popular Patristics 62. St. Vladimir's Seminary Press, 2022.

Julius Africanus. *Chronographiae: The Extant Fragment*. Edited by Martin Wallraff. De Gruyter, 2007.

Justin Martyr. *Writings of Saint Justin Martyr*. Translated by Thomas B. Falls. Fathers of the Church. Christian Heritage, 1948.

Klumpenhouwer, Samuel J., trans. *Biblia cum Glossa Ordinaria: The Great Medieval Commentary on Sacred Scripture; Genesis*. Emmaus Academic, 2023.

Kramer, Samuel N., ed. and trans. *Gilgamesh and the Huluppu-Tree*. University of Chicago Press, 1938.

Levison, John R. "The Life of Adam and Eve." In volume 1 of *Early Jewish Literature: An Anthology*, edited by Brad Embry, Ronald Herms, and Archie T. Wright, 445–61. 2 vols. Eerdmans, 2018.

Lightfoot, J. B. *The Apostolic Fathers*. 2nd ed. 5 vols. in 2 parts. MacMillan, 1889–1890. Reprint, Baker, 1981.

Lucan. *The Civil War*. Translated by J. D. Duff. Loeb Classical Library. Harvard University Press, 1928.

Melito of Sardis. *On Pascha and Fragments*. Edited and translated by Stuart George Hall. Clarendon, 1979.

Meyer, Marvin, ed. *The Nag Hammadi Scriptures: The International Edition*. HarperOne, 2007.

Midrash Rabbah. 10 vols. 3rd ed. Soncino, 1983.

Nickelsburg, George W. E., and James C. VanderKam, trans. *1 Enoch: The Hermeneia Translation*. Fortress, 2012.

Origen. *Commentary on the Song of Songs*. Translated by R. P. Lawson. Ancient Christian Writers 26. Newman, 1957.

———. *Contra Celsum libri viii*. Edited by M. Marcovich. Brill, 2001.

———. *Contra Celsum*. Translated by Henry Chadwick. Cambridge University Press, 1953.

———. *Homilies on Genesis and Exodus*. Translated by Ronald E. Heine. Fathers of the Church. Catholic University of America Press, 1982.

———. *Homilies on Luke; Fragments on Luke*. Translated by Joseph T. Lienhard. Fathers of the Church 94. Catholic University of America Press, 1996.

———. *On First Principles: A Reader's Edition*. Translated by John Behr. Oxford University Press, 2019.

Pamphilus and Rufinus. *Apology for Origen; On the Falsification of the Books of Origen*. Translated by Thomas P. Scheck. Fathers of the Church. Catholic University of America Press, 2010.

Pausanias. *Description of Greece*. 5 vols. Translated by W. H. S. Jones. Loeb Classical Library. Harvard University Press, 1918–1935.

Philo. 12 vols. Translated by F. H. Colson, G. H. Whitaker, and Ralph Marcus. Loeb Classical Library. Harvard University Press, 1929–1962.

Plato. 12 vols. Loeb Classical Library. Harvard University Press, 1914–1935.

Plutarch. *Moralia*. 16 vols. Loeb Classical Library. Harvard University Press, 1927–2004.

Qimron, Elisha, and James H. Charlesworth, eds. and trans. *Rule of the Community and Related Documents*. Princeton Theological Seminary Dead Sea Scrolls Project 1. Westminster John Knox, 1994.

The Qur'an. Translated by M. H. Shakir. 11th ed. Tahrike Tarsile Qur'an, 1999.

Sanders, J. A., ed. and trans. *The Dead Sea Psalms Scroll*. Cornell University Press, 1967.

Schroeder, Joy A., ed. and trans. *The Book of Genesis*. The Bible in Medieval Tradition. Eerdmans, 2015.

Sifré to Numbers: An American Translation and Explanation. Translated by Jacob Neusner. 2 vols. Scholars Press, 1986.

Stern, David, and Mark Jay Mirsky, trans. "The Alphabet of Ben Sira." In *Rabbinic Fantasies: Imaginative Narratives from Classical Hebrew Literature*, 167–202. Yale University Press, 1990.

Tertullian. *Adversus Marcionem*. Edited and translated by Ernest Evans. 2 vols. Clarendon, 1972.

———. *Disciplinary, Moral, and Ascetical Works*. Translated by Rudolph Arbesmann, Emily Joseph Daly, and Edwin A. Quain. Fathers of the Church. Catholic University of America Press, 1959.

Theodoret of Cyrus. *The Questions on the Octateuch*. Volume 1: *On Genesis and Exodus*. Translated by Robert C. Hill. Library of Early Christianity. Catholic University of America Press, 2007.

Theophilus of Antioch. *Ad Autolycum*. Edited and translated by Robert M. Grant. Clarendon, 1970.

Tromp, Johannes, ed. *The Assumption of Moses: A Critical Edition with Commentary*. Brill, 1993.

Vergil. *The Aeneid*. Translated by Sarah Ruden. 2nd ed. Yale University Press, 2021.

Wise, Michael, Martin Abegg Jr., and Edward Cook, trans. *The Dead Sea Scrolls: A New Translation*. 2nd ed. HarperSanFrancisco, 2005.

Wyatt, N. *Religious Texts from Ugarit*. 2nd ed. Sheffield Academic, 2002.

MODERN WORKS

Albani, Matthias. "The Downfall of Helel, the Son of Dawn: Aspects of Royal Ideology in Isa 14:12–13." In *The Fall of the Angels*, edited by Christoph Auffarth and Loren T. Stuckenbruck, 62–86. Brill, 2004.

Alexander, Philip S. "The Targumim and Early Exegesis of 'Sons of God' in Genesis 6." *Journal of Jewish Studies* 23 (1972): 60–71.

Andersen, Francis I. *Job*. Tyndale Old Testament Commentaries. IVP, 1976.

Anderson, Gary A. "The Original Form of the *Life of Adam and Eve*: A Proposal." In *Literature on Adam and Eve: Collected Essays*, edited by Gary Anderson, Michael Stone, and Johannes Tromp, 215–31. Brill, 2000.

———. *Sin: A History*. Yale University Press, 2009.

Angelini, Anna. "Is Azazel a Goat, Place, Demon, or Deity?" Torah.com, 2021. https://www.thetorah.com/article/is-azazel-a-goat-place-demon-or-deity.

———. "Δαίμονες and Demons in Hellenistic Judaism: Continuities and Transformations." In *Demons in Early Judaism and Christianity: Characters and Characteristics*, edited by Hector M. Patmore and Josef Lössl, 54–73. Brill, 2022.

———. *L'imaginaire du démoniaque dans la Septante: Une analyse comparée de la notion de "démon" dans la Septante et dans la Bible Hébraïque*. Brill, 2021.

Assmann, Jan. "Re." In *Dictionary of Deities and Demons in the Bible*, edited by van der Toorn, Becking, and van der Horst, 689–92.

Aulén, Gustaf. *Christus Victor: An Historical Study of the Three Main Types of the Idea of Atonement*. MacMillan, 1938.

Aune, David E. *Revelation*. 3 vols. Word Biblical Commentary. Thomas Nelson, 1997–1998.

Barth, Karl. *Church Dogmatics*. Volume 3: *The Doctrine of Creation*, pt. 3. T&T Clark, 1960.

Barton, John. *Ethics in Ancient Israel*. Oxford University Press, 2014.

Bauckham, Richard. *Jesus and the God of Israel: God Crucified and Other Studies on the New Testament's Christology of Divine Identity*. Eerdmans, 2008.

———. *Jude and the Relatives of Jesus in the Early Church*. T&T Clark, 1990.

———. *"Son of Man."* Volume 1 of *Early Jewish Literature*. Eerdmans, 2023.

Bazzana, Giovanni B. *Having the Spirit of Christ: Spirit Possession and Exorcism in the Early Christ Groups*. Yale University Press, 2020.

Becking, Bob. "Rapha." In *Dictionary of Deities and Demons in the Bible*, edited by van der Toorn, Becking, and van der Horst, 687–88.

Bell, Richard H. "Demon, Devil, Satan." In *Dictionary of Jesus and the Gospels*, edited by Joel B. Green, Jeannine K. Brown, and Nicholas Perrin, 193–202. 2nd ed. IVP, 2013.

Ben-Amos, Dan. "From Eden to Ednah—Lilith in the Garden." *Biblical Archaeology Review* (May/June 2016).

Bernat, David. "Circumcision: Is the Foreskin a Defect?" TheTorah.com, 2017. https://www.thetorah.com/article/circumcision-is-the-foreskin-a-defect.

Blair, Judit M. De-Demonising *the Old Testament: An Investigation of Azazel, Lilith, Deber, Qeteb and Reshef in the Hebrew Bible*. Mohr Siebeck, 2009.

Blenkinsopp, Joseph. *Ezekiel*. Interpretation. John Knox, 1990.

Block, Daniel I. *The Book of Ezekiel: Chapters 25–48*. New International Commentary on the Old Testament. Eerdmans, 1998.

———. *The Gods of the Nations: A Study in Ancient Near Eastern National Theology*. 2nd ed. Baker, 2000.

Bonino, Serge-Thomas. *Angels and Demons: A Catholic Introduction*. Catholic University of America Press, 2016.

Boring, M. Eugene. *Disciples and the Bible: A History of Disciples Biblical Interpretation in North America*. Chalice, 1997.

Brayford, Susan. *Genesis*. Septuagint Commentary Series. Brill, 2007.

Brown, Derek R. *The God of This Age: Satan in the Churches and Letters of the Apostle Paul*. Mohr Siebeck, 2015.

Brown, Francis, S. R. Driver, and Charles A. Briggs. *A Hebrew and English Lexicon of the Old Testament*. Clarendon, 1906.

Brown, Peter. *Augustine of Hippo: A Biography*. Faber & Faber, 1967.

Bruk Ayele Asale. *1 Enoch as Christian Scripture: A Study in the Reception and Appropriation of 1 Enoch in Jude and the Ethiopian Orthodox Tewahedo Church*. Pickwick, 2020.

Buck, Pearl S. *The Good Earth*. John Day, 1931.

Calder, Todd. "The Concept of Evil." *The Stanford Encyclopedia of Philosophy* (Winter 2022 Edition). Edited by Edward N. Zalta and Uri Nodelman. https://plato.stanford.edu/archives/win2022/entries/concept-evil/.

Calvin, John. *Institutes of the Christian Religion* (1559). Translated by Ford Lewis Battles. Edited by John T. McNeil. 2 vols. Westminster, 1960.

Campbell, Alexander. "Demonology." *Millennial Harbinger* (Oct. 1841): 457–80. Reprint. Pages 379–402 in *Popular Lectures and Addresses*. James Challen, 1863.

———. *Familiar Lectures on the Pentateuch*. Edited by W. T. Moore. Bosworth, 1867.

Carasik, Michael, ed. and trans. *The Commentators' Bible: The Rubin JPS Miqra'ot Gedolot*. 5 vols. Jewish Publication Society, 2005–2018.

Cardozo Mindiola, Cristian. "Fabricating the Fall of Satan: Revelation 12:7–9 and Its Interpretation in Early Christianity." *Journal of Theological Studies* 74 (2023): 240–73.

Carson, D. A. "2 Peter." In *Commentary on the New Testament Use of the Old Testament*, edited by G. K. Beale and D. A. Carson, 1047–61. Baker, 2007.

Carter, Warren. *The Roman Empire and the New Testament: An Essential Guide*. Abingdon, 2006.

Chadwick, John. *Lexicographica Graeca: Contributions to the Lexicography of Ancient Greek*. Clarendon, 1996.

Chapman, Stephen B. *1 Samuel as Christian Scripture: A Theological Commentary*. Eerdmans, 2016.

Charlesworth, James H., ed. *Damascus Document, War Scroll, and Related Documents*. Princeton Theological Seminary Dead Sea Scrolls Project 2. Westminster John Knox, 1995.

Clark, Elizabeth A. *The Origenist Controversy: The Cultural Construction of an Early Christian Debate*. Princeton University Press, 1992.

Clines, David J. A., ed. *The Dictionary of Classical Hebrew*. 9 vols. Sheffield Phoenix, 1993–2016. Volume 1 revised in 2018.

Coblentz Bautch, Kelley. "The Fall and Fate of Renegade Angels: The Intersection of Watchers Traditions and the Book of Revelation." In *The Fallen Angels Traditions: Second Temple Developments and Reception History*, edited by Angela Kim Harkins, Kelley Coblentz Bautch, and John C. Enders, 69–93. Catholic Biblical Association of America, 2014.

Collins, John J. *The Apocalyptic Imagination: An Introduction to Jewish Apocalyptic Literature*. 3rd ed. Eerdmans, 2016.

Collins, John J., and James Nati. *The Rule of the Association and Related Texts*. Oxford University Press, 2024.

Comer, John Mark. *Practicing the Way*. Waterbrook, 2024.
Cook, Edward M. *Dictionary of Qumran Aramaic*. Eisenbrauns, 2015.
Cooper, Lamar Eugene, Sr. *Ezekiel*. New American Commentary. Broadman and Holman, 1994.
Cousland, J. R. C. "Adam and Evel: Did Satan Sleep with Eve in the Greek and Latin Lives of Adam and Eve?" *Journal of Theological Studies* 71 (2020): 134–57.
Crouzel, Henri. "A Letter from Origen 'To Friends in Alexandria.'" In *The Heritage of the Early Church: Essays in Honor of the Very Reverend Georges Vasilievich Florovsky*, edited by David Nieman and Margaret Schatkin. Pontifical Oriental Institute, 1973.
Daley, Brian E. *The Hope of the Early Church: A Handbook of Patristic Eschatology*. Cambridge University Press, 1991.
Daniélou, Jean. *The Angels and Their Mission: According to the Fathers of the Church*. Newman, 1957.
Danker, Frederick William, ed. *A Greek-English Lexicon of the New Testament and Other Early Christian Literature*. University of Chicago Press, 2000.
Daoust, Francis. "Belial in the Dead Sea Scrolls: From Worthless to Stumbling Block to Archenemy." In *New Vistas on Early Judaism and Christianity: From Enoch to Montreal and Back*, edited by Lorenzo DiTommaso and Gerbern S. Oegema, 217–33. Bloomsbury T&T Clark, 2016.
Davila, James R. *The Provenance of the Pseudepigrapha: Jewish, Christian, or Other?* Brill, 2005.
Day, John. *From Creation to Babel: Studies in Genesis 1–11*. Bloomsbury, 2013.
———. "The Sons of God and the Daughters of Men and the Giants: Disputed Points in the Interpretation of Genesis 6:1–4." *Hebrew Bible and Ancient Israel* 1 (2012): 427–47.
deSilva, David A. *4 Maccabees*. Septuagint Commentary Series. Brill, 2006.
Diggle, J., ed. *The Cambridge Greek Lexicon*. 2 vols. Cambridge University Press, 2021.
Doedens, Jaap. *The Sons of God in Genesis 6:1–4: Analysis and History of Exegesis*. Brill, 2019.
Dolansky, Shawna. "How the Serpent in the Garden Became Satan." *Bible History Daily*, April 8, 2016. https://www.biblicalarchaeology.org/daily/biblical-topics/bible-interpretation/how-the-serpent-in-the-garden-became-satan/.
Douthat, Ross. *Believe: Why Everyone Should Be Religious*. Zondervan, 2025.
Driver, S. R. *Deuteronomy*. 3rd ed. International Critical Commentary. T&T Clark, 1895.

Earl, Douglas S. *Reading Old Testament Narrative as Christian Scripture*. Eisenbrauns, 2017.

Edelstein, Gershon. "Rephaim, Valley of (Place)." In volume 5 of *Anchor Bible Dictionary*. Edited by David Noel Freedman, 676–77. 6 vols. Doubleday, 1992.

Elder, Nicholas A. "Of Porcine and Polluted Spirits: Reading the Gerasene Demoniac (Mark 5:1–20) with the Book of Watchers (*1 Enoch* 1–36)." *Catholic Biblical Quarterly* 78 (2016): 430–46.

Embry, Brad, Ronald Herms, and Archie T. Wright. *Early Jewish Literature: An Anthology*. 2 vols. Eerdmans, 2018.

Evans, C. F. *Saint Luke*. SCM, 1990.

Evans, J. M. *Paradise Lost and the Genesis Tradition*. Clarendon, 1968.

Farrar, Thomas J. "The Intimate and Ultimate Adversary: Satanology in Early Second-Century Christian Literature." *Journal of Early Christian Studies* 26 (2018): 517–46.

———. "New Testament Satanology and Leading Suprahuman Opponents in Second Temple Jewish Literature: A Religion-Historical Analysis." *Journal of Theological Studies* 70 (2019): 21–68.

Farrar, Thomas J., and Guy J. Williams. "Diabolical Data: A Critical Inventory of New Testament Satanology." *Journal for the Study of the New Testament* 39 (2016): 40–71.

———. "Talk of the Devil: Unpacking the Language of New Testament Satanology." *Journal for the Study of the New Testament* 39 (2016): 72–96.

Feldman, Louis H. *Flavius Josephus: Judean Antiquities 1–4*. Brill, 2000.

Feldman, Louis H., James L. Kugel, and Lawrence H. Schiffman, eds. *Outside the Bible*. 3 vols. Jewish Publication Society, 2013.

Ferguson, Everett. *Demonology of the Early Christian World*. Edwin Mellen, 1984.

———. *Early Christians Speak: Faith and Life in the First Three Centuries*. Volume 2. Abilene Christian University Press, 2002.

Fitzmyer, Joseph A. *Tobit*. De Gruyter, 2003.

Fornberg, Tord. "Baal-Zevul—the History of a Name." In *L'adversaire de Dieu—Der Widersacher Gottes*, edited by Michael Tilly, Matthias Morgenstern, and Volker Henning Drecoll, 95–106. WUNT 364. Mohr Siebeck, 2016.

Forsyth, Neil. *The Satanic Epic*. Princeton University Press, 2003.

Foster, Douglas A. *A Life of Alexander Campbell*. Eerdmans, 2020.

Fraade, Steven D. *The Damascus Document*. Oxford University Press, 2021.

Frankfurter, David. "Master-Demons, Local Spirits, and Demonology in the Roman Mediterranean World: An Afterword to Rita Lucarelli." *Journal of Ancient Near Eastern Religions* 11 (2011): 126–31.

Freeman, Austin M. *Tolkien Dogmatics: Theology through Mythology with the Maker of Middle-Earth*. Lexham, 2022.

Friedman, Richard Elliott. *The Exodus: How It Happened and Why It Matters*. HarperOne, 2017.

Fröhlich, Ida, and Erkki Koskenniemi, eds. *Evil and the Devil*. T&T Clark, 2013.

Gaines, Janet Howe. "Lilith: Seductress, Heroine or Murderer?" *Bible History Daily* (blog). Biblical Archaeology Society, last updated September 15, 2024. https://www.biblicalarchaeology.org/daily/biblical-topics/hebrew-bible/lilith-in-the-bible-and-mythology/.

Gallagher, Edmon L. *The Apocrypha through History: The Canonical Reception of the Deuterocanonical Literature*. Oxford University Press, 2025.

———. *The Book of Exodus: Explorations in Christian Theology*. Cypress Bible Studies. Heritage Christian University Press, 2020.

———. *Translation of the Seventy: History, Reception, and Contemporary Use of the Septuagint*. Abilene Christian University Press, 2021.

Garr, W. Randall. *In His Own Image and Likeness: Humanity, Divinity, and Monotheism*. Brill, 2003.

Ginzberg, Louis. *Legends of the Jews*. 7 vols. Jewish Publication Society, 1909–1938.

Glare, P. G. W., ed. *Oxford Latin Dictionary*. Clarendon, 1982.

Glaser, Samuel Z. "Demigods and the Birth of Noah." The Torah.com, 2020. https://www.thetorah.com/article/demigods-and-the-birth-of-noah.

Glover, Daniel B. "Mark's Demonic Christology: Reevaluating the *Daimonic* Confessions of Jesus's Messiahship." *Journal of Theological Studies* 75 (2024): 46–62.

Gordon, Cyrus H. "['Elohim] אלהים in Its Reputed Meaning of Rulers, Judges." *Journal of Biblical Literature* 54 (1935): 139–44.

Greenberg, Moshe. *Ezekiel 21–37*. Anchor Bible. Doubleday, 1997.

———. *Understanding Exodus: A Holistic Commentary on Exodus 1–11*. 1969. Edited by Jeffrey H. Tigay. 2nd ed. Cascade, 2013.

Gurtner, Daniel M. *Introducing the Pseudepigrapha of Second Temple Judaism: Message, Context, and Significance*. Baker, 2020.

Hamori, Esther J. "The Spirit of Falsehood." *Catholic Biblical Quarterly* 72 (2010): 15–30.

Haring, James W. "Origen and the Council of YHWH: A Case Study in Theological-Critical Interpretation." *Pro Ecclesia* 25 (2016): 475–95.

Hayward, C. T. R. *Saint Jerome's Hebrew Questions on Genesis*. Clarendon, 1995.

Heine, Ronald E. *Origen: Scholarship in the Service of the Church*. Oxford University Press, 2010.

Heiser, Michael S. *The Unseen Realm: Recovering the Supernatural Worldview of the Bible*. Lexham, 2015.

Hendel, Ronald. "God and the Gods in the Tetrateuch." In *The Origins of Yahwism*, edited by Jürgen Oorschot and Markus Witte, 239–66. De Gruyter, 2017.

Henze, Matthias. *Mind the Gap: How the Jewish Writings between the Old and New Testament Help Us Understand Jesus*. Fortress, 2017.

Herrmann, Wolfgang. "Baal Zebub." In *Dictionary of Deities and Demons in the Bible*, edited by van der Toorn, Becking, and van der Horst, 154–56.

———. "El." In *Dictionary of Deities and Demons in the Bible*, edited by van der Toorn, Becking, and van der Horst, 274–80.

Hughes, Richard T., and James L. Gorman. *Reviving the Ancient Faith: The Story of Churches of Christ in America*. 3rd ed. Eerdmans, 2024.

Hummel, Horace D. *Ezekiel 21–48*. Concordia Commentary. Concordia, 2007.

Hutter, Manfred. "Lilith." In *Dictionary of Deities and Demons in the Bible*, edited by van der Toorn, Becking, and van der Horst, 520–21.

Jacobson, Howard. "Ezekiel the Tragedian and the Primeval Serpent." *American Journal of Philology* 102 (1981): 316–20.

James. *Daemonologie*. 1597.

Janowski, Bernd. "Azazel." In *Dictionary of Deities and Demons in the Bible*, edited by van der Toorn, Becking, and van der Horst, 128–31.

Japhet, Sara. *I & II Chronicles: A Commentary*. Old Testament Library. Westminster John Knox, 1993.

Jastrow, Marcus. *A Dictionary of the Targumim, the Talmud Babli and Yerushalmi, and the Midrashic Literature*. Putnam's, 1903.

Jensen, Robert W. *Ezekiel*. Brazos Theological Commentary. Brazos, 2009.

Kaiser, Otto. *Isaiah 13–39: A Commentary*. Old Testament Library. Westminster, 1974.

Kautzsch, E., and A. E. Cowley. *Gesenius' Hebrew Grammar*. 2nd ed. Oxford University Press, 1910.

Keel, Othmar, and Christoph Uehlinger. *Gods, Goddesses, and Images of God in Ancient Israel*. Fortress, 1998.

Keener, Craig S. *Miracles: The Credibility of the New Testament Accounts*. 2 vols. Baker, 2011.

Keith, Chris, and Loren T. Stuckenbruck, eds. *Evil in Second Temple Judaism and Early Christianity*. Mohr Siebeck, 2016.

Kelly, Henry Ansgar. *Satan: A Biography*. Cambridge University Press, 2006.

Koskenniemi, Erkki. "Miracles of the Devil and His Assistants in Early Judaism and Their Influence on the Gospel of Matthew." In *Evil and the Devil*, edited by Ida Fröhlich and Erkki Koskenniemi, 84–97. T&T Clark, 2013.

Kuemmerlin-McLean, Joanne K. "Demons: Old Testament." In volume 2 of *Anchor Bible Dictionary*, edited by David Noel Freedman, 138–40. 6 vols. Doubleday, 1992.

Kugel, James L. *The Bible As It Was*. Belknap, 1997.

Laato, Antti. "The Devil in the Old Testament." In *Evil and the Devil*, edited by Ida Fröhlich and Erkki Koskenniemi, 1–22. T&T Clark, 2013.

Lange, Armin. "Satanic Verses: The Adversary in the Qumran Manuscripts and Elsewhere." *Revue de Qumran* 24 (2009): 35–48.

Levenson, Jon D. *Resurrection and the Restoration of Israel: The Ultimate Victory of the God of Life*. Yale University Press, 2006.

Levison, John R. *The Greek Life of Adam and Eve*. Commentaries on Early Jewish Literature. De Gruyter, 2023.

Lewis, C. S. *The Lion, the Witch and the Wardrobe*. HarperCollins, 1950.

———. *Mere Christianity*. Macmillan, 1952.

———. *A Preface to Paradise Lost*. Oxford University Press, 1961.

———. *The Screwtape Letters*. Geoffrey Bles, 1942.

Lewis, Charlton T., and Charles Short, eds. *A New Latin Dictionary*. American Book Company, 1879.

Liddell, Henry George, and Robert Scott, with Henry Stuart Jones and Roderick McKenzie, eds. *A Greek-English Lexicon*. 9th ed. Clarendon, 1940/1996.

Lipscomb, David. *Civil Government: Its Origin, Mission, and Destiny, and the Christian's Relation to It*. Gospel Advocate, 1889.

Litwa, M. David. *The Evil Creator: Origins of an Early Christian Idea*. Oxford University Press, 2021.

Luther, Martin. *Against Hanswurst*. 1541. Translated by Eric W. Gritsch. In *Church and Ministry III*, edited by Eric W. Gritsch, 179–256. Luther's Works 41. Fortress, 1966.

———. *Lectures on Genesis*. Translated by George V. Schick. Luther's Works 1. Concordia, 1958.

———. "Our God He Is a Castle Strong." In *Liturgy and Hymns*, edited by Ulrich S. Leupold, 283–85. Luther's Works 53. Fortress, 1965. German: In volume 35 of *D. Martin Luthers Werke*, 455–57. Hermann Böhlau, 1923.

Lynch, Matthew J. *First Isaiah and the Disappearance of the Gods*. Eisenbrauns, 2021.

———. "Mapping Monotheism: Modes of Monotheistic Rhetoric in the Hebrew Bible." *Vetus Testamentum* 64 (2004): 47–68.

Macaskill, Grant. "2 Enoch: Manuscripts, Recensions, and Original Language." In *New Perspectives on 2 Enoch: No Longer Slavonic Only*, edited by Andrei A. Orlov and Gabriele Boccaccini, 83–101. Brill, 2012.

———. *The Entangled Enoch: 2 Enoch and the Cultures of Late Antiquity*. Brill, 2024.

MacDonald, Nathan. *Deuteronomy and the Meaning of "Monotheism."* 2nd ed. Mohr Siebeck, 2012.

Machinist, Peter. "How Gods Die, Biblically and Otherwise: A Problem of Cosmic Restructuring." In *Reconsidering the Concept of Revolutionary Monotheism*, edited by Beate Pongratz-Leisten, 189–240. Eisenbrauns, 2011.

Martens, Matthew T. *Reforming Criminal Justice: A Christian Proposal*. Crossway, 2023.

Martin, Dale Basil. *The Corinthian Body*. Yale University Press, 1995.

———. "When Did Angels Become Demons?" *Journal of Biblical Literature* 129 (2010): 657–77.

Martin, R. A. "The Earliest Messianic Interpretation of Genesis 3:15." *Journal of Biblical Literature* 84 (1965): 425–27.

McClellan, Daniel. "The Gods-Complaint: Psalm 82 as a Psalm of Complaint." *Journal of Biblical Literature* 137 (2018): 833–51.

McClymond, Michael J. *The Devil's Redemption: A New History of Christian Universalism*. 2 vols. Baker, 2018.

Milgrom, Jacob. *Leviticus*. 3 vols. Anchor Bible. Doubleday, 1991–2000.

Milton, John. *Paradise Lost*. 1667. Reprint, Oxford University Press, 2004.

Moberly, R. W. L. *The God of the Old Testament: Encountering the Divine in Christian Scripture*. Baker, 2020.

———. *Old Testament Theology: Reading the Hebrew Bible as Christian Scripture*. Baker, 2013.

Moffitt David M. *Rethinking the Atonement: New Perspectives on Jesus's Death, Resurrection, and Ascension*. Baker, 2022.

Montanari, Franco, ed. *The Brill Dictionary of Ancient Greek*. Brill, 2014.

Moore, George Foot. *Judaism in the First Centuries of the Christian Era: The Age of the Tannaim*. 3 vols. Harvard University Press, 1927–1930.

Muraoka, T. *A Greek-English Lexicon of the Septuagint*. Peeters, 2009.

Nickelsburg, George W. E., and James C. VanderKam. *1 Enoch 2: A Commentary on the Book of 1 Enoch Chapters 37–82*. Hermeneia. Fortress, 2012.

Niehoff, Maren. *Philo of Alexandria: An Intellectual Biography*. Yale University Press, 2018.

Orlov, Andrei A. *Supernal Serpent: Mysteries of Leviathan in Judaism and Christianity*. Oxford University Press, 2023.

Orlov, Andrei A., and Gabriele Boccaccini, eds. *New Perspectives on 2 Enoch: No Longer Slavonic Only*. Brill, 2012.

Orr, D. Alan. "'God's Hangman': James VI, the Divine Right of Kings, and the Devil." *Reformation and Renaissance Review* 18 (2016): 137–54.

Papaioannou, Kim. "The Sin of the Angels in 2 Peter 2:4 and Jude 6." *Journal of Biblical Literature* 140 (2021): 391–408.

Parker, Simon B. "Council." In *Dictionary of Deities and Demons in the Bible*, edited by van der Toorn, Becking, and van der Horst, 204–8.

Patmore, Hector M. *Adam, Satan, and the King of Tyre: The Interpretation of Ezekiel 28:11–19 in Late Antiquity*. Brill, 2012.

Poobalan, Ivor Gerard. "Who Is the 'God of This Age' in 2 Corinthians 4:4?" PhD diss., University of Cape Town, 2015.

Pope, Marvin H. *Job*. Anchor Bible. Doubleday, 1965.

Provan, Iain. *The Reformation and the Right Reading of Scripture*. Baylor University Press, 2017.

Quack, Joachim Friedrich. "Demons, Demonology: Ancient Near East; Egypt." In *Encyclopedia of the Bible and Its Reception*, 6:531–34. De Gruyter, 2013.

Reed, Annette Yoshiko. "When Did *Daimones* Become Demons? Revisiting Septuagintal Data for Ancient Jewish Demonology." *Harvard Theological Review* 116 (2023): 340–75.

Reeg, Gottfried. "The Devil in Rabbinic Literature." In *Evil and the Devil*, edited by Ida Fröhlich and Erkki Koskenniemi, 71–83. T&T Clark, 2013.

Riley, Greg J. "Demon." In *Dictionary of Deities and Demons in the Bible*, edited by van der Toorn, Becking, and van der Horst, 235–40.

Roberts, J. J. M. *First Isaiah*. Hermeneia. Fortress, 2015.

Römer, Thomas. "Lilith: Ancient Near East and Hebrew Bible/Old Testament." In *Encyclopedia of the Bible and Its Reception*, 16:661–63. De Gruyter, 2018.

Ronis, Sara. *Demons in the Details: Demonic Discourse and Rabbinic Culture in Late Antique Babylonia*. University of California Press, 2022.

Routledge, Robin. "The Nephilim: A Tall Story? Who Were the Nephilim and How Did They Survive the Flood?" *Tyndale Bulletin* 66 (2015): 19–40.

Runia, David T. *On the Creation of the Cosmos according to Moses: Introduction, Translation and Commentary*. Philo of Alexandria Commentary Series. Brill, 2001.

Russell, Jeffrey Burton. *The Devil: Perceptions of Evil from Antiquity to Primitive Christianity*. Cornell University Press, 1977.

———. *Lucifer: The Devil in the Middle Ages*. Cornell University Press, 1984.

———. *Mephistopheles: The Devil in the Modern World*. Cornell University Press, 1986.

———. *Satan: The Early Christian Tradition*. Cornell University Press, 1981.

Sawyer, John F. A. *Isaiah through the Centuries*. Wiley, 2018.

Scott, Alan. *Origen and the Life of the Stars: A History of an Idea*. Clarendon, 1991.

Segal, Alan F. *Two Powers in Heaven: Early Rabbinic Reports about Christianity and Gnosticism*. Brill, 1977.

Shipp, R. Mark. *Of Dead Kings and Dirges: Myth and Meaning in Isaiah 14:4b–21*. Society of Biblical Literature, 2002.

Siebenthal, Heinrich von. *Ancient Greek Grammar for the Study of the New Testament*. Peter Lang, 2019.

Skehan, Patrick W., and Alexander A. Di Lella. *The Wisdom of Ben Sira*. Anchor Bible. Doubleday, 1987.

Skinner, John. *A Critical and Exegetical Commentary on Genesis*. 2nd ed. International Critical Commentary. T&T Clark, 1930.

Smith, Gregory A. "How Thin Is a Demon?" *Journal of Early Christian Studies* 16 (2008): 479–512.

Smith, Mark S. *The Origins of Biblical Monotheism: Israel's Polytheistic Background and the Ugaritic Texts*. Oxford University Press, 2001.

———. "Rephaim." In volume 5 of *Anchor Bible Dictionary*, edited by David Noel Freedman, 674–76. 6 vols. Doubleday, 1992.

Sommer, Benjamin D. *The Bodies of God and the World of Ancient Israel*. Cambridge University Press, 2009.

Sperling, S. David. "Belial." In *Dictionary of Deities and Demons in the Bible*, edited by van der Toorn, Becking, and van der Horst, 169–71.

Stokes, Ryan E. *The Satan: How God's Executioner Became the Enemy*. Eerdmans, 2019.

———. "Satan, YHWH's Executioner." *Journal of Biblical Literature* 133 (2014): 251–70.

Stuckenbruck, Loren T. "The Demonic World of the Dead Sea Scrolls." In *Evil and the Devil*, edited by Ida Fröhlich and Erkki Koskenniemi, 51–70. Bloomsbury, 2013.

———. *The Myth of Rebellious Angels: Studies in Second Temple Judaism and New Testament Texts*. Mohr Siebeck, 2014.

———. "Why Should Women Cover Their Heads Because of the Angels (1 Corinthians 11:10)?" *Stone-Campbell Journal* 4 (2001): 205–34.

Susnow, Matthew. *The Practice of Canaanite Cult: The Middle and Late Bronze Ages*. Zaphon, 2021.

Termini, Cristina. "Philo's Thought within the Context of Middle Judaism." In *The Cambridge Companion to Philo*, edited by Adam Kamesar, 95–123. Cambridge University Press, 2009.

Thiessen, Matthew. "A Buried Pentateuchal Allusion to the Resurrection in Mark 12:25." *Catholic Biblical Quarterly* 76 (2014): 273–90.

———. *Jesus and the Forces of Death: The Gospels' Portrayal of Ritual Impurity within First-Century Judaism*. Baker, 2020.

Thompson, Shane M. "Local Manifestations of YHWH within El's Divine Council: Psalm 82 in the Context of Israelite Religion." *Journal of Biblical Literature* 143 (2024): 245–65.

Tigay, Jeffrey H. *Deuteronomy*. The JPS Torah Commentary. Jewish Publication Society, 1996.

Tilly, Michael, Matthias Morgenstern, and Volker Henning Drecoll, eds. *L'adversaire de Dieu—Der Widersacher Gottes*. Mohr Siebeck, 2016.

Tolkien, J. R. R. *The Lord of the Rings*. 3 vols. Allen & Unwin, 1954–1955.

Tov, Emanuel. *Textual Criticism of the Hebrew Bible*. 3rd ed. Fortress, 2012 / 4th ed. Fortress, 2022.

Travers, P. L. *Mary Poppins*. HarperCollins, 1934.

VanderKam, James C. "1 Enoch, Enochic Motifs, and Enoch in Early Christian Literature." In *The Jewish Apocalyptic Heritage in Early Christianity*, edited by James C. VanderKam and William Adler, 33–101. Fortress, 1996.

———. "Genesis 6:1–4 and the Angel Stories in the *Book of the Watchers* (*I Enoch* 1–36)." In *The Fallen Angels Traditions: Second Temple Developments and Reception History*, edited by Angela Kim Harkins, Kelley Coblentz Bautch, and John C. Endres, 1–7. Catholic Biblical Association, 2014.

———. *Jubilees: A Commentary in Two Volumes*. Hermeneia. Fortress, 2018.

van der Toorn, Karel, Bob Becking, and Pieter W. van der Horst, eds. *Dictionary of Deities and Demons in the Bible*. 2nd ed. Brill, 1999.

van der Toorn, Karel, and Pieter W. van der Horst. "Nimrod before and after the Bible." *Harvard Theological Review* 83 (1990): 1–29.

von Rad, Gerhard. *Old Testament Theology*. 2 vols. Harper & Row, 1962.

Waldman, Felicia. "Lilith: Judaism." In *Encyclopedia of the Bible and Its Reception*, 16:663–65. De Gruyter, 2018.

Walton, John H. "Demons in Mesopotamia and Israel: Exploring the Category of Non-Divine but Supernatural Beings." In *Windows to the Ancient World of the Hebrew Bible: Essays in Honor of Samuel Greengus*, edited by Bill T. Arnold, Nancy L. Erickson, and John H. Walton, 229–46. Eisenbrauns, 2014.

Walton, John H., and J. Harvey Walton. *Demons and Spirits in Biblical Theology: Reading the Biblical Text in Its Cultural and Literary Context*. Cascade, 2019.

Wassen, Cecilia. "'Because of the Angels': Reading 1 Corinthians 11:2–16 in Light of Angelology in the Dead Sea Scrolls." In volume 2 of *The Dead Sea Scrolls in Context*, edited by Armin Lange, Emanuel Tov, and Matthias Weigold, 734–54. 2 vols. Brill, 2011.

Watson, Wilfred G. E. "Helel." In *Dictionary of Deities and Demons in the Bible*, edited by van der Toorn, Becking, and van der Horst, 392–94.

West, Earl Irvin. *The Search for the Ancient Order: A History of the Restoration Movement 1849–1950*. 4 vols. Religious Book Service, 1949–87.

Wevers, John William. *Notes on the Greek Text of Deuteronomy*. Scholars Press, 1995.

———. *Notes on the Greek Text of Genesis*. Scholars Press, 1993.

———. *Notes on the Greek Text of Leviticus*. Scholars Press, 1997.

Wickham, L. R. "The Sons of God and Daughters of Men: Genesis vi 2 in Early Christian Exegesis." In *Language and Meaning: Studies in Hebrew Language and Biblical Exegesis*, edited by A. S. van der Woude, 135–47. Brill, 1974.

Wiebe, Gregory D. *Fallen Angels in the Theology of St Augustine*. Oxford University Press, 2021.

Wieger, Madeleine. "'Celui qu'on appelle διάβολος' (Apocalypse 12,9): L'histoire du nom grec de l'Adversaire." In *L'adversaire de Dieu—Der Widersacher Gottes*, edited by Michael Tilly, Matthias Morgenstern, and Volker Henning Drecoll, 201–18. Mohr Siebeck, 2016.

Wildeberger, Hans. *Isaiah 13–27: A Continental Commentary*. Fortress, 1997.

Williams, Guy. *The Spirit World in the Letters of Paul the Apostle: A Critical Examination of the Role of Spiritual Beings in the Authentic Pauline Epistles*. Vandenhoeck & Ruprecht, 2009.

Williams, Travis B., and David G. Horrell. *1 Peter*. 2 vols. International Critical Commentary. T&T Clark, 2023.

Wright, Archie T. *The Origin of Evil Spirits: The Reception of Genesis 6:1–4 in Early Jewish Literature*. 2nd ed. Mohr Siebeck, 2013.

———. *Satan and the Problem of Evil: From the Bible to the Early Church Fathers*. Fortress, 2022.

Wright, Christopher. *Deuteronomy*. New International Biblical Commentary. Hendrickson, 1996.

———. *The Mission of God: Unlocking the Bible's Grand Narrative*. IVP, 2006.

Wright, David P. *Inventing God's Law: How the Covenant Code of the Bible Used and Revised the Laws of Hammurabi*. Oxford University Press, 2009.

Yogev, Jonathan. *The Rephaim: Sons of the Gods*. Brill, 2021.

Zimmerli, Walther. *Ezekiel 2*. Hermeneia. Fortress, 1983.

Zurawski, Jason. "Separating the Devil from the *Diabolos*: A Fresh Reading of Wisdom of Solomon 2.24." *Journal for the Study of the Pseudepigrapha* 21 (2012): 366–99.